T0135696

Studien zur Mustererkennung

herausgegeben von:

Prof. Dr.-Ing. Heinrich Niemann
Prof. Dr.-Ing. Elmar Nöth

Bibliografische Information der Deutschen Nationalbibliothek

Die Deutsche Nationalbibliothek verzeichnet diese Publikation in der
Deutschen Nationalbibliografie; detaillierte bibliografische Daten sind
im Internet über http://dnb.d-nb.de abrufbar.

©Copyright Logos Verlag Berlin GmbH 2017
Alle Rechte vorbehalten.

ISBN 978-3-8325-4567-3
ISSN 1617-0695

Logos Verlag Berlin GmbH
Comeniushof
Gubener Str. 47
10243 Berlin
Tel.: +49 030 42 85 10 90
Fax: +49 030 42 85 10 92
INTERNET: http://www.logos-verlag.de

Automatic Assessment of Prosody in Second Language Learning

Automatische Bewertung von Prosodie beim Fremdsprachenlernen

Der Technischen Fakultät
der Friedrich-Alexander-Universität
Erlangen-Nürnberg

zur

Erlangung des Doktorgrades Dr.-Ing.

vorgelegt von

Florian Thomas Hönig
aus
Neuendettelsau

Als Dissertation genehmigt
von der Technischen Fakultät
der Friedrich-Alexander-Universität Erlangen-Nürnberg

Tag der mündlichen Prüfung: 16.12.2016
Vorsitzender des Promotionsorgans: Prof. Dr.-Ing. Reinhard Lerch
Gutachter: Prof. Dr.-Ing. Elmar Nöth
     Prof. Dr.-Ing. Björn Schuller

Acknowledgment

This thesis would not have been possible without the generous help of many people. First of all, I would like to thank Dr.-Ing. Georg Stemmer, for kindling my interest in pattern recognition in general and automatic speech processing specifically, and for patiently teaching me the tools and tricks of the trade. Further, I am grateful to Prof. Dr.-Ing. habil. Elmar Nöth, Prof. em. Dr.-Ing. Heinrich Niemann, Prof. Dr.-Ing. Joachim Hornegger, and Prof. Dr.-Ing. habil. Andreas Maier for making it possible for me to do my PhD at the Pattern Recognition Lab, and to my colleagues who wrote grant applications involved (among others, Dr.-Ing. Christian Hacker, Dr. phil. Anton Batliner, and Dr.-Ing. Stefan Steidl). I am further indebted to the federal ministry of education and research (BMBF), the European commission, the federal ministry for economic affairs and energy (BMWi), the German research foundation (DFG), and Hessen Agentur, for funding in the research projects Smart-Web (BMBF 01IMD01F), HUMAINE (NoE IST-2002-507422), C-AuDiT (BMBF 01IS07014B), AUWL (BMWi KF2027104ED0), SLEDS (DFG KR 3698/4-1), and ASSIST I/II (Hessen Agentur 397/13-36 and 463/15-05).

I would further like to thank Prof. Dr.-Ing. habil. Elmar Nöth for supervising this thesis, for giving me not only comprehensive scientific but also personal advice and support throughout all the time. I also owe to his being the 'soul' of the lab—contributing crucially to making it a pleasant, inspiring, and humane place to learn, research and work.

I also would like to thank Dr. phil. Anton Batliner for his extensive and excellent scientific guidance and support throughout this thesis and the research projects, data collections, and scientific papers that contributed to it.

Further I would like to thank my colleagues for help, scientific discussions, and their contribution to a great and rewarding time while doing my PhD at the lab, among others Dr.-Ing. Christian Hacker, Dr.-Ing. Stefan Steidl, PD Dr.-Ing. Tino Haderlein, Axel Horndasch, Dr.-Ing. Viktor Zeißler, Prof. Dr.-Ing. habil. Andreas Maier, Dr.-Ing. Martin Kraus, Prof. Dr. Björn Eskofier, Dr. Tobias Bocklet, Prof. Dr.-Ing. Korbinian Riedhammer, Dr.-Ing. Dirk Kolb, Dr.-Ing. Johannes Feulner, Dr.-Ing. Johannes Jordan, Caroline Kaufhold, Martin Gropp, Vincent Christlein, Christine Martindale, and Prof. Dr.-Ing. Juan Rafael Orozco-Arroyave.

I also would like to thank Kristina Müller and Iris Koppe for not only giving friendly and competent support for all organizational matters, but also helping in the organizing of the funds for my position. Further, I would like to thank Fritz Popp and Sven Grünke, and the colleagues in charge of the system administration task for supporting me in hardware and software matters.

I also would like to thank Prof. Dr.-Ing. habil. Björn Schuller for being my second reviewer, Prof. Dr.-Ing. Walter Kellermann for being my external examiner, and Prof. Dr.-Ing. habil. Andreas Maier for being chairman of the examination committee.

Further I would like to thank Freddy Ertl and Dr. Karl Weilhammer from digital publishing for the great cooperation and support in the C-AuDiT project. Further thanks go to all labellers, among others Susanne Burger, Susanne Waltl, Juliane

Kappes, Tania Ellbogen, Jessica Siddins, and Dr. Catherine Dickie, and to all speakers donating their speech for the databases used.

I also would like to thank Dr. Alexander Wolff von Gudenberg, Dr. Harald Moll-berg, Frank Jassens and Lea Mahlberg from the Kassel Stuttering Therapy for their support during the last stages of writing the thesis.

Finally, I would like to thank my parents Ernst and Elisabeth for enabling me to do a PhD in the first place (by affording me the necessary prior education), and my wife Gudrun (for taking the lion's share of parenting in favour of my full-time position).

Erlangen, September 2017
Florian Hönig

Abstract

The present thesis studies methods for automatically assessing the prosody of non-native speakers for the purpose of computer-assisted pronunciation training. We study the detection of word accent errors, and the general assessment of the appropriateness of a speaker's rhythm. We propose a flexible, generic approach that is (a) very successful on these tasks, (b) competitive to other state-of-the-art result, and at the same time (c) flexible and easily adapted to new tasks.

For word accent error detection, we derive a measure for the *probability of acceptable pronunciation* which is ideal for a well-grounded decision whether or not to provide error feedback to the learner. Our best system achieves a true positive rate (TPR) of 71.5 % at a false positive rate (FPR) of 5 %, which is a result very competitive to the state-of-the art, and not too far away from human performance (TPR 61.9 % at 3.2 % FPR).

For scoring general prosody, we obtain a Spearman correlation of $\rho = 0.773$ to the human reference scores on the C-AuDiT database (sentences read by non-native speakers); this is slightly better than the average labeller on that data (comparable quality measure for machine performance: $r = 0.71$ vs. 0.66 for human performance). On speaker level, performance is more stable with $\rho = 0.854$. On AUWL (non-native speakers practising dialogues), the task is much harder for both human and machine. Our best system achieves a correlation of $\rho = 0.619$ to the reference scores; here, humans are better than the system (quality measure for humans: $r = 0.58$ vs. 0.51 for machine performance). On speaker level, correlation rises to $\rho = 0.821$. On both databases, the obtained results are competitive to the state-of-the-art.

Kurzdarstellung

Die vorliegende Arbeit beschäftigt sich mit Methoden für die automatische Auswertung der Prosodie nicht-nativer Sprecher für Zwecke des computergestützten Aussprachetrainings. Untersucht werden die Detektion von fehlerhaften Wortakzenten und eine allgemeine Bewertung des Sprachrhythmus. Der vorgeschlagene generische Ansatz zeichnet sich dadurch aus, dass er (a) sehr gute Ergebnisse für die genannten Aufgabenstellungen erzielt, (b) mindestens die Zuverlässigkeit anderer aktueller Ansätze erreicht, und (c) gleichzeitig flexibel ist und sich einfach an neue Aufgabenstellungen anpassen lässt.

Für die Detektion fehlerhafter Wortakzente leiten wir ein Maß für die *Wahrscheinlichkeit akzeptabler Aussprache* her, dass sich bestens als fundierte Entscheidungsgrundlage dafür eignet, ob ein Fehler an den Lernenden zurückgemeldet werden soll oder nicht. Das beste System erreicht eine Trefferquote von 71.5 % bei 5 % Fehlalarm, was ein sehr gutes Resultat im Vergleich mit dem Stand der Technik ist, und nicht allzuweit entfernt von Zuverlässigkeit eines Menschen ist (61.9 % Trefferquote bei 3.2 % Fehlalarm).

Für die allgemeine Bewertung der Prosodie wird bei der C-AuDiT-Stichprobe (nicht-native Sprecher lesen Sätze vor) eine Spearman-Korrelation von $\rho = 0.773$ zu den menschlichen Referenzbewertungen erzielt. Das ist etwas besser als der durchschnittliche menschliche Bewerter bei diesen Daten (vergleichbare Messzahl für die Maschine: $r = 0.71$ vs. 0.66 für den Mensch). Auf Sprecher-Ebene steigt die Leistung des Systems auf $\rho = 0.854$. Bei der AUWL-Stichprobe (nicht-native Sprecher üben Dialoge) ist die Aufgabenstellung sowohl für Mensch und Maschine deutlich schwieriger. Das beste System erreicht eine Korrelation von $\rho = 0.619$ zu den Referenz-Bewertungen; hier sind die menschlichen Bewerter besser als die Maschine (vergleichbare Messzahl für Menschen: $r = 0.58$ vs. 0.51 für die Maschine). Auf Sprecher-Ebene steigt die Korrelation auf $\rho = 0.821$. Die Ergebnisse bei beiden Stichproben sind kompetitiv zum Stand der Technik.

Contents

1

Introduction

1.1 Motivation

One only needs to go to an international scientific conference to be—sometimes painfully—reminded how great the need for improving second language skills is. Here, researchers from a variety of language backgrounds use English as a *lingua franca* to exchange ideas, but all too often, *non-native* speakers such as the author of this thesis, who were not so lucky as to grow up with that language, find themselves giving talks that require a sustained high listening effort or that are in whole or in part unintelligible, failing to convey the meaning of their questions and answers, or having difficulties establishing social contacts. As in all situations where a second language is involved, insufficient proficiency[1] constitutes a major impediment to communication.

Many non-native speakers have deficiencies in vocabulary, syntax and grammar, but what primarily makes listening hard and understanding difficult is often a *pronunciation* that deviates strongly from native speech. (Even when intelligibility is not affected, a *non-native accent* can stigmatize the speaker, and the listener may jump to conclusions about actual language proficiency, social skills, intellectual capability, and even credibility of the talker [Glus 10, Lev 10].) The perceived deviation from native pronunciation is usually attributed mainly to the difficulties of producing the individual phonemes of the language, which is especially pertinent for phonemes that do not exist in the native language of the speaker. Just as important however, and often underestimated, are the deviations in *prosodic* properties of speech, such as word accent position, syntactic-prosodic boundaries, and especially rhythm, which help listeners to process syntactic, semantic and pragmatic content. How important the structuring function of prosody is for understanding speech, one can envision by trying to read text from which all structure, i.e. capitalization, spaces, and punctuation has been removed [Batl 10]:

pleasecallstellaaskhertobringthesethingswithherfromthestoresixspoonsoffr
eshsnowpeasfivethickslabsofbluecheeseandmaybeasnackforherbrotherbob

---

[1]This refers to proficiency in speech *production*. Deficiencies in perception constitute an impediment as well, especially in noise [McAl 98], but production is more important as it affects all one's listeners, while perception only affects oneself.

Thus failing to produce adequate prosody can result not only in speech that sounds strange, but also in degraded intelligibility, up to the point where a listener who is neither acquainted with the speaker, nor with the native language of the speaker, may have a hard time understanding anything the speaker is trying to convey.

Practice makes perfect, yet with traditional textbooks, pronunciation is hardly approachable. Audio-visual media offer some help, but they are relatively unwieldy and do not offer feedback. In typical classroom instruction, little time is spent on pronunciation, and for prosody the situation is even worse. Also, there is hardly time for individual problems, and sometimes the pronunciation of the teacher is a problem in itself. Intuitively, one-to-one lessons by a highly qualified teacher are the ideal method to teach pronunciation. And there is indeed some evidence: Bloom found a striking difference in test scores of students when comparing one-to-one tutoring with conventional learning in a class with about 30 students per teacher, the so-called *2 sigma problem*: "The average student under tutoring was about two standard deviations above the average of the control class (the average tutored student was above 98 % of the students in the control class)." [Bloo 84] Although Bloom was measuring general performance in school, there is every reason to assume similar effects for language learning and pronunciation learning in particular.

Only few learners can afford one-to-one tutoring, and the number of qualified personnel is limited. Bloom and others therefore tried to "[. . .] solve the 2 sigma problem" [Bloo 84], i. e. approach the effectiveness of one-to-one tutoring, by developing improved group teaching methods such as mastery learning [Leyt 83]. A different and possibly complementary approach is to use computer technology to *simulate and automate* aspects of human one-to-one tutoring. This is part of *Computer assisted language learning* (CALL).

In general, CALL holds the promise to help learners and teachers in all aspects of language learning, including acquisition or improvement of written and perceptual skills, with all the obvious advantages of the technology: scalability with respect to learners, curriculum and languages, tireless and patient instruction at any time, objective and reproducible assessment, and with the advent of powerful, network-connected mobile devices in recent years also ubiquity of access. Also, CALL can benefit students who are not willing to speak or be corrected in front of the class for social reasons. For pronunciation learning, the potential of CALL is especially striking, since it usually comes off badly in traditional classroom instruction: tackling pronunciation problems of the individual students is highly time-demanding for teachers, and when the native language of the teacher is very different from the taught language in terms of rhythm or phonology, the teacher's expertise often is not sufficient [Moed 08]. This sub-area of CALL concerned with pronunciation learning is called *Computer-assisted pronunciation training* (CAPT).

It is evident that any CAPT software, in order to help pronunciation learning, requires a component to automatically analyse the student's pronunciation. This can comprise the detection of concrete, individual errors (*error detection, pinpointing*), or the gradual appraisal of the quality of the uttered speech (*rating, grading, assessment*). This is precisely the topic of this thesis, albeit with the restriction to prosodic aspects: *to study methods for the automatic detection of prosodic errors, and the automatic assessment of the prosodic quality in non-native speech.* As a basis, the remainder of this chapter introduces relevant aspects of prosody, second language learning, and CALL, and outlines the structure of the thesis. Note that here and throughout the text, terms that are well-known and non-controversial in the pertinent fields of phonetics/linguistics, pedagogics, and machine learning/pattern recognition are not necessarily formally introduced/defined.

1.2 Prosody

1.2.1 Segmental versus suprasegmental aspects

When analysing language, it is useful to distinguish between *segmental* and *suprasegmental* aspects. A *segment* here in general refers to "[...] any discrete [classifiable] unit" [Crys 03, p. 408] the object of analysis (written text, spoken utterance, etc.) can be *segmented*, i. e. subdivided into. Syllables, words and even whole sentences can constitute such segments. In the narrow sense of phonetics and phonology, which we will adopt here, these units correspond to phones or phonemes. Thus, a segmental feature of speech relates to properties *within the boundaries of a single segment* [Crys 03, p. 408]. A *segmental error* a German learner of English might make, for instance, is confusing the dental fricative /θ/[2] with the coronal sibilant /s/; a general tendency to mispronounce certain phonemes could be called a *non-native segmental trait*. Suprasegmental features, on the other hand, extend over multiple segments. For example, producing a wrong word accent pattern, say, *en*-ter-*tain*-ment /ˈɛntə̩teɪnmənt/ instead of *en*-ter-***tain***-ment /ˌɛntəˈteɪnmənt/ is a *suprasegmental error* a learner might make; a non-native rhythm could be called *non-native suprasegmental trait*.

Given the effects that coarticulation can have on the actual realization and perception of the segments, i. e. the phonemes, this division seems over-simplistic, or even contradictory: although the identity of a phoneme is certainly a segmental feature, its influence usually goes *beyond* its boundaries. Still, coarticulation is mainly confined to the immediate neighbours of a phoneme, and most segmental features are indeed located within a segment, and most of them can also be produced or observed in isolated segments. So, the division into segmentals and suprasegmentals remains a useful mode of description, but should not be taken too literally.

1.2.2 Definition

We can now define *prosody* as the suprasegmental aspects of loudness, pitch and duration (of both speech segments and pauses)[3]. Thus we include rhythm, tempo, word accent (also called word stress), phrase accent, phrase boundaries, sentence mood, intonation[4], and exclude segmental aspects such as intrinsic vowel duration (e. g. the

---

[2]For denoting phonemic and phonetic transcriptions, the conventions of the International Phonetic Association (IPA) are used [Asso 99].

[3] There "[...] is no universal consensus among phonologist about either the nature of prosodic features themselves or the general framework for their description" [Fox 00, p. 1]. For a comprehensive discussion, see [Kies 97].

[4]Intonation is used in the narrow sense of suprasegmental pitch variations; see [Kies 97, p. 9] for a discussion.

vowel in beat /biːt/ is longer than in bit /bɪt/), intrinsic vowel loudness (e.g. the vowel in bat /bæt/ is louder than in bit /bɪt/) and lexical tone in tone languages (e.g. in Mandarin Chinese, /mā/, i.e. with a high, level tone, means *mother*, but /mǎ/, i.e. with a low, dipping tone, means *horse* [Shen 90]). Again, the actual realization (and perception) of segmental aspects such as vowel length or tone will heavily depend on context, yet, they can even be produced and observed in isolated segments, so there is good reason to treat them as segmentals. Word accent is clearly suprasegmental; isolated segments, e.g., cannot constitute different accent patterns. On the other hand, it encodes lexical information, which is usually encoded by segmental features. In so far, word accent 'misbehaves', but it is a sacrifice we are willing to make, especially because it is useful to include it as suprasegmental aspect in this thesis: it definitely is an issue in second language learning, and it is also intimately related to phrase accent and rhythm.

By restricting prosody—as common in linguistics—to loudness, pitch and duration, we exclude voice quality, although sometimes aspects of voice quality are relevant for prosody. For example, some speakers use laryngealization to mark phrase boundaries [Lehi 76]. Campbell proposed the normalized amplitude quotient, a measure of how pressed (or breathy, on the other end of the scale) the voice is, as the '[...] 4th prosodic dimension', as it has "[...] significant correlations with interlocutor, speaking-style, and speech-act." [Camp 03a] Campbell observes that the degree of breathiness seems to reflect "[...] the degree of 'care' taken in the speech" to the interlocutor [Camp 03a].

Most aspects of voice quality, however, are not relevant for prosody: some are outside of the speaker's control, and most others are either relatively constant over longer stretches of time, or used to signal emotional (para-linguistic) information rather than linguistic-prosodic information. This could also be claimed for the normalized amplitude quotient of Campbell (breathiness, see above). Last but not least, voice quality is not a major issue in second language learning.

By characterizing prosody as 'suprasegmental', we have defined it referring to structure. One can, at least partly, separate prosodic from non-prosodic features in terms of phonetic criteria, too:

> "It is convenient to distinguish three components of the physiology of speaking: the *subglottal*[5] component, the *larynx*, and the *supralaryngeal* component. [...] Most of the segmental [i.e. non-prosodic] features of speech are produced by the supralaryngeal component. Place and manner of articulation depend on the postures and movements of the tongue, velum, jaw, and so on. The one exception to this generalization is voice, which, as we have noted, is generated in the larynx, along with other laryngeal features such as aspiration and glottalization. By contrast, prosodic features can be seen *primarily* as the result of laryngeal or subglottal activity. Tone and intonation are based on pitch, which is controlled by the laryngeal muscles, while accentual features are often attributed to the activity of the respiratory muscles." [Fox 00, p. 3–4].

---

[5]Unless stated otherwise, emphasis in quotations is true to the original.

It is important to note that the prosodic and non-prosodic aspects of duration, loudness and pitch cannot be produced or observed independently: All speech organs closely cooperate to produce speech, and the laryngeal and subglottal system, although mainly responsible for prosody, fulfils segmental, i. e. non-prosodic aspects, too. Thus, the duration, loudness and pitch observations are the product of a complex interplay of both segmental and suprasegmental functions. This is one reason why prosody presents a challenge for language learners on the one hand, and for automatic error analysis on the other hand, as we will see later.

1.2.3 Prosodic functions

With just the three parameters loudness, pitch and duration, a multitude of *prosodic functions* can be associated: structuring on basic (rhythmical) level, linguistic functions such as indicating lexical, syntactic, semantic and pragmatic information, but also paralinguistic information such as attitude, emotional, physiological and mental state of the speaker, and idiosyncratic speaker characteristics. Here, we will confine ourselves to those most relevant to language learning, namely, those used for structuring speech: *word accent, phrase accent, (prosodic-syntactic) phrase boundaries, and rhythm.* They will be covered in more detail in Section 2.1. Note that we do not attempt to deal with intonation beyond its role in phrase accents and boundaries, as (native) intonation is highly variable and thus difficult to model, and although the impact of intonation on sounding 'non-native' can be large, the impact on intelligibility is limited.

1.3 Second language learning

While children seem to learn the language they grow up with—their *native* or *first language* (L1)—effortlessly to perfection, learning a new language—a *foreign* or *second language* (L2)—after a certain age is hard, and few succeed in complete, native-like mastery. This can be explained in part simply by the fact that many L2 learners are not immersed in the learned language, and undergo only limited exposure, e. g. in classroom teaching. However, also non-native speakers who live for decades immersed in a second language, often significantly fall short of the proficiency of native speakers, and people who were not exposed to (any) language during childhood show pathologic language deficiencies. A wide-spread explanation for this is the *critical period hypothesis* put forward by Penfield [Penf 59] and Lenneberg [Lenn 67], see Sections 2.1.1 and 2.2.1. Although it is unquestioned that language "[...] proficiency declines with age of initial acquisition" [Bial 99, p. 172], empirically, proofs for a clearly delimited critical period have not been found. That is encouraging for second language learners: mechanisms that govern native language acquisition can also be utilized for second language learning. Also, there are examples of late learners who do acquire near-native competence [Bird 92], and many more acquire at least a fluency that allows them to communicate in the learned language without any restrictions.

1.3.1   Second language acquisition

The scientific study of describing and explaining the process of L2 acquisition is called *second language acquisition* (SLA) [Elli 97] or SLA research. Second language does not necessarily refer to a single, or a foreign language, rather, it refers to "[...] any language learned subsequent to the mother tongue." [Elli 97, p. 3] Although one cannot define a precise starting date, SLA research seems to have been kindled by two seminal contributions, Corder's *The significance of learners' errors* [Cord 67] and Selinker's *interlanguage* [Seli 72].

Corder refutes behaviourist explanations for SLA in favour of internal linguistic processes: "[...] the learner's possession of his native language is facilitative and [...] errors are not to be regarded as signs of inhibition, but simply as evidence of his strategies of learning. [...] We may be able to allow the learner's innate strategies to dictate our practice and determine our syllabus; we may learn to adapt ourselves to *his* needs rather than impose upon him *our* preconception of *how* he ought to learn, *what* he ought to learn and *when* he ought to learn it." [Cord 67]

Selinker argues for an "[...] internal linguistic system worthy of study in its own [...] neither the L1 nor the L2, but something in-between that the learner was building from environmental data." [Van 10, p. 2-3] Errors in learners' productions in the target language (TL) are not random; rather, they are expression of the rules of the learner's imperfect version of the target language, the *interlanguage* (IL). The triangle of native language (NL), TL, and IL provides a useful theoretical framework for the study of the principles behind second language learning. One approach is studying NL and IL utterances by the learner, and TL utterances by a native speaker, where all three utterances are trying to express the same meaning. Selinker also extends the interlanguage concept to groups of speakers, where "[...] fossilized IL competences may be the normal situation" [Seli 72, p. 217], e. g. Indian English. The interlanguage framework accounts for *fossilization* of errors, "[...] which speakers will tend to keep in their IL productive performance, no matter what the age of the learner or the amount of instruction he receives in the TL." [Seli 72] Fossilizations "[...] tend to remain [...] even when seemingly eradicated. Many of these phenomena reappear in IL performance when the learner's attention is focused upon new and difficult intellectual subject matter or when he is in a state of anxiety or other excitement" [Seli 72, p. 215]. Interlanguage provides a theoretical framework for various aspects of SLA:

- *L2 transfer*: Rules of the NL are inappropriately overtaken for the IL by the learners, e. g. "[...] French uvular /r/ in their English IL, American English retroflex /r/ in their French IL, English rhythm in the IL relative to Spanish, German *Time-place* order after the verb in the English IL of German speakers" [Seli 72, p. 215].

- *Overgeneralization* of rules of the TL: "Speakers of many languages could produce a sentence of the following kind in their English IL: 'What did he intended to say?' where the past tense morpheme *-ed* is extended to an environment in which, to the learner, it could logically apply, but just does not." [Seli 72, p. 218] In the light of interlanguage, overgeneralization is the result of the learner's attempts to learn grammatical constraints or rules, often without explicit explanation or instruction.

- Fossilized errors can partly be explained by the learner's *strategy of second language communication*: "This strategy of communication dictates to them [. . .] that they know enough of the TL in order to communicate. And they stop learning." [Seli 72, p. 217]

- Another source of errors is the *strategy of second language learning* which often exhibits "[. . .] a tendency on part on the learners to reduce the TL to a simpler system." [Seli 72, p. 219]

Stephen Krashen's *Input hypothesis* [Kras 82, Kras 85] aims at explaining the mechanisms behind successful acquisition. "The Input Hypothesis [. . .] assumes that we acquire language by understanding messages. [. . .] More precisely, comprehensible input is the essential environmental ingredient [. . .] language is subconsciously acquired—while you are acquiring, you don't know you are acquiring; your conscious focus is on the message, not the form." [Kras 89] The input hypothesis contrasts with the *Skill-building hypothesis* ("[. . .] we learn language by first consciously learning individual rules or items, and gradually, through drills and exercises, make these rules [automatic] " [Kras 89]) and the *Output hypothesis* ("[. . .] we learn language by producing it. [. . .] we learn rules and items by trying them out in production. If we experience communicative success, our (conscious) hypothesis about the rule or items is confirmed. If we experience communication failure, or correction, our hypothesis is disconfirmed and we alter it." [Kras 89]). While leaving "[. . .] a good amount of acquisition unexplained" [Van 10, p. 3], Krashen's input hypothesis turned out to be generally true and was very influential on teaching methods.

Parallel to these linguistic approaches, cognitive psychology has created its own views on second language acquisition. "In general learning, cognitive theory is one in which psychologists attempt to understand how humans create and use knowledge." [Van 10, p. 71] The *cognitive approach* to SLA accordingly sees language learning in the context of the general human capacity for learning, and ignores or even denies that language is anything special: "[. . .] if indeed the learner had any mental representation that could be called language, it was an artefact of learning, a latent structure that emerged based on data the learner encountered in the environment." [Van 10, p. 5] The cognitive approach focusses on "[. . .] the learning factors that affect acquisition such as how learners come to understand the nature of a particular feature and what strategies learners go about to master a concept. Under the umbrella of cognitive theory, then would fall *individual differences* such as aptitude, motivation, memory." [Van 10, p. 71] The denial of the special role of language learning is in strong contrast [Van 10, 71] to the *innateness hypothesis* [Chom 62] widespread in linguistic theory which implies "[. . .] that the human brain is 'programmed' at birth in some quite *specific* and *structured* aspects of human natural language." [Putn 67] Generally, it is observed that "[as] a discipline, it [SLA] is splintered, with certain camps not in dialogue with others. Both linguistic and cognitive approaches continue to dominate the field and we do not envision this changing in the near future" [Van 10, p. 5].

1.3.2   Second language teaching methods

"It has been estimated that some 60 percent of today's world population is multilingual. From both a contemporary and a historical perspective, bilingualism or
multilingualism is the norm rather than the exception. It is fair, then, to say that
throughout history foreign language learning has always been an important practical
concern." [Rich 01, p. 3] Nevertheless, it was not until the early twentieth century
that "Language teaching came into its own as a profession" [Rich 01, p. 1] and as a
scientific discipline.

A common framework for describing and comparing ways of teaching language
is given by Anthony's *approach, method and technique* model [Anth 63][6]. At the
highest level of abstraction, the *approach* relates to theoretical assumptions about
the nature of language and learning, referring to linguistic as well as psychological
aspects. More concretely, the *method* defines how an approach will be substantiated.
It is "[...] an overall plan for the orderly presentation of language material, no part of
which contradicts, and all of which is based upon, the selected approach" [Anth 63],
thus defining the "[...] skills to be taught, the content to be taught" [Rich 01, p. 19].
The *technique* relates to the practical implementation of a method in the classroom,
"[...] a particular trick, strategem or contrivance used [...] consistent with a method,
and therefore in harmony with an approach as well." [Anth 63] We will be concerned
mainly with methods here: their theoretical basis, the approach, is less relevant to
us, just like the details of its implementation, the technique.

Over time, "[...] teaching methods [...] have reflected recognition of changes in
the kind of proficiency learners need, such as a move toward oral proficiency rather
then reading comprehension as the goal of language study" [Rich 01, p. 3]. During
the twentieth century, language teaching "[...] was characterized by frequent change
and innovation and by the development of sometimes competing language teaching
ideologies; they have also reflected changes in theories of the nature of language
and language learning." [Rich 01, p. 1] It is however worth noting that "[...] many
current issues in language teaching are not particularly new. Today's controversies
reflect contemporary responses to questions that have been asked often throughout
the history of language teaching." [Rich 01, p. 3, referring to [Kell 69, Howa 84]] In
the following, some important language teaching methods are outlined.

Grammar-translation method: When Latin began to lose its role as a lingua
    franca in the western world in the sixteenth century, gradually becoming a
    'dead' language, its study "[...] took on a different function. [...] Latin was said
    to develop intellectual abilities, and the study of Latin grammar became an end
    in itself." [Rich 01, p. 3–4] The instructions were given in the student's native
    language, and consisted of "[...] abstract grammar rules, lists of vocabulary"
    [Rich 01, p. 5], and "mechanical translation" [Tito 68, p. 27] exercises. Oral
    practice was minimal and did not aim at communicative skills. This approach
    came to be known as the *Grammar-translation method* and was the standard
    approach for teaching also other foreign languages in Europe in the eighteenth
    and nineteenth century [Rich 01, p. 4].

---

[6]Richards and Rogers suggested a refinement, the *approach, design, and procedure* model
[Rich 82], but it seems that Anthony's original formulation prevails [Hall 11, p. 77].

Direct method: Many reformers saw the shortcomings of the Grammar-translation method. François Gouin was one of first to "[...] attempt to build a methodology around observation of child language learning." [Rich 01, p. 11] Being a Latin teacher, Gouin had intensively tried to teach himself German according to the traditional Grammar-translation method but failed completely to communicate once he arrived in Germany. On the other hand, he was stunned by the success his three-year-old nephew made in learning to speak (his mother tongue) [Dill 78]. Following that experience, he designed his *series method* [Goui 80], which can be regarded as a precursor to the *direct* or *natural method*, which assumes that second language learning should be more like first language learning: "[...] a foreign language could be taught without translation or the use of the learner's native language if meaning was conveyed directly through demonstration and action." [Rich 01, p. 11] It concentrates "[...] upon good pronunciation, oral work, inductive teaching of grammar, genuine reading, and [...] realita." [Krau 16, p. 53] A representative for the direct method is Maximilian Berlitz (1852-1921); he did not claim originality, and others developed similar methods under different names [Dill 78].

Audio-lingual method: US Government's need for fluent speakers of other languages than English around World War II contributed to the development of the *oral approach* [Rich 01, p. 53], which was later, during the space race in the 1950s, refined to the *audio-lingual* method. It is strongly influenced by the structural linguistics and behaviourist theory and can be seen as a "[...] contemporary version of the direct method with a new emphasis on the *communicative value* of the foreign language taught in class." [Muka 05, p. 78-79] The audio-lingual method "drills students in the use of grammatical sentence patterns" [Lars 00, p. 35]. In the classroom, typically a short dialogue item is introduced, either by the teacher, or with an audio recording, and then repeated and/or systematically varied by the class. According to the behaviourist theory, the learner is trained with reinforcement, i. e. immediate feedback on correct or incorrect productions. The use of the student's native language was deprecated.

Although the theoretical foundations of the audio-lingual method were later questioned [Chom 59], and the efficiency shown to be sub-optimal, at least parts of the method are still used in today's classrooms and textbooks.

Communicative language teaching: Like all modern languages teaching methods, *communicative language teaching* (CLT) has the goal of communicative competence, but "[...] the implications of this goal have been explored more thoroughly and explicitly than before" [Litt 81, p. x] by the communicative movement. It "[...] pays systematic attention to functional as well as structural aspects of language" [Litt 81, p. 1] and emphasizes interaction as a means of learning. Typical classroom activities are role-plays, discussions, problem-solving tasks, simulations, projects and games. Fluency is more important than accuracy.

With its comprehensive claim it is generally seen as an approach rather than a method. This approach can be interpreted in a strong and weak fashion: "The weak version which has become more or less standard practice in the last ten years, stresses the importance of providing learners [of English] with opportunities to use their English for communicative purposes and, characteristically, attempts to integrate such activities into a wider program of language teaching. [...] The 'strong' version of communicative teaching, on the other hand, advances the claim that language is acquired through communication, so that it is not merely a question of activating an existing but inert knowledge of the language, but of stimulating the development of the language itself. If the former could be described as 'learning to use' English, the latter entails 'using English to learn it'." [Howa 84, p. 279]

CLT, and especially its refinement *Task-based language teaching* (TBLT), are supposed to overcome problems of many classical approaches, such as all approaches that apply a synthetic syllabus, i.e. break up language into "[...] discrete linguistic items for presentation one at a time" [Long 92, p. 28], such as words or verb tenses. SLA "[...] research shows that people do not learn isolated items in the L2 one at a time, in additive, linear fashion, but as parts of complex mappings of groups of form-function relationships. Nor, in principle, could languages be learned in that way given that many items share a symbiotic relationship: Learning English negation, for example, entails knowing something about word order, auxiliaries, and how to mark verbs for time, person, and number. Progress in one area depends on progress in the others." [Long 92, p. 31] In TBLT, on the other hand, "[...] students are given functional tasks that invite them to focus primarily on meaning exchange and to use language for real-world, non-linguistic purposes." [Bran 06, p. 12] The tasks "[...] provide a vehicle for the presentation of appropriate target language samples to learners—input which they will inevitably reshape via application of general cognitive processing capacities—and for the delivery of comprehension and production opportunities of negotiable difficulty." [Long 92, p. 43] A special characteristic of TBLT is that in spite of the abandonment of a synthetic syllabus, an *occasional* focus on form is encouraged [Long 92] to "[...] deal with its known shortcomings, particularly rate of development and incompleteness where grammatical accuracy is concerned." [Long 00, p. 599] As tasks are to be selected and modified according to the needs and skills of the students, TBLT makes high demands on the skills of the teacher.

1.3.3   Goals of second language education

What exactly should be the aim of second language teaching: Is it native-like mastery, or just the ability to freely communicate in the L2? This question is especially pertinent to pronunciation skills:

> "Is it really necessary for most language learners to acquire a perfect pronunciation? Intending secret agents and intending teachers have to, of course, but most other language learners need no more than a comfortably intelligible pronunciation (and by 'comfortably' intelligible, I mean a pronunciation which can be understood with little or no conscious effort

on the part of the listener). I believe that pronunciation teaching should have, not a goal which must of necessity be normally an unrealised ideal, but a limited purpose which will be completely fulfilled; the attainment of intelligibility." [Aber 49]

There may of course be individual deviations from that guideline, and there are also aspects beyond intelligibility to consider, e. g. the fact that a foreign accent makes speakers seem less truthful to listeners [Lev 10]. Nevertheless, there seems to be a general consensus that *intelligibility* is a goal fair enough.

If this is agreed, the next question is, especially for English as a second language (ESL), *who* should be able to understand the learner comfortably? Asked the other way around, which accent should be taught? Traditionally, the answer would have been some sort of standardized British or American accent, but with globalization, the role of English as a lingua franca makes things more complicated [Dewe 07]: "[. . .] there are more than 300 million non-native English speakers (NNSs) who may regularly use English to communicate more with each other than with native English speakers (NSs). These speakers have no need of a near-native accent and should not be forced to choose between two models or 'brands' of English that they may not want to identify with" [Daue 11, referring to [Jenk 00] and [McAr 02]].

The *English as an international language* movement acknowledges this: the non-native speakers of English are "[. . .] language users in their own right" [Seid 04] and there is a need for "[. . .] a description of salient features of English as a lingua franca (ELF), alongside English as a native language (ENL)." [Seid 04] As a key contribution in this field, Jenkins proposed the *lingua franca core* (LFC) [Jenk 98, Jenk 00, Jenk 02] which is a list of simplified pronunciation rules for which "[. . .] intelligibility for NNS rather than for native speaker (NS) receivers is the primary motivation." [Jenk 02] "The LFC departs from current pronunciation methodology by emphasizing segmentals (consonants and vowels) and downplaying the importance of suprasegmentals (rhythm, word stress, and intonation). Many current texts written from a NS orientation [. . .], emphasize the teaching of prosody as the most efficient way of achieving some measure of fluency, which seems to be highly correlated with NSs' perceptions of intelligibility and thus is important for scoring well on oral proficiency tests." [Daue 11] In contrast, Jenkins says "[. . .] for EIL, and especially for NBESs [nonbilingual English speakers, commonly known as non-native speakers], the greatest phonological obstacles to mutual intelligibility appear to be deviant core sounds in combination with misplaced and/or misproduced nuclear stress." [Jenk 00, p. 155] Some examples of these simplified pronunciation rules are:

- word stress may be changed, but nuclear and contrastive stress must be produced and placed correctly;

- intelligible substitutions of /θ/ and /ð/ are acceptable, such as /f/ and /v/, respectively;

- vowels may be added to consonant clusters: 'product', e. g., may be pronounced as /pərˈɒdʌkʊtɔ/.

The LFC has met with considerable criticism. Dauer, for instance, points out several inconsistencies and defects [Daue 11], for example, the difficulty of teaching correct placement of nuclear stress when the concept of word stress has not been introduced to the students, and even questions that the LFC is more teachable or learnable. She agrees however, that

- "A 'foreign accent' is okay [...] and teachers, test makers, and the wider public should [...] be more tolerant of it, as we should of all varieties of English. [...]

- Intelligibility should not be defined exclusively in relation to NSs [native speakers] [...]

- Fluency is rewarded on speaking tests, possibly more than it should be in relation to accuracy and clarity." [Daue 11]

1.3.4   Role of learner

Not only the goals of second language education may be different for each learner, but also the means for achieving these goals best. Besides individual differences such as motivation or learning styles [Pask 72] that should ideally be taken into account, one can identify characteristic needs of certain groups of learners.

A decisive factor is the L1 of the learner. Abercrombie argues that for the goal of comfortably intelligible pronunciation, the syllabus should focus on aspects that are important for intelligibility and difficult for the targeted learners; aspects less important for intelligibility should only be included if they do not present a major difficulty [Aber 49, p. 121]. This also applies for suprasegmental aspects [Miss 99b], and the rhythm class of L1 and L2 plays an important role: "Rhythm need not concern, for example, a German, but very possibly speakers of French should give attention to it before they tackle anything else." [Aber 49, p. 122]

Other aspects that can be important are the age of the learner, and the purpose of learning the L2. For instance, pupils learning languages in school as part of their general education may have different competences, needs and motivations than adults who have to improve their language competences for professional purposes in corporate training programs. The latter often have considerable written competence but clear deficiencies in pronunciation, with *fossilized* errors that might need special attention in the instruction program.

1.3.5   Segmental and suprasegmental aspects

There is nowadays a general consensus on the importance of teaching intelligible pronunciation. The relative importance of segmental and suprasegmental aspects, however, is subject of a lively debate. "[...] for many years, and especially in the formative period of modern linguistic theory in the second quarter of the twentieth century, the study of these [prosodic] features suffered from relative neglect. With some exceptions, phonological descriptions were based primarily on 'segments'—vowels and consonants—and prosodic features were either ignored or forced into an inappropriate segmental mould." [Fox 00, p. 1] This deficiency was also present in second language education, and numerous authors have pointed out the important role of prosody for communication, and argued that more attention should be given to teaching suprasegmental aspects. "Suprasegmentals provide the framework for utterances, they direct the listener's attention to important information in the discourse, and they help to establish cultural harmony between the speaker and listener." [Ande 92] "Suprasegmental features are manifested in terms of acoustic cues and convey important information about linguistic and information structures. Hence, L2 learners must harness appropriate suprasegmental productions for effective communication." [Meng 09] Some authors even hold the view that "[...] prosodic deviations have a more negative influence on the communicative effect of speech acts than segmental mistakes." [Miss 07]

Teaching prosody is difficult: "However, in spite of their importance in communication, suprasegmentals often elude ESL students. When listening to spoken discourse, students so often focus on comprehension at the lexical level that they do not attend to the overriding melody and rhythm of utterances, and, because they do not hear these features of speech, they have difficulty producing them" [Ande 92]. A number of techniques have been suggested to draw the student's attention to suprasegmental aspects: "[...] techniques for isolating intonation from lexical meaning are the use of hand movements [...], drawing intonation contours [...], and humming. Rhythm can be similarly isolated by tapping [...], clapping, or whispering" [Ande 92]. Gilbert suggests to use musical equipment—a *kazoo*[7]:

> "Second language learners don't hear intonation very well. [...] they are powerfully distracted from paying attention to the 'music' because they are struggling to understand strange sounds, word meaning, and difficult grammar. [...] My suggestion is that we should offer him a speech model stripped of everything but melody and rhythm. [...] For a [...] practical approach, I recommend the kazoo." [Gilb 91, p. 319]

Prosodic training indeed seems to have a positive influence on the learner's communicative competences: "In fact, it is [...] a combined, intensive focus on suprasegmental aspects of pronunciation and on general speech characteristics [...] that appears to be most effective in improving learner's intelligibility over time" [Kenn 09, p. 133]. Interestingly, prosodic training also seems to help on the segmental level: "Experimental data (Missaglia 1997) showed that correct pronunciation is largely dependent on the self-control of intonation—also in L1—and on the correct accentuation [...]. Once the learners acquired a rudimentary prosodic competence, many phonological interferences disappeared [...]. Correct prosodic perception or production have proved to have positive consequences on the segmental level." [Miss 07, referring to [Miss 97]]

The trend towards emphasizing suprasegmental aspects in second language education has not remained uncriticised. Firstly, some suprasegmental aspects (such as word accent or intonation) vary considerably between different dialects of an L2, and are also subject to change over time [Crys 94]. "Word stress patterns differ quite markedly among L1 varieties of English, most notably RP [received pronunciation] and GA [general American], with no great subsequent loss of intelligibility. In addition, stress patterns may change over time with the dictates of fashion [...]. All this suggests that L1 speakers are capable of a fair degree of flexibility in this

---

[7]a small and inexpensive membranophone, a wind instrument which can be sung or spoken into, modifying the voice by means of a vibrating membrane

area." [Jenk 00, p. 40] Secondly, not all suprasegmental aspects contribute much to intelligibility, especially in an *English as a lingua franca* setting (cf. Section 1.3.3). Care has also to be taken not to equate fluency with intelligibility, although the first "[...] seems to be highly correlated with NSs' perceptions of intelligibility and thus is important for scoring well on oral proficiency tests." [Daue 11]

Altogether, it seems that a compromise should be made: A considerable part of the instruction should focus on phrase accent and phrase boundaries ([Chel 08]: "[...] division of the stretch of speech into *meaningful chunks*"; [Jenk 00, p. 159]: "Nuclear stress production and placement and division of speech stream into word groups."), and also rhythm if the learners' L1 does not belong to the rhythm class of L2 ([Aber 49, p. 122]; [Chel 08]; [Daue 11]: "[...] vowel reduction may be very important for the [learner]"). Also the teaching of word accent seems advisable [Daue 11]. Thus, our selection of prosodic functions in 1.2.3 is definitely justifiable.

1.3.6   Perception and production

Competences and deficiencies in language production are not independent of *perception*. In fact, "Incorrect pronunciation is mainly to be attributed to the learners' distorted perception(!) of L2 sounds and intonation, i. e. a perception filtered by the mother tongue's characteristics, rather than to defective speech, i. e. to a deficit in the speakers' phonatory apparatus." [Miss 99a] Consider, e. g. the difficulties of Japanese learners in correctly producing the English sounds /r/ and /l/ if they have not learned yet to perceive that these form a phonemic contrast—which is not present in their native language [Slaw 99]. Indeed, perception training can improve learner's productions [Eske 09, Haza 05], and foreign accent is correlated to perception performance (comprehension ability) [McAl 98]. Perception training also works for prosody: "[...] training in the perception of intonation resulted in a statistically significant improvement in the production of English intonation patterns." [Bot 82]

1.3.7   Tests

A number of language tests have been developed to measure the proficiency of a speaker in a standardized, objective way. Often, universities, authorities and other employees require applicants to pass a certain test for admittance. The most widespread test for English is the *Test of English as a foreign language* (TOEFL®). It has been developed to test the language competences of applicants to U.S. universities, and comprises reading, listening, speaking and writing tasks which are evaluated by human raters. TOEFL is administered and developed further by the non-profit organization *Educational testing service* (ETS). The current version, the "TOEFL iBT test is the most widely accepted English language assessment, used for admissions purposes in more than 130 countries including the United Kingdom, Canada, Australia, New Zealand and the United States." [Educ 11] ETS is conducting a comprehensive research program[8] around TOEFL, including validity and *washback*, i. e. the feedback effects on teaching of a widely deployed test [Educ 11].

---

[8]`http://www.ets.org/toefl/research` (last visited September 8th, 2017)

1.4 Computer-assisted language learning

Computer-assisted language learning (CALL) has been defined tersely as "[...] the search for and study of applications of the computer in language teaching and learning." [Levy 97, p. 1] As such, it is in principle concerned with helping the learner in every aspect of language learning, by the use of computer technologies such as audio/video reproduction, synthesis, and analysis or connecting learners/teachers via the internet. Although this could apply to all sorts of language learners, such as adolescent or handicapped native speakers, CALL usually refers to learning a second language. Nevertheless, many issues and techniques of CALL are likewise found, e. g. in technology for diagnosis and therapy of speech pathologies such as dysarthria, laryngectomy, and cleft lip and palate [Schu 06, Maie 09b]: The needs of speakers who have a congenital or acquired deficiency in language production and perception will have a high overlap with those of non-native learners.

Given the deficiencies of traditional instruction (space, time, and economical restrictions; possible shortcomings of teacher), CALL systems have a huge potential for supporting the language learner, e. g. by simulating aspects of one-to-one tutoring, or aspects of first language acquisition such as the exposure to large amounts of L2 speech. Many existing CALL systems, however, cannot be called much more than the digitalization of existing textbook language courses with a few attached grammar and pronunciation exercises. Yet recently, dedicated suppliers of CALL software have developed impressive comprehensive systems (cf. 1.4.1), and it will be interesting to see which CALL systems the next decade will give birth to, given the lasting demand from the private, industrial, and also military sector for second language learning, plus the technological progress in adjacent fields such as automatic speech recognition (ASR).

Alternative names for CALL are CALI (Computer-assisted language instruction), CALT (Computer-assisted language technologies), and TELL (Technology-enhanced language learning). SLaTE (Speech and language technology in education) focusses on technological aspects. A little confusingly, SLATE (Spoken language technology for education; note the capital 'A') has been used for the sub-area of *spoken* language and thus excludes non-spoken language processing [Eske 09]. CAPT (Computer-Assisted Pronunciation Training) is further restricted to the use of automatic analysis of pronunciation and suitable feedback. Non-spoken language, i. e. grammar and lexicon, is the realm of intelligent language tutoring systems (ILTS) [Schw 90], more recently known as ICALL ("Intelligent CALL") [Matt 92]. Here, methods and conceptualizations from natural language processing (NLP) and general artificial intelligence (AI) are applied.

CALL is embedded in the field of general E-learning (alias online learning, online education or computer-assisted instruction), where currently a trend can be observed towards applying crowd-sourcing techniques in order to personalize education, not only with respect to instruction and grading, but also to the curriculum [Weld 12]. Such approaches might be particularly suitable for second language learning. The related term *augmented learning* specifically emphasizes that the learning is adapting to the learner.

Blended or hybrid learning refers to the combination of CALL with traditional classroom-based instruction or one-to-one human tutoring. MALL (Mobile assisted language learning) focusses on aspects of ubiquitous access and collaborative learning [Chin 06]. Different names for CALL and related fields reflect its history and interdisciplinarity: The older term CALI (from general CAI, computer-assisted instruction) was superseded by CALL when CALI was suspected of an outdated focus on teacher/instruction. Related fields like ICALL have their roots in different areas and may have slightly different aims, sometimes more specific than the name suggests (e. g. the focus of ICALL on grammar).

CALL is highly interdisciplinary. It inherits the interdisciplinarity of SLA we have discussed above: a given CALL system may need to account for psychological, linguistic and pedagogic principles. In addition, on the technical side, it will depend on the available computer hard- and software, and potentially on signal processing, computer graphics, and artificial intelligence, in particular machine learning, ASR, and natural language processing. It is evident that throughout the history of CALL, existing systems have been a mirror of the progress in these areas [Levy 97, p. 1]. The presentation of material evolved from text-only displays to rich multimedia, and interaction grew from typing only to include the use of speech and gestures. CALL has also been reflecting progress and fashion in second language pedagogy: curriculum-driven systems are being substituted by systems that adapt to the capabilities and learning style of the user; drill and isolated exercises are being superseded by task-based learning units and communicative approaches, e. g. the embedding of the learner in virtual environments to interact with virtual characters.

One of the most obvious domains of CALL is *pronunciation*: It is usually difficult to tackle for L2 learners, vital for intelligibility and often under-represented in language instruction. *Computer-assisted pronunciation training* (CAPT), on the other hand, can provide "[...] a private, stress-free environment with virtually unlimited access to input and self-paced practice" and "[...] individualized, instantaneous feedback." [Neri 02] CAPT is one of the most challenging technical aspect of CALL, as it necessitates the automatic analysis of the learner's productions in order to decode content and meaning, and to detect pronunciation errors.

Second language pronunciation competence is closely linked to perception (cf. Section 1.3.6). Consequently pronunciation training is often complemented by perception training in CALL systems, e. g. in the form of identification exercises for phonemic contrasts, or word accent position. Note that perception training comes at very little cost compared to pronunciation training with—possibly erroneous—feedback. The only possible source of errors are the reference speakers, but that can be neglected when qualified native speakers are employed.

1.4.1   State of the art in computer-assisted language learning

During the last decade, CALL has evolved remarkably. Still in 1998 Ehsani and Knodt noted that "[...] the practical impact of CALL in the field of foreign language education has been rather modest." [Ehsa 98] From the pedagogical side, they identified criticism about the "[...] lack of a unified theoretical framework for designing and evaluating CALL systems" [Ehsa 98], and "[...] the absence of conclusive empirical evidence for the pedagogical benefits of computers in language learning" [Ehsa 98]. The field was also blamed of technology push: "[. . .] many commercial systems tend to prefer technological novelties that do not always comply with pedagogical criteria" [Neri 02]. There were (and still are) also limitations of the involved technology: ASR will make errors, much more often than a human does. As of 2009, the "[. . .] man-machine-gap in terms of the signal-to-noise ratio (SNR) was estimated to be 15 dB, i. e., the masking level in ASR has to be lowered by 15 dB to achieve the same performance as human listeners." [Meye 09] Ehsani and Knodt, however, object to the fatalistic view expressed in some pedagogical publications (e. g. [Higg 88, Sala 96]) poignantly paraphrased as "Because speech technology isn't perfect, it is of no use at all." [Ehsa 98] On the contrary, speech technology as an "[. . .] essential component of CALL [. . .] is, in fact, ready to be deployed successfully in second language education, provided that the current limitations of the technology are understood and systems are designed in ways that work around these limitations." [Ehsa 98]

Ehsani and Knodt were quite right: Today we see mature and commercially successful CALL systems that are used widely in the private, educational, industrial and military sector. The benefit of both research and commercial CALL systems for learner progress has now been proven in a number of studies [Eske 07, Hard 04, Hans 13, Neri 08, Cucc 09]. Two prominent examples of successful commercial systems are Alelo's Language and Culture Training System[9] [John 08] and Rosetta Stone's ReFLEX system [Pell 12].

Alelo's Language and Culture Training System: In Alelo's training system, students first have to master course material on the target language, and also on the culture of the target country. This is done in the form of "[. . .] interactive lessons, each of which focuses on communicative tasks." [John 08] These skills are then further developed by means of a serious game: The learner is placed into a virtual environment and has to accomplish tasks by communicating with game characters in the target language. Also some basic non-verbal communication training is included: Where appropriate, the learner has to select (from a menu) a gesture to be performed (e. g. bowing). Feedback on language performance is either "[. . .] organic feedback, meaning that it is intrinsic to the behavior of the characters in the simulation" [John 12], e. g. the learner is misunderstood by the game character if speech input was not intelligible. More details on the learner's performance, e. g. on vocabulary usage or pronunciation is only given after a unit has been completed because "[. . .] such feedback would tend to break the sense of immersion in the simulation and turn it into a pronunciation exercise." [John 12] Generally, pronunciation skills of the learner are considered relevant but subordinate to the development of communicative competence.

ASR technology is imperfect, and recognizing non-native speech is especially error-prone. One might therefore wonder how Alelo's system manages to conduct the conversations between learners and game characters at all. In fact, the system seems to be a successful realization of Ehsani and Knodt's suggestions of "[. . .] how to create robust interactive learning environments that exploit the strengths of speech technology while working around its limitations." [Ehsa 98] Primarily, we can identify

---

[9]https://www.alelo.com/tilts (last visited September 8th, 2017)

two measures: the adaptation of speech technology to the specific group of targeted learners, and the adaptation to the specific domain language of the dialogues. For example, Alelo trains their "[...] speech recognition models using a mixture of native speech and learner speech. The incorporation of learner speech helps to ensure that the input system is relatively tolerant of variability in accent." [John 12] Thus, speech recognition is acoustically tailored for a certain L1 group. A complementary measure is to restrict the words and phrases to be recognized during the dialogue to the covered course material, which reduces the opportunities for recognition errors. This may first seem over-simplistic and prejudiced, but is very effective especially for beginners, who otherwise would hardly be understood at all by an ASR system. Besides, the underlying assumption of no prior exposure to the target language can be a reasonable one for certain learner groups, such as US American soldiers learning Iraqi Arabic. And as soon as the learner progresses, the perplexity of the speech input considered is increased, effectively "[...] increasing the accuracy threshold for the learner's speech" [John 12]. Outside the virtual dialogues, the detection of pronunciation and other errors is desired. This is "[...] achieved by incorporating common learner errors into the language model." [John 12] Again, we see here that the chances of false alarms are reduced by restricting the errors to be detected to those frequent in the targeted L1 group.

Rosetta Stone's ReFLEX: ReFLEX has been designed by Rosetta Stone, the market leader in CALL software, specifically for Korean learners of English. Passing English exams is very important for university admission and career steps in Korea, which explains why outstanding amounts of time and money are invested into English education. For a variety of reasons, many learners have advanced skills in grammar, reading and vocabulary, but their oral skills fall far behind, and often they are practically unable to converse with native English speakers [Pell 12]. ReFLEX addresses the two main problems pronunciation and oral practice. Training is scheduled as a daily 30-minute session, comprising practising sound skills, rehearsing conversational dialogues, and a short one-to-one conversation practice with a native American tutor via an internet audio/video connection.

Sound skill training consists of perceiving and producing challenging sound contrasts in game-like activities. Rehearsing conversation is done by means of pre-scripted dialogues, which are first presented by replaying recordings of native speakers. The learner then practices the dialogue by repeating the utterances of one of the dialogue partners. After having mastered that, the learner has to manage his or her part of the dialogue without prompting. Depending on the dialogue state, the learner can also deviate from the originally provided utterances. To enhance the sense of reality, the dialogues are implemented in a 3D virtual world. Similar to the conversation training of Alelo, there is no feedback on errors during the dialogues; speech processing is restricted to understanding what the learner tries to say.

Technically, ReFLEX uses non-native data to train the acoustic models used for the dialogues, i.e. it adapts to the targeted Korean learners. Additionally, the acoustic parameters are adapted over time to the characteristics of the individual user's speech. The chance of misrecognitions is further reduced by restricting the speech to be recognized to the phrases of the current dialogue plus those the learner has presumably acquired in previous dialogue sessions (a dedicated module keeps track of the learner's progress in that respect).

The acoustic models used for phoneme error detection and identification are solely estimated using native speech. However, the errors to be detected are restricted to those common in Korean learners. These errors are modelled in a principled, data-driven way: a statistical machine translation model is estimated with a corpus of canonical and transcribed non-native pronunciations. Likely errors are then obtained by automatically translating from canonical to non-native pronunciation. The statistical translation model can generate multiple translation hypotheses; only the first few are considered to restrict the possibly identified errors to the most frequent ones. Again, this is a strong specialization of a CALL system to the targeted L1 group of learners.

The specialization of these two systems to the Learner's L1 is the key for success in implementing such ambitious features as (semi-free) spoken dialogue or phoneme error identification. It is also in accord with the idea that a teacher should "[...] have a knowledge of [...] his pupils' native language" [Aber 49], since "[...] speakers of different L1s have different problems for any given target language (L2)." [Eske 09] It has to be noted, however, that this specialization requires a high effort during system development and deployment and may not be commercially worthwhile for many L1/L2 pairs (cf. Section 1.4.4). A way out of this misery might be new algorithms that lower the amount of required manual annotation (e. g. based on unsupervised learning [Glas 12, Jans 13]).

1.4.2 Analysing the learner's productions

Central to ambitious CALL systems are components that are able to automatically assess the quality of the learner's language. This assessment can be specified with respect to a number of factors:

Scope: The learner's language can be assessed on a global, more long-term scale[10]. Examples for global assessment are holistic pronunciation quality across a sentence, and vocabulary richness within an essay. Local assessment, on the other hand, relates to the pronunciation of individual items such as phrases, words, syllables, or phonemes. Generally, global assessment will be easier and more reliable, and local assessment more difficult and less reliable. As a rationale, consider that regardless of whether a human or a machine is rating, assessments will always include a certain amount of error due to noise in the speech signal and rater deficiencies (e. g. fatigue in the case of the human, or imperfection of the model used or of the parameters estimated in case of the machine). In the case of global assessment, however, decisions will be more stable: for human assessors, several local impressions are (at least unconsciously) aggregated to form a more reliable decision; algorithms for automatic assessment similarly use more stable acoustic features (characteristics) that are averaged over several local contexts, or they combine local decisions whose errors tend to cancel out because they are often occurring independently of each other.

---

[10]This long-term assessment has been called *pronunciation assessment* [Eske 09]. Note that we use assessment in a broader sense.

Granularity : Assessment can further be characterized as either gradual or discrete. In the first case, quality is holistic, essentially a continuum—even when the labels given by human raters are often selected from a finite set such as an (ordinal) Likert scale. Discrete assessments are classifications of learner output into a (not necessarily ordinal) set of choices like 'correct' or 'wrong'. Usually, global assessments are gradual: the overall pronunciation quality of a sentence is clearly a continuous quantity; classifying it just as either right or wrong would not be very adequate. Local assessments, on the other hand, are often discrete: the realization of a phoneme can well be classified as either acceptable or not. Even though the realization itself is a continuous process, and the borderline between right and wrong cannot be clearly defined, a gradual appraisal of such a local phenomenon would be very laborious for human raters, and of limited use for the learner. Discrete assessment can further be subdivided into *error detection* and *error identification*. Error detection has to decide whether a particular item is acceptable or not; error identification additionally has to specify which error has been made, e. g. which article is missing, or which phoneme substitution has occurred. As an exception to the rule above, *error diagnosis*, i. e. the identification of frequent errors of an individual learner, is global and yet discrete.

Object: Regarding the object of analysis, one can either assess the uttered words (vocabulary, morphology, syntax, pragmatics), or the manner of production, i. e. pronunciation. Grammar exercises are common in CALL systems, however, in "[. . .] the majority of these systems the learner's output is provided in the written modality, by means of a keyboard and/or a mouse (clicking, drag & drop, etc.). Although this way of practicing may be successful for learning the grammar of the target language, it is questionable whether the knowledge thus acquired really contributes to speaking the target language more correctly." [Stri 10] Few systems have attempted to analyse non-native speech with respect to grammatical correctness. Strik et al. lay one foundation for analysing syntax in non-native speech [Stri 10]: Since it is not straightforward how to determine syntactic errors, they propose a method for automatically generating an inventory of common errors from a suitably annotated corpus of non-native speech. This corpus comprises transcriptions plus corresponding target utterances, i. e. what the speakers presumably have been trying to say. The method uses part-of-speech (POS) tagging and aligns the erroneous non-native transcriptions to the correct target utterances. Each deletion, insertion, and substitution then constitutes—together with the identified POS category—a certain error type (e. g. omission of an article, or using the wrong verb). Automatically assessing the pronunciation of non-native speech is much more common in CALL, and, at least for segmental aspects, established in commercial products at a profound level (cf. Section 1.4.1).

Once the desired assessment has been specified in the above terms, the next step is to design algorithms that are capable of such automatic assessments. Here, the *pattern recognition* approach turned out particularly effective: collect *annotated data* (i. e. speech items plus associated labels indicating learners' errors or pronunciation quality), develop procedures to automatically compute suitable *features* (i. e. acoustic parameters of the speech items), and create classification or regression systems that map the computed features to error classes or scores, using *machine learning* techniques, i. e. constructing these models automatically from the annotated data in a statistical, data-driven way. One can distinguish two main approaches to applying pattern recognition techniques for pronunciation modelling [Hön 12a]:

Generative or indirect: The model only describes what is *acceptable*, and a distance measure is used to derive a score or to decide for 'correct' or 'error'. The advantage is that data collection is far easier: We can use native speech, and more importantly, when neglecting the few errors that native speakers make as well, we do not need the expensive error annotations to build the model. For example, when detecting mispronounced phonemes, we can use just transcribed native speech to build models for correctly produced phonemes, and use the *probability* according to the model that the observed speech signal corresponds to the target phoneme sequence as a similarity measure. For *evaluating* how well such an approach works on non-native data, we do, however, need annotated data from non-native speakers that includes examples of both good and bad speaking performance. Yet, the sample can be much smaller than the one needed for building the model. The most well-known generative approach is probably the Goodness of Pronunciation (GOP) score [Witt 99], which is an efficient approximation of the probability of the target phonemes.

Discriminative or direct: Here we model *both* acceptable and unacceptable pronunciations (or the decision boundary between them). The pronunciation score, or the decision 'correct' or 'wrong', is a direct output of the classification or regression module. This approach has the potential for maximum accuracy, as the data-driven methods are estimated with the 'real thing'—the actual target outputs—and thus can play to their strengths. However, data collection is much more expensive, as enough *annotated* non-native speech comprising both good and bad pronunciations is needed to get good performance—*much* more than for the evaluation of generative approaches. For the example of identifying mispronounced phonemes, this is practically infeasible in the general case due to data sparsity resulting from coarticulation effects and different L1s. For modelling frequent errors of a certain target L1, however, such as $[\theta] \rightarrow [s]$ and $[\eth] \rightarrow [z]$ for German learners of English, it may be the method of choice. Examples of the discriminative approach are [Tsub 02] and [Truo 05], where classifiers such as linear discriminant analysis or decision trees are used to distinguish between correctly pronounced phonemes and frequent error patterns.

In practice, both approaches are often mixed to reach satisfying accuracy at manageable cost, e. g. a generative model is used for correctly pronounced phonemes but information is included about likely phoneme substitutions of the target learners in order to identify errors, as we have seen in both state-of-the-art systems in Section 1.4.1.

For creating reference annotations, "[...] human judgment [...] is used as the gold standard" [Eske 09]. Individual decisions of human raters may be error-prone, especially for local assessment. This can be alleviated by employing multiple raters

and combining their votes. The object of analysis determines whether experts need
to be employed: for identifying phoneme substitutions, we need phoneticians; for a
more global assessment of pronunciation quality, naïve raters can suffice, as long as
they are native speakers of the target language [Hön 11]. In economic terms, it can
be favourable to hire a larger number of naïve raters instead of a smaller number
of experts in order to reach a certain reliability for the combined annotation. Naïve
labellers can be acquired easily and inexpensively with *crowdsourcing*[11] techniques,
although "[...] the incoming data must go through quality assessment" [Eske 13,
p. xv] or be intelligently combined [Rayk 12], and parts of the data may even have to
be processed by a trusted annotator [Penn 12]. Also employee rights should be taken
into account[12] [Fels 11].

As a substitute for expensive annotations, one can also collect data from both
native and non-native speakers and use just the information of whether a speaker is
native or not as a reference [Tepp 10]. While this is a good method to generate large
quantities of training data for machine learning algorithms, one should additionally
define which aspect of pronunciation is targeted and manually annotate at least a
small subset of the non-native data accordingly—in the same sense as the suitability
of generative approaches needs to be evaluated with non-native data. In the general
case, due to the varying proficiency among non-native speakers, nativeness alone
cannot be expected to be a particular precise and suitable reference.

1.4.3   Feedback

The ability to give feedback about the learner's productions is central to CALL systems and can be a great help for second language learning. Although humans acquire
their first language to perfection with little explicit feedback about pronunciation or
grammar, and to a large part in an unsupervised manner, the case is quite different
for second language learning. As discussed earlier, insufficient L2 exposure, declin-
ing acquisition ability with age, and interfering L1 phonology and grammar form
obstacles. *Corrective* or *negative* feedback, i. e. any "[...] indication to the learners
that their use of the target language is incorrect" [Ligh 99, p. 71], can therefore contribute considerably to learners' progress [Prec 00, Neri 06]: with the help of this
supervision, the learner can enhance his or her interlanguage (internal representation
of the target language, cf. Section 1.3.1), sharpen perception, tune his or her internal
production-perception feedback loops [Cass 10], and notice fossilized errors. "Feedback has to be genuinely responsive, so that learners are allowed to experience the
effect of what they utter as a guide in their subsequent output" [Camp 03b]. Also,
feedback should be locally confined so that the learner is able to trace the source
of an error (e. g. pinpointing a certain phoneme that is mispronounced, instead of a
whole word).

At what points in the curriculum of CALL systems is feedback useful? One
rule seems to be not to exaggerate. For example, there is a consensus that only

---

[11] A portmanteau made from 'outsourcing to the crowd': "[...] the act of a company or institution
taking a function once performed by employees and outsourcing it to an undefined (and generally
large) network of people in the form of an open call." [Howe 06]

[12] The website `http://faircrowd.work` lists fairness ratings for different cloud service providers;
a cloud worker organization can be found on `http://www.wearedynamo.org`.

one error should be pointed out at a time. Also, feedback should not disturb other goals: it is no coincidence that both commercial CALL systems described above (cf. Section 1.4.1) intentionally avoid giving any feedback on pronunciation (or on form) during communicative competence training. There is only implicit feedback on intelligibility: the virtual dialogue partners understand the learner's utterance or not. This is also owed to the fact that at least currently, sufficiently reliable pronunciation (or grammar) error detection on top of the already highly challenging non-native ASR is beyond the state of the art. It is conceivable that with further technical progress, there might be situations even during dialogue training where feedback is useful, e. g. to point out which part of an utterance makes it unintelligible or mistakable. During other parts of the curriculum such as skill-building exercises, feedback is of course an integral part, and can be used without further consideration, e. g. reporting 'correct'/'incorrect' in minimal pairs production or perception exercises.

Ideally, feedback should also be highly adjusted to the competences of the learner: using suitable "pronunciation error gravity hierarchies" [Neri 02], only severe errors should be fed back to beginners; conversely, for the advanced learners one can try to tackle the more subtle issues (given sufficient reliability of detection). Feedback mechanisms should also be intelligent enough not to report a certain error over and over again; instead, a suitable skill-building exercise should be offered.

Given the possibility of recognition errors, feedback should also be modest. It may be possible to utilize the confidence of the error detection module for deciding whether to report a supposed learner error. Here, an important question arises: When in doubt, should a possible error rather be suppressed or reported? In the literature [Bach 90, Eske 09], the pertinent terms are defined as follows:

> "There are two types of errors. The system can determine that the user pronounced a correct sound or word when in reality the sound was incorrect. This is called a *false positive*. On the other hand, the system can determine that the user pronounced an incorrect sound or word when in reality it was correct. This is called a *false negative*." [Eske 09]

This definition is somewhat of a misnomer, since generally, in a detection task *falsely detecting the item to detect* (i. e. the error) is called a false positive. We will therefore use the clearer terms *false alarm* for wrongly reporting an error, and *hit (or miss)* for identifying (or missing) a real error [Hön 09, Aria 10, Ferr 15]. So the question is, what are the relative costs of false alarms and a misses? There seems to be a general consensus that false alarms are more harmful than missing errors [Eske 09]. Dissenting, Bachmann argues that "[...] during learning, false positives [i. e. misses] may be more costly (might lead to errors fossilizing) than false negatives [i. e. false alarms] (which will just lead to redundant instructions, less likely to impair learning)." [Bach 90] Only for important graduation or employment tests, Bachmann deems false alarms more costly. This view, however, does not take into account the dissatisfaction and confusion which false alarms will create. Also it would then logically follow that all presumable errors of an utterance should be reported; this would clearly exceed the learner's comprehension.

Once it has been determined that the learner should receive corrective feedback at a particular point, how should it be given? One distinction can be made according to either *explicit* or *implicit* feedback:

Explicit feedback means that the learner is given concrete information on whether a specified part of produced output is correct or not, or how good it is on some quality scale. Also meta-linguistic explanation about in what way something is wrong, and possibly suggesting a remedy, is useful [Neri 02], e. g. identifying a mispronounced sound as an L1 phone, and giving hints on how to use the articulators to produce the correct L2 sound. Adapting these explanations and remedies to the L1 of the learner is helpful, too.

Implicit feedback also gives the learner information that something is wrong with his or her output, however in an indirect way, without interrupting the communicative situation by telling the learner "You just made a mistake!" or resorting to a meta-linguistic level. It is therefore more in accord with the communicative approach to language teaching. For an automatic system, giving implicit feedback is also less difficult—because predicting that *something* is wrong with a non-native utterance is less risky than pinpointing and characterizing the error. For this reason, using implicit feedback has been suggested in order to reduce the impact of false alarms [Wach 99]. Implicit feedback includes elicitation (e. g. pausing to let the learner complete the teacher's utterance [Lyst 97]), "[...] confirmation checks, repetitions, recasts, clarification requests, silence, and even facial expressions that express confusion." [El T 06] Recasting, i. e. uttering a corrected version of what the speaker has been trying to say, seems to be the feedback technique most commonly chosen by teachers [Lyst 97, Suzu 05]; recasts are also frequent in child-parent interaction. Locality can be increased by selecting a smaller sub-part of the utterance around the corrected item; explicitness can be increased by putting emphasis on the corrected item.

As to the effectiveness of different types of feedback, one can distinguish between uptake (i. e. any response of the learner to the feedback at all) and repair (response with successful repair). Findings about the relative effectiveness of different corrective feedback types regarding uptake and repair yielded partly contradicting results [Lyst 97, Suzu 05], and whether "[...] the rate of uptake correlates with second language learning still remains an empirical question." [Suzu 05] Obviously, optimal feedback also depends on the teaching approach, the teacher and the learner; besides, is seems likely that feedback in CALL should comprise a mix of available feedback techniques and should be adaptive to the needs of the learner [Vrie 10] both in long and short term.

Both types of feedback can be realized, or supported, by audio playback (recorded or synthesized recasts, speech transfer for illustrating mistakes in the tutor's voice or corrections in the learner's voice) and visual displays (text, recorded or synthesized videos of a target speaker, waveforms, pitch curves, loudness curves, sagittal sections, anatomic models with the skin removed to show articulatory organs). While a number of these techniques have been shown to be useful for teaching particular aspects [Fleg 88, Bot 83, Ande 92, Haza 98, Haza 05], is seems wise to strongly limit the usage of such techniques, e. g. to specific skill-building exercises. Many of these displays are not easily interpretable [Neri 02] and will confuse and distract rather than help the learner. For example, it is questionable whether a learner who does not happen to be a phonetician will benefit from seeing a sagittal section or anatomical models.

Indeed, most commercial CALL systems rely mainly on the most natural of such displays: a video recording of a talking native speaker. This is justified by the "multisensory nature of speech perception" [Bern 96], [McGu 76]; it has been shown that "[...] word identification accuracy under noisy acoustic conditions improves when the listener can also see the talker" [Bern 96], so the benefit for non-native listeners seems obvious. Less obvious is perhaps the fact that also "[...] rhythmic and timing characteristics" [Mark 96] improve when learners have access to video information on top of audio. It is worth noting that commercial providers of CALL software seem hesitant to integrate virtual tutors. For example, *Digital publishing*[13], a major German CALL system supplier, resorts to video recordings of a real tutor. A probable reason is that the virtual tutors are, at least for the time being, not realistic enough. This view is supported by the finding of Hazan et al. that adding visual cues only helped when natural visual cues were used [Haza 05].

Real-time, i.e. live feedback about the learner's speech is an especially interesting candidate for pronunciation training. It is actually a special case of *biofeedback*. Here, physiological processes are measured and presented concurrently to a person in an intuitive way, e.g. with a visual display. With that feedback loop, the person can learn to control the underlying physiological process, even if below conscious awareness and voluntary control, and often this control can be retained after feedback is withdrawn. An important field of application for biofeedback is, e.g. muscle re-training in rehabilitation [Fern 78]; but it is also used in speech therapy [Eule 09]. For learning pronunciation, which is partly below voluntary control, biofeedback is an interesting possibility: to instantaneously supply the learner with augmented information extracted live from the audio signal. For instance, one can display the first two formants to train vowel pronunciation [Dowd 98] or the pitch to train intonation [Jame 76, Bot 83]. However, there are mixed findings regarding performance beyond the training sessions [Care 04]. Indeed, there are general doubts about the usefulness of real-time feedback for learning:

> "On the surface, continuous feedback appears to be effective for learning because it guides the learner powerfully to the correct response, minimizes errors, and holds behavior on target. The problem is that the performance gains during practice are seldom carried over to retention or transfer tests in which the augmented feedback is withdrawn. The usual finding is that people who have practiced with concurrent continuous feedback often perform worse on no-feedback retention tests than do people who have practiced without such feedback." [Schm 97]

There are, however, also positive counterexamples. The "[...] reasons for these contradictory patterns of results are unclear, and further work seems warranted to understand the nature of these effects." [Schm 97] Summing up, real-time feedback remains a fascinating possibility to help the learner's awareness of his own articulatory possibilities, but the exercises or learning games should be carefully designed, and the learner should be given ample opportunity to train his or her own feedback skills based on "audition and proprioception" [Bord 79] without being distracted by augmented, artificial feedback.

---

[13]`https://www.digitalpublishing.de`, last visited September 8th, 2017

1.4.4   Economic considerations

We have seen above that taking into account the L1 of the learner is important for giving appropriate pedagogical guidance as well as for obtaining adequate performance
for automatic error detection. Tasks as delicate as pinpointing and characterizing segmental pronunciation errors are only possible if the L1 is explicitly modelled. This is
economically feasible when working in a research project, or when the target group
is large enough, as the Korean learners of English in the case of Rosetta Stone's Re-
FLEX (cf. Section 1.4.1). But consider a company targeting the European market,
offering a number of L2s for a number of L1s, with a limited number of learners (and
expected sales) per L1/L2 pair. Here, data collection for each *pair* is usually not
affordable, at least if manual annotation is involved:

> "One of the most needed resources [...] is large corpora of non-native
> transcribed speech data, of both read and conversational speech. Since
> accents vary depending on the student's first language, separate data-
> bases must either be collected for each L1 subgroup, or a representative
> sample of speakers of different languages must be included in the data-
> base. Creating such databases is extremely labour and cost intensive—a
> phone level transcription of spontaneous conversational data can cost up
> to one dollar per phone." [Ehsa 98]

Also note that simple approaches like modelling the L1 influence on phoneme productions by a closed set of possible substitution sounds may not work for the more
advanced learner: "The disparity in level of competence by the speakers resulted in
many different mistakes, mostly not representable by very general rules." [Bona 00]

Thus, a company serving the general language learning market may have to limit
automatic feedback to tasks which can be solved in an L1-independent manner. This
also has to be taken into account when evaluating the system. For example, if no
assumptions can be made about the L1 of the learner, the reliability of the system
has to be evaluated in an L1-independent manner (i.e. for all collected L1s, test with
a system that was constructed without data from that L1).

A general strategy to mitigate the problem of L1 adaptation may be to *separately*
model the targeted L1s, and derive a combined L1-L2-model automatically. For
example, one could try to suggest exercises based on the L1 of the learner [Husb 11]
or guess likely pronunciation errors, by acoustically comparing the phoneme set of
L1 and L2 [Kore 11] and identifying likely substitutions.

1.5   Contribution of this work

The aim of this work is to develop algorithms that can automatically assess the
quality of a non-native utterance with respect to its *prosody*. Individual errors such
as wrong placement of word accents are treated as well as a gradual assessment of
the general quality of the prosody of the learner's output. The chosen route to reach
this goal is the application of pattern recognition methods:

- Signal processing methods are used to compute acoustic *features* capable of
  compactly representing the speech properties we are interested in,

- *machine learning* algorithms are used to model these properties in a statistical, data-driven way for classification and regression, and

- native and non-native *labelled (annotated) speech material* is collected to 'learn', i. e. to estimate the free parameters of the classification and regression modules.

It will be analysed in how far the developed methods are independent of the L1 of the learner, and in how far they can be applied to new text material not covered by the speech databases used for constructing the models. The reliability of the algorithms is evaluated in a speaker-independent manner, i. e. tests are always conducted on speech from speakers who were previously not known to the system. The methods are applied to non-native English speech, but should be largely language independent in the sense that given an annotated database of a different new L2, they should be applicable with minimal changes (e. g. regarding language specificities about accents).

Not in the scope of this work is the pedagogic design of exercises; neither is the generation or presentation of suitable feedback. The focus of this work is on the automatic analysis of the learner's utterances with the aim of giving short-term and local feedback, yet neither real-time (concurrent) feedback on the one hand nor long-term diagnosis or language tests on the other hand. Nevertheless, the developed algorithms may also be applied for long-term diagnosis or language tests. For text-dependent analyses where the learner is expected to speak a certain, previously known sequence of words, we assume a cooperative learner, and assume that the expected words of each exercise have actually been spoken. In other words, utterance verification will not be covered here.

1.6 Structure of this work

The remainder of this thesis is structured as follows:

Chapter 2 will discuss prosody in native speech, and then analyse its role in second language acquisition.

Chapter 3 will review the state of the art in the automatic assessment of non-native prosody.

Chapter 4 will cover the pertinent mathematical and technological foundations, comprising automatic speech recognition for segmentation (localization), and the automatic computation of prosodic parameters such as the pitch contour over time, which will be the basis for the computation of acoustic features. Further, the automatic classification and regression techniques used are described.

Chapter 5 will present the corpora of audio recordings that were collected, including both native reference speakers and non-native learners.

Chapter 6 will detail the manual annotations that have been collected for the audio corpora, i. e. which categories have been defined, and how the labelling was realized. Further, comparing labeller performance and merging multiple labellers to improve reliability are discussed.

Chapter 7 will present the procedures for computing acoustic features, and the models and algorithms that have been developed for automatic error detection and prosody assessment.

Chapter 8 comprises the detailed experimental evaluation of the approaches proposed for automatic assessment, analysing the contribution of the different prosodic properties, looking at error detection and gradual assessment, and covering different scenarios such as application on known or unknown texts/exercises.

Chapter 9 will analyse, discuss and interpret the results obtained in the preceding Chapter.

Chapter 10 will summarize the main results of this work.

2

The role of prosody in first and second language

We have already seen that prosody is a vital aspect of speech, and consequently also of second language learning. While the proponents of a strong focus on prosody in general language instruction [McNe 92, Miss 99a, Miss 07] are probably too extreme, suggesting to downplay prosody (e. g. word stress errors [Jenk 00]) is not helpful either (cf. [Daue 11], Section 1.3.3). Although today "[...] we see signs that pronunciation instruction is moving away from the segmental/suprasegmental debate and toward a more balanced view" [Celc 96], it seems that prosody still tends to be underrepresented in human instruction and all the more in CALL.

To lay the ground for the methods presented for automatic prosody assessment later, in this Chapter, we will detail the relevant prosodic concepts, starting with their role in native language, defining their prototypical properties, and then analyse aspects of prosody that are specific with respect to second language learning.

2.1   Prosody in first language

Prosody provides the structural basis upon which segmentals are realized, and contributes highly to transmitting information through speech beyond that of phonemes. "The role of prosody in human speech communication cannot be overemphasized. The linguistic function of prosody covers lexical, syntactic, semantic and pragmatic information that supplements information carried by individual segments [...] A speaker expresses, either consciously or unconsciously, his/her intentions, attitude, emotion, and even physical conditions that may or may not be related to the linguistic content of the utterance" [Fuji 94, Foreword].

Prosody is such an integral part of speech that there have been speculations that speech evolved in fact from a 'proto-language' mainly characterized by pitch rather than segmentals [Darw 71, Pink 90, Fitc 00, Fitc 05, Fitc 10, Chri 03, Falk 04]. These theories are, however, hardly verifiable. What we can study, however, is how prosody is involved when an individual human develops the ability to perceive, understand, and produce speech from birth on, and even earlier in utero. This topic is highly fascinating in itself, but it might also give us relevant clues for problems and solutions in second language acquisition later.

2.1.1   Language acquisition

It is still a puzzle how children manage to acquire their native language over time
to perfection, given that there is comparatively little explicit instruction involved or
even possible. One of the first steps is learning to segregate speech from other environmental noises, and to discover regularities among the utterances of the native language [Mehl 88]. But how do children manage this even in a bilingual environment?
This question was the motivation for Mehler's studies on language discrimination
[Mehl 88]. He found out that infants as young as four days "distinguish utterances in
their native languages from those of another language." [Mehl 88] It is hardly imagin-
able that this is possible without some familiarity with the native language; this view
was also backed up by control experiments [Mehl 88]. That is, some learning has to
take place in utero. Hearing develops very early in embryos, and although limited in
amplitude, it is now established that embryos can hear the surrounding sound quite
well. (And discriminating the voice of the mother from other voices, and thus the
native language from a possible different language in the surrounding, should be facilitated by the direct sound conduction over the mother's tissue.) However, the tissue
and water surrounding the embryo act as a low-pass filter, so Mehler assumed that
"[...] much of the information necessary for distinguishing among phonetic segments
is not available prenatally." [Mehl 88] Thus, the embryo would have to rely on "[...]
prosodic characteristics such as rhythm, stress and intonation" [Mehl 88]. Indeed,
Mehler found the results in general confirmed when low-pass-filtering the stimuli at
400 Hz. Meanwhile it has been established that the filtering in utero is not too strong
[Busn 92], and that also vowels can be discriminated by embryos in utero [Part 13].
But it has also been shown that newborns do recognize speech rhythm, since they
are able to discriminate not only languages, but also language rhythm classes (stress-
timed vs. syllable-timed, cf. Section 2.1.3), even for unknown languages [Nazz 98].

  Mehler and others interpreted these findings in the light of the innateness hypothesis of Chomsky [Chom 62]: "[...] speakers of different languages use different
segmentation units, and [...] rhythm is the cue that allows the infant to select the
correct unit" ([Ramu 99] referring to [Cutl 86, Mehl 96, Otak 93]), or more generally,
"[...] each language has principles governing the structure that its syllables may take.
We hypothesize that an early determination of rhythm type may allow the child to
set some of these principles." [Ramu 99] The innateness hypothesis implies "[...] that
the human brain is 'programmed' at birth in some quite *specific* and *structured* aspects of human natural language." [Putn 67] The plausibility of that, however, has
been questioned, especially from an evolutionary point of view: It is difficult to ima-
gine how such 'template' structures for language should have evolved. It seems likely
that more general learning capabilities are responsible for speech acquisition. These
general learning capabilities are able to utilize prosodic cues, and rhythmic structures, but the ability to discriminate different rhythmic properties is probably more
basic than the ability to learn speech: It has been demonstrated that other mam-
mals like cotton-top tamarins, but also rats show the ability to discriminate language
rhythm [Toro 05]. Thus, rhythm doesn't seem to play as explicit a role for language
acquisition as hypothesized by Ramus [Ramu 99].

  More convincingly, Kuhl introduces a computational model of speech acquisition based on statistical and prosodic cues, e.g. (co)occurrence frequencies, accents

and boundaries [Kuhl 00, Kuhl 04], mediated by social interaction (e. g. *motherese*, a special speaking-style in infant-directed speech [Thie 05]): "The learning strategies—demonstrating pattern perception, as well as statistical (probabilistic and distributional) computational skills—are not predicted by historical theories. The results lead to a new view of language acquisition, one that accounts for both the initial state of linguistic knowledge in infants and infants' extraordinary ability to learn simply by listening to ambient language. The new view reinterprets the critical period for language and helps explain certain paradoxes—why infants, for example, with their immature cognitive systems, far surpass adults in acquiring a new language." [Kuhl 00]

Accents and boundaries play an important role in helping the infant segment the incoming speech. This is straightforward for pauses, which can be used to isolate words, possibly together with a referential gesture. When listening to continuous speech, the infant is faced with the challenge to segment words from the connected stream of sounds. Here, word accent can be utilized as a cue: "About 90 % of English multisyllabic words in conversational speech begin with linguistic stress on the first syllable, as in the words 'pencil' and 'stapler' [. . .]. At 7.5 months of age, English-learning infants can segment words from speech that reflect the strong–weak pattern, but not the weak–strong pattern—when such infants hear 'guitar is' they perceive 'taris' as the word-like unit, because it begins with a stressed syllable." [Kuhl 04] It is important to note, however, that the infant first has to learn the correlation between stress and word boundaries, which probably happens after or at least together with learning to use spectral cues (formant transition probabilities) for segmentation [Thie 07].

2.1.2   Word accent, phrase accents and phrase boundaries

We will now have a closer look at the most tangible aspects of prosody: word accent, phrase accents and phrase boundaries. They are pertinent for this thesis because (1) they can be associated with clear linguistic functions, and are therefore important for intelligibility, and (2) they can be characterized clearly enough to attempt the detection and diagnosis of concrete, locatable learner errors. The conceptualizations used here focus on *function* rather than on *form* (concrete phonetic realization): We do not use any intermediate phonological layer as in the *Tones and Break Indices* (ToBI) approach [Silv 92] which, for example, not only describes the presence or absence of accents but also their particular realization (pitch movement). The reason for this is that

> "All these models introduce a phonological level of description that is intermediate between *(abstract) function* and *(concrete) phonetic form*: tone sequences, holistic contours, etc. [. . .] Phonological systems like the ToBI approach [. . .] only introduce a quantisation error: the whole variety of F_0 values available in acoustics is reduced to a mere binary opposition L vs. H, and to some few additional, diacritic distinctions. This fact alone prevents tone levels (or any other *phonological prosodic* concepts such as, e. g.,the one developed within the IPO approach) from being a meaningful step that automatic processing should be based on; it seems

better to leave it up to a large feature vector and to statistical classifiers to find the form to the function." [Batl 05]

(As an example, cf. [Guin 11] where raw prosodic features outperformed automatically estimated ToBI labels.)

In line with this, *accent* here refers to "[...] the linguistic phenomenon in which a particular element of the chain of speech is singled out in relation to surrounding elements, irrespective of the means by which it is achieved." [Fox 00, p. 115] As a consequence, we use accent as a cover term for both *pitch-accent*[1] which is almost exclusively realized by pitch variation (e. g. in Japanese), and *stress-accent*, which is realized by varying duration and loudness as well (e. g. in English or German) [Fox 00, Beck 86]. As pitch-accent is rare, "[...] the terms 'accent' and 'stress' can often be used interchangeably." [Fox 00, p. 127]

Word accent: In most languages, *word accent* serves to structure the syllables within multisyllabic words. By definition, exactly one syllable bears the *primary* stress, e. g.

| able | *a*-ble | /ˈeɪ . bəl/ |
| about | a-*bout* | /ə . ˈbaʊt/, |

while the remaining syllables are either unstressed or may bear (especially in compounds) a secondary stress, e. g.

| situation | *sit*-u-*a*-tion | /ˌsɪtʃ . uː . ˈeɪ . ʃən/ |
| airport | *air*-port | /ˈɛr . ˌpɔːrt/. |

In some languages, there are fixed, simple rules for the primary word accent position. This if often referred to as *non-free word accent*. For example in French, it is always the last syllable that is stressed, unless it contains a schwa. In other languages, e. g. English, the word accent is *free* in so far as every word accent position is conceivable. For a particular word, the word accent pattern is usually fixed, although it may change over time. In British English, there are only few words such as 'controversy' or 'kilometre' for which more than one pattern is currently in use and intelligible [Jenk 00, p. 40]. In Germanic languages such as English or German, vowels in unstressed syllables are *centralized* (weakened, reduced, 'schwa-isized'), i. e. have the tendency to approach /ə/.

Research by Kenworthy, Brown, Dalton and Seidlhofer [Kenw 87, Brow 90, Dalt 94] suggests that "[...] speakers from childhood onwards identify words in the first place through their stress patterns" [Jenk 00, p. 40], perhaps comparable to the role the gross shape of printed words plays in reading for the visual identification of the words. Word accent also seems to play a role in speech acquisition by infants [Kuhl 04] (see Section 2.1.1). In this view, word accent primarily has a structuring function that eases the recognition of spoken words

---

[1]Sometimes, 'pitch accent' is used to refer to accent in the English language. This usage is, however, outdated and misleading: "Contrary to textbooks and common assumption, fundamental frequency (f_0) [plays] a minor role in distinguishing prominent syllables from the rest of the utterance." [Koch 05]; [Cutl 81, Batl 99, Batl 01]

for the listener. In some cases, word accent can even disambiguate between otherwise ambiguous segmental information: For instance, the English word 'transfer' can either be a verb, /trænts'fɜːʳ/ or a noun, /'træntsfɜːʳ/, solely discriminated by the position of the word accent. Usually, however, in English a shift of word accent is accompanied by changes in vowel quality, up to phoneme substitutions. Strong vowels in accented syllables commonly become weaker vowels when the accent is removed, e. g. /ɒ/ → /ə/ in the noun **pro**-duce /'prɒdjuːs/ and the verb pro-**duce** /prə'djuːs/ (British English, [Jone 06]).

Even if word accent is normally immutable, it is not as set in stone as normally perceived. Word accent might be realized weakly or not at all in words which do not receive phrase accents (cf. below) [Lehi 70, p. 70], [Ladd 96]. Native speakers sometimes do put word accent on non-canonical positions [Waib 86]. In Germany, one can occasionally observe a (bad) habit in the media towards wrongly placing the word accent on the first syllable (for words which canonically have a different accent position). This could be interpreted as Germanization [Zirp 08], but if done as consistently as by some politicians, it could be regarded a rhetoric technique aimed at conveying decisiveness and control, e. g.

> "Es ist für die Zukunft unserer **Demm**okratie **un**verzichtbar, die **finn**anziellen **Konn**sequenzen der **demm**ografischen **Re**volution zu **katt**alogisieren — sonst droht uns eine **Katt**astrophe." [Leic 07]
>
> (it should be Demokra**tie**, unver**zicht**bar, finanzi**ell**en, etc.).

Also the perception of actually realized word stress, even for native speakers and listeners, is subjective to some extent. For example, the perceived accent positions in word pairs such as **re**-cord vs. re-**cord** were not unanimous in as much as 12 % of the cases in [Lieb 60] (word embedded in sentence, native speakers, four ratings from two native raters).

Phrase accents: Accent can also be used to single out a particular word within the *whole phrase*. We will call that phenomenon here *phrase accent*; terms with similar meaning are 'dynamic accent' and 'nuclear stress', where nucleus relates to "[...] the most prominent syllable in any group of words." [Jenk 00, p. 42] Thus, phrase accent is a phenomenon very similar to word accent—its only the scope within prominence is determined that is larger than a word.

Phrase accents are primarily used to structure the stream of words within utterances. Phrase accents are usually put on content words, and with some exceptions, realized on the syllable bearing the primary word accent [Cutl 84, p. 77]. We discriminate here between *primary* and *secondary* phrase accents; each phrase delimited by a phrase boundary (see below) contains by definition exactly one **primary** phrase accent, and may contain multiple *secondary* phrase accents, e. g.:

> I'll *speak* to him **today**
> **excuse** me ‖ can **you** *tell* me | *how* to *get* to the **city** *museum*

In contrast to word accent there is often a number of different, equally acceptable configurations of phrase accents (and boundaries) for a given piece of written text. By indicating the most important piece of information, parsing and understanding is facilitated for the listener. For example, the sentence[2]

The old man the boat.

will usually be a bit difficult to understand [Cont 89, p. 72] during reading, as most readers will find themselves expecting something like

A man, who is old ...

i. e. their tentative parsing hypothesis (S=sentence, NP=noun phrase) will look like this:

But having read until the end of the sentence without a meaningful interpretation for this parse, the reader will restart, and eventually make out the meaning, with 'old' as a noun and 'man' as a verb:

The old [warriors, or the like] enter the boat and take their places.

with the final syntax parse (VP=verb phrase)

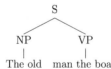

When one hears this sentence being spoken, however, prosody conveys enough syntactic information to avoid any confusion about possible parses in the first place. In particular, there will be an accent on 'old', revealing it as a noun:

The **old** man the **boat**.

The initial, wrong hypothesis of above would never be considered by the listener, because 'The old **man**' as a noun phrase would have an accent on 'man'. As there is no accent on man, this parsing hypothesis can be excluded at an early stage.

In some cases, phrase accents can even distinguish between otherwise ambiguous sentences, such as

They are hunting dogs.

with the two admissible interpretations [Mill 65, p. 16]

---

[2]Such 'Garden path sentences' have been used to study human parsing strategies, see e. g. [Meng 00].

> *They* are *hunting **dogs***. i. e. the dogs are being hunted, and
> *They* are ***hunting** dogs*. i. e. they are dogs trained for hunting

As in these examples, typesetting can be used in written language as a substitute for cues about accent that are conveyed via prosody in spoken language. In normal prose, however, this is usually confined to *contrastive* [Boli 61] or *emphatic* accents, i. e. accents with a particularly strong emphasis, e. g.

> I said *got*, not goat.

Similar to the perception of word accent, also the perceived phrase accent is to some extent subjective. For example in [Lea 73b], phonetically trained listeners were to identify stressed syllables within spoken sentences. This differs a bit from our definition of phrase accent, since stresses were assigned to syllables instead of words, and listeners were not required to discriminate primary from secondary accents. Still, in about 5 % of the cases, the listeners disagreed, even though each listener's decision was taken as the majority vote over multiple intra-rater sessions.

Phrase boundaries: Complementary to phrase accents, *phrase boundaries* structure spoken utterances into phrases and sub-phrases, facilitating segmentation and parsing, and thus understanding. Again, our focus is on function, not form: boundaries can delimit "syntactic, semantic, or dialogue units" [Batl 05], and like accents, boundaries can be realized by the speaker using various means. Most often, timing is used: boundaries are preceded by deceleration (so-called pre-final lengthening), or manifested in the form of pauses, but periods of laryngealization, or different intonation contours are sometimes also used [Lehi 76].

Boundaries can be classified according to their strength: the ToBI approach [Silv 92] distinguishes four levels; here, we follow the convention of Batliner et al. [Batl 98, Batl 00] and just discriminate between

B3 "full intonational boundary with strong intonational marking with/without lengthening or change in speech tempo" [Batl 98]; here marked by '||', and

B2 "minor (intermediate) phrase boundary with rather weak intonational marking" [Batl 98]; here marked by '|',

B0 all other word boundaries,

e. g.

> yes | of course || come in || take a seat.

In written language, punctuation is used as a substitute for boundaries that are conveyed via prosody in spoken language. Even with that, there are often different, equally acceptable boundary configurations for a given piece of written text:

> "Yes, of course! Come in. Take a seat."

is perfectly conceivable both with and without a minor phrase boundary after 'Yes'. When categorizing prosodic boundaries on an ordinal 5-point scale, Campbell [Camp 93] found the realizations of different speakers to correlate just with (Pearson correlation) r=0.48. Especially around function words, the positioning of boundaries seems to be flexible, so that one could conceptualize the boundary "[...] to be at the function word location itself, rather than at one or other side of the word." [Camp 93]

Boundaries can sometimes disambiguate otherwise ambiguous sentences. Consider the sentence

> The hostess greeted the girl with a smile.

Who was smiling? Phrase boundaries, here indicated by a vertical bar (|) can give a clue:

> The hostess | greeted the girl with a smile.   i.e. the girl smiled vs.
> The hostess | greeted the girl | with a smile.   i.e. the hostess smiled

with the respective syntax trees (PP=prepositional phrase)

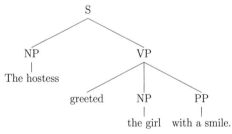

and

Note that the difference in actual realizations might be small and not clearly discernible; at least, Lehiste found listeners to perform better than chance level when trying to identify the meaning the speaker had intended [Lehi 73], and found a significant effect when manipulating durations [Lehi 76].

In the following German example [Till 97],

> Kohl sagte Strauß wird nie Kanzler.

the difference between the two admissible readings is more pronounced:

> Kohl ‖ sagte Strauß ‖ wird nie Kanzler vs.
> Kohl sagte ‖ Strauß wird nie Kanzler.

The same also works in English:

> Livingston said Boris Johnson will never be Prime Minister.

with the two readings

> Livingston ‖ said Boris Johnson ‖ will never be Prime Minister vs.
> Livingston said ‖ Boris Johnson will never be Prime Minister.

In 'real life', such cases where phrase accents or boundaries are really necessary to distinguish otherwise ambiguous or meaningless interpretations are rare, since the context usually reveals what is missing. However, these examples illustrate the mechanism of encoding syntactic structure by prosodic means. The main purpose of phrase accents and boundaries is not disambiguation but a *redundant* coding of information on syntactic structure. How important this information is for the human listener when decoding and trying to understand speech, one realizes when reading text from which all punctuation and emphasis has been removed (cf. 1.1), or when listening to synthetic speech with inappropriate prosody, to speech from novice readers, or to non-native speakers with poor prosody.

2.1.3 Rhythm

Besides word/phrase accents and boundaries, speech is also structured by its *rhythm*. As we will see in this section, speech rhythm cannot be characterized as clearly as above accents and boundaries; neither is its linguistic purpose as clear. Still, rhythm is pertinent for this thesis as it is very important for the goal of speaking in a comfortably intelligible manner. Due to the difficulty of pinpointing concrete, local learner errors or making suggestions for improvement, we will restrict ourselves in Chapter 7 to scoring the appropriateness of the learner's rhythm on a continuous rating scale in the medium- to long-term range (see 1.4.2).

Rhythm in general can be defined as a "[...] movement marked by the regulated succession of strong and weak elements, or of opposite or different conditions." [Murr 71, II, p. 2537] Speech rhythm relates thus to the way contrasting speech segments, e. g. accented and unaccented syllables, are distributed over time. This is a little similar to the way notes of different emphasis and duration are produced in music, although speech rhythm is much less regular. (Rhythm is often more regular and pronounced in read poetry and sung speech.) Indeed, concepts and notations borrowed from music have been used in early descriptions of speech rhythm, cf. Figure 2.1. (For a contemporary approach, the reader is referred to [Niem 13].) How does rhythm emerge when speech is produced? We will later on discuss what distinguishes the rhythm of different languages; as to the basic phenomenon, we will

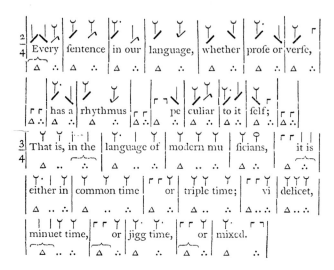

Figure 2.1: An example of Steele's system of describing rhythm and intonation [Stee 75, p. 28].

contend ourselves with the observation "[...] it seems that well-organized motor sequences require precise and predictable timing (Lashley, 1951). Language is a very special motor behaviour but there is every reason to expect it to have a rhythmical organization comparable to that found in other motor skills such as walking or typing." [Ramu 99, referring to [Lash 51]]

There is still much debate about the exact nature of speech rhythm; we will not attempt to contribute to this debate. Rhythm seems to be a phenomenon where we can find a common pre-theoretical core of understanding. Yet, it becomes difficult when trying to operationalise a precise definition by using measures of signal characteristics. Such measures, however, seem to work fairly well when used within an automatic regression approach, correlating signal characteristics with assessments of native listeners in perception experiments. The rather informal description of rhythm that we use here and for labelling (cf. Capter 6) may not be the theoretically most satisfying one, but it was shown to work also with naïve listeners [Hön 10a, Hön 11], and we think it is hard to come up with a better one. Naïve listeners are important because "in the vast majority of cases learners will be communicating with non-experts; therefore, it is important that the perception of errors by non-experts not be ignored in favor of experts' perception." [Vaki 15]

English speech rhythm has often been characterized negatively: together with languages like Dutch, German or Russian, it sounds very different than the rhythm of languages like French, Spanish or Hindi. The first group has been described as exhibiting a "Morse code rhythm" [Jame 40, p. 25], while the latter shows a "machine-gun rhythm" [Jame 40, p. 25]. Pike [Pike 45, p. 35] and Abercrombie [Aber 67, p. 97] termed *stress-timed* for the first group, where *stressed* (accented) syllables occur

English: The next local elections will take place during the winter

cVcVccccVcVcVcVcccVcccVccVVcccVVcccVVcVccVcVccV

Italian: Le prossime elezioni locali avranno luogo in inverno

cVccVcVcVVcVccVVcVcVcVcVVccVcVcVVcVVcVccVccV

Japanese: Tsugi no chiho senkyo wa haruni okonawareru daro

ccVcVcVccVcVcVccVVcVcVcVcVVcVcVcVcVcVcVcV

Figure 2.2: Structure of vocalic (V) and consonantal (c) segments for a sentence translated from English (stress-timed) to Italian (syllable-timed) and Japanese (mora-timed), from [Nesp 03, with corrections].

isochronously, and *syllable-timed* for the second group, where *every* syllable tends to be realized isochronously.

Strikingly enough, the wide-spread notion of stress/syllable isochrony was proven wrong when actual durations were measured and analysed in a number of experimental studies in the 1970s and 1980s. For instance, Dauer [Daue 83] showed that there is a universal tendency for stress timing in all languages, independent of the classical division into stress/syllable-timed. What really adds up to the impression of "syllable-timed" and "stress-timed" are differences in the phonology of a language, such as syllable structure or whether unaccented vowels are reduced. The terms "syllable-timed" and "stress-timed" are still in use, because they describe the true phenomenon of different rhythms, although wrongly referring to timing as a correlate. It took another 20 years before Ramus et al. [Ramu 99] and Grabe and Low [Grab 02] came up with simple phonetic parameters (e. g. ratio of vocalic intervals %V, or standard deviation of the duration of consonantal segments ΔC, see [Louk 11] for a comprehensive analysis, and [Koch 10] for an alternative approach based on predictability) that reflect perceived rhythm well and are on the whole conform with the classic categorization of language rhythms. It is still debated whether language rhythm is a gradual or categorical phenomenon as claimed by Abercrombie [Aber 67]. Additional to the two classes proposed by Abercrombie, *mora-timed* languages are generally recognized as a third rhythm class [Hoeq 83], perhaps with Japanese as the most prominent member. A *mora* is a unit to subdivide syllables; usually, one or two (in some languages up to three) morae form a syllable. Although empirically, mora isochrony has not been found, the mora plays a similar role for rhythm as the syllable does in syllable-timed languages. Two more potential rhythm classes are hypothesized, one between syllable- and mora-timed, and one beyond mora-timing [Ramu 99].

The phonological difference between rhythm classes [Daue 83, Ramu 99, Grab 02] can be illustrated when comparing the vowel/consonant structure of the respective languages, see Figure 2.2. Here it is evident that syllabic complexity decreases from stress-timing (English) to syllable-timing (Italian) and is even lower for mora-timing (Japanese). One may also see in Figure 2.2 how simple acoustic parameters [Ramu 99, Grab 02] such as the standard deviation of the duration of consonantal segments can capture these characteristics.

It is instructive to note that the vowel/consonant structure, and thus the rhythm, is also reflected in the *lexical structure* of a language: First, consonants are the main carriers of lexically discriminative information [Nesp 03]. Now syllable-timed languages with their simpler syllable structure and thus fewer consonants per syllable, need more syllables on average to form words; for mora-timed languages this is even more pronounced. The number of consonants per word, on the other hand, tends to be similar across rhythm classes [Nesp 03].

Rhythm is important for basic segmentation and parsing, and thus understanding of speech for the human listener. This is supported by the hypothesis in cognitive science that rhythm plays an essential role for children acquiring the phonology (e. g. syllable structure) of their mother tongue (see Chapter 2.1.1). Rhythm forms the *basis* upon which the structuring elements of prosody (accents and boundaries) are realized: "Rhythm is hierarchical in nature. While the %V is proposed to define rhythm at the lowest level, at all the levels above it, the rhythmic flow is determined by alternations in prominence among the different phonological constituents." [Nesp 03] Ghitza goes even further and argues that rhythmicity within certain bounds is necessary for decoding speech due to (brain-)physiological restrictions [Ghit 11, Ghit 12, Powe 12].

2.1.4   Paralinguistic aspects

"'Paralinguistics' means 'alongside linguistics' [...]; thus the phenomena in question are not typical linguistic phenomena such as the structure of a language, its phonetics, its grammar (syntax, morphology), or its semantics. It is concerned with *how* you say something rather than *what* you say." [Schu 13] These phenomena include long-term *traits* of the speaker such as gender, age, pathologies, and personality, and short-term *states* such as sleepiness, friendliness, affect and emotion [Schu 13]. With the pivotal exception of *non-native traits*, these phenomena are not the topic of this thesis, but it is worthwhile mentioning them, because they interfere with the above-mentioned *linguistic functions* of prosody [Fox 00, p. 10]—word accent, phrase accents, phrase boundaries and rhythm—because they can affect all channels of prosody: loudness, pitch, and durations. (Paralinguistic phenomena can also affect voice quality, but this is not our concern here as we excluded that from our definition of prosody, cf. Section 1.2.2.)

As a result, language-specific rhythm or intonation patterns can be misinterpreted as affective traits by a non-native listener who is not acquainted with these patterns: "British female voices, in general relatively high-pitched, tend to sound aggressive or over-excited to the German hearer, and, conversely, German males may sound 'bored' or 'unfriendly' to the British hearer." [Gibb 98, p. 89] Such impressions are rather superficial and fade with increasing knowledge of the respective language and person [Town 85], but they illustrate how linguistic and paralinguistic functions of prosody interfere. Another example is that bilingual speakers partly change "[...]

their personality as perceived by the self and by others, depending on which of the two languages they were speaking" [Schu 13, p. 131].

While this interference between different linguistic and paralinguistic functions of prosody is certainly a source of difficulties for automatic processing, it also means that the same modelling techniques can be useful for both fields. For example, it could be worthwhile to use features developed for emotion classification for assessing rhythm (and vice versa).

2.2 Prosody in second language acquisition

After having detailed the aspects of prosody most pertinent for this thesis, we will now discuss their role in second language learning. We will follow the same structure as used above for first language, i.e. start with Language Acquisition (Section 2.2.1), treat the linguistic functions word accent, phrase accents, and phrase boundaries (Section 2.2.2), and rhythm (Section 2.2.3), and conclude with paralinguistic aspects (Section 2.2.4).

2.2.1 Language acquisition

We have already mentioned above (Section 1.3) the critical period hypothesis (CPH) put forward by Penfield [Penf 59] and Lenneberg [Lenn 67], originally relating to loss of neuroplasticity with growing age. "In its most succinct and theory-neutral formulation, the CPH states that there is a limited developmental period during which it is possible to acquire a language, be it L1 or L2, to normal, nativelike levels. Once this window of opportunity is passed, however, the ability to learn languages declines." [Bird 99] It is unquestioned that language "[...] proficiency declines with age of initial acquisition" [Bial 99, p. 172]. A strong CPH as an explanation has been challenged, however, first, because contrary to predictions of the CPH, no *sudden* drop in language acquisition competence with increasing age has been observed empirically, and second, there are alternative explanations: "[...] social factors [...] ease the effort for young children by providing a nurturing environment, simplified input, educational opportunities, cooperative peers, and other supportive aspects of a social context that facilitate the acquisition of any language." [Bial 99] Also, Birdsongs's results suggest "[...] that [even] postpubertal learners can acquire native competence." [Bird 92]

The brain, especially the young brain, develops in response to sensory input. As was shown when cochlear implants were introduced, missing exposure to auditory stimuli within early childhood has dramatic and irreversible consequences on the development of hearing and speech understanding [Kral 12]. The apparent contradiction between studies showing brain immutability after a certain age, and accounts of late second language acquisition to native-like levels could be reconciled like this: as long as a child is exposed to *some* audio and language content, the brain can develop the basic structures needed to process speech in general. Therefore, later acquisition of a second language is possible, but it is constrained by *neural commitment*, the "[...] initial mapping that has taken place." [Kuhl 00] For example, infants can initially discriminate a wide range of language-independent phonetic contrasts, but within the first year of life, they lose the ability to perceive contrasts that are not present in their native language [Werk 84]—i. e. they are learning phonetic equivalence classes. This explains why "[...] certain phonetic distinctions are notoriously difficult to master [for L2 learners] both in speech perception and production, as shown, for example, by the difficulty of the /r-l/ distinction for native speakers of Japanese, even after training." [Kuhl 00] So neural commitment explains why learning a second language is difficult, but it also gives hope to the learners: There is no reason why the brain cannot learn new mappings adapted to the new language, and even without feedback or reinforcement, the right kind of listening experience helps L2 learners to train the perceptual mapping for the new language [Kuhl 00], with positive effects not only of perception but also production [Kuhl 00, p. 113]. Newer brain-physiologic studies emphasize the role of actually acquired proficiency rather than the age of acquisition (AoA): "[...] there is little evidence for a strict critical period in the domain of late acquired second language (L2) morphosyntax. As illustrated by data from our lab and others, proficiency rather than AoA seems to predict brain activity patterns in L2 processing, including native-like activity at very high levels of proficiency. Further, a strict distinction between linguistic structures that late L2 learners can vs. cannot learn to process in a native-like manner [...] may not be warranted. Instead, morpho-syntactic real-time processing in general seems to undergo dramatic, but systematic, changes with increasing proficiency levels." [Stei 09]

The acquisition of prosody seems to be no exception regarding the critical period hypothesis: Native patterns and learned equivalence classes impede learning to perceive and produce the prosody of a second language. For instance, "Italian learners of German, beginners and students with high level L2 competence [...] are not equipped to discriminate elements of German prosody and tend to carry incompatible Italian intonation patterns over into German contexts." [Miss 99a, referring to [Miss 97]] But similarly to segmental aspects, there is no barrier that principally prevents learners from acquiring native-like prosody: Native-like brain processing patterns have been demonstrated for second language learners processing prosodic information [Nick 13]. The condition for learning suprasegmentals might even be more favourable than for segmentals: "Results suggest that the acquisition of the L2 prosody is not constrained by the age of first exposure to the L2 as is the acquisition of segments." [Kagl 10]

In order to be able to acquire natural and lively prosody in a second language at all, it seems, however, important to be exposed to sufficiently rich (native) prosodic input when growing up. For example, the child can thus learn to use and interpret the role of pauses and intonation for turn taking [Brun 08]. Especially if some hearing impairment is present, children are in danger of developing prosodic deficits if the parents do not talk to them in their native language but instead in a prosodically impoverished second language [Batl 10] such as the language of the host country of immigrants. Similarly harmful seems to be the *early oral tradition* where hearing-impaired children were exposed to overly simplified and exaggerated prosody [Clar 06, p. 127].

2.2.2 Word accent, phrase accents and phrase boundaries

For learners of a second language, there are two principle sources of problems: First, "[. . .] language learners do not have the same mentally stored motor patterns for the activity of muscles involved in the production of a particular sound sequence, or cannot execute these patterns as fast as a native speaker can." [Gut 09, p. 98] Second, "[. . .] learners, whose first language (L1) requires different phonological representations of phonological units and rules from the second language (L2) might [. . .] inappropriately use these units and rules in the L2" [Gut 09, p. 98], which is called L1 interference, L1 transfer, or negative transfer. The motor patterns are arguably not the major problem for learning prosody, as the 'building blocks' (loudness, pitch, and duration, and their variation over time) are not as intricate as and more language-universal than segmentals. L1 transfer, on the other hand, presents a major difficulty for the different prosodic functions, as we will detail below. L1 transfer is exacerbated by the perceptual mapping (cf. Section 2.2.1) which heavily affects prosody, too, so there is always the danger that a particular aspect cannot be mastered in production until it is grasped perceptually (although explicit training seems to be able to help nevertheless [Schn 06]). The role these aspects play in second language learning varies according to the different linguistic functions of prosody.

Word accent: Word accent is comparatively easy to master. Most of the errors come from falsely applying fixed L1 stress rules, lexical ignorance or 'false friends', i. e. words that are similar in the L1 but happen to possess a different word accent position in the L2, e. g. the German A-na-*ly*-se versus the English a-*na*-ly-sis. Additionally, differences in phonology (syllable structure) can create problems [Juff 90]. Also, there are specific L1-L2 combinations which make it harder: In different languages, accents are realized by different means, e. g. in Japanese, almost exclusively pitch is used, and in some Indian languages, stress is associated with a lower instead of higher pitch [Dyru 01]. In Germanic languages, vowels of unstressed syllables should be centralized to a considerable extent. So although a non-native speaker "[. . .] may place word stress correctly, it may not be perceived as such, especially by an L1 receiver" [Jenk 00, p. 40]; see also [Fleg 89].

Wrong word accents are stumbling blocks for the listener, as "[. . .] false stress information leads to difficulty of word recognition" [Cutl 84, p. 80]. However, if not accompanied with by other mistakes on the "[. . .] level of sounds, syllable structure, nuclear placement [i. e. phrase accent], or various combinations of these" [Jenk 00, p. 41], pure word accent errors are not an important impediment to intelligibility [Jenk 00, p. 41]. Still, many word stress errors occur together with phonetic errors [Jenk 00, p. 41], and then definitely add to problems for intelligibility: "Generally more serious, however, were word stress deviations which occurred in combination with consonant deletions and which, in spite of contextual cues, rendered words totally unintelligible to all listeners. For example, the words 'product' and 'expenditure' were pronounced by a Taiwanese-English speaker as [pɒdˈʌk] [. . .] and [epeʔ ˈdɪʃɔ]" [Jenk 00, p. 42], see also [Benr 97]. So all in all, mastering word stresses seems worthwhile indeed, also because usually it is the basis for realizing phrase accents as these are realized on word accents in most languages.

Phrase accents: Phrase accents imply prominence just like word accents, so their realization can present the same difficulties to language learners as word accents. Another difficulty arises from the fact that assigning prominence with prosodic means is less important in languages where prominence can be expressed by word order. "For example, in English, a language with a rather fixed order of phrases, the location of the main prominence is quite variable. Thus in a sentence like *I gave a book to John*, the main prominence falls either on *John* or on *a book*, depending on which phrase carries new information in a given context. In Italian, instead, a language in which phrases are allowed to occupy different positions in a sentence, the phrase carrying new information is final, whenever possible, and so is the main prominence. In Italian, the two word orders corresponding to the English sentence above are *Ho dato un libro a Giovanni*, when *Giovanni* is new information, but *Ho dato a Giovanni un libro*, when *libro* is new information." [Nesp 03] That means that a native speaker of a language with variable word order might not see the necessity of putting a focus onto important words, resulting in difficulties with appropriate placing of phrase accents.

In line with that, wrongly placed or missing phrase accents are harmful, more so than wrong word accent [Jenk 00, p. 42]. Although there is a lot of variability regarding acceptable configurations of phrase accent (and boundaries) in case of reading out a given text, "[a] reader cannot do just anything if he is to produce an intelligible spoken realization of the text" [Braz 84, p. 46]. Inappropriate accent placement "[. . .] makes nonsense of what is being read; indeed we often claim that it shows in some way that the reader has not grasped . . . [the] import [of the text]." [Braz 84, p. 46] Similarly, accent placement in free speech is important for the speaker to make herself or himself understood: "When listening to speech with correct primary stress, the participants recalled significantly more content and evaluated the speaker significantly more favourably than when primary stress was aberrant or missing. Listeners also tended to process discourse more easily when primary stress was correct" [Hahn 04]. A further consequence of wrong phrase accents is that their function for easing decoding and parsing is lost, resulting in increased mental effort for the listener.

Phrase boundaries: The production of phrase boundaries should present the least technical difficulty to non-native speakers, as pauses and deceleration are the main means for signalling boundaries. For some L1/L2 pairs, again, things can be more difficult. For example in French, boundaries (except for the end of a declarative statement) are preceded by a pitch rise. This might be difficult to produce for non-native speakers of French; conversely, French natives transferring that pattern to another language will sound a little strange, although not necessarily failing to produce perceivable boundaries. More trivially, hesitations, which frequently occur in non-fluent learners, can produce inappropriately placed boundaries.

Inappropriate phrasing will have a negative impact on intelligibility: "Word groups also tend to coincide with syntactic boundaries, so that failure to divide the speech stream into these units can result in grammatical ambiguity and misinterpretation." [Jenk00, p. 45] A part of the problem is that false boundaries can also corrupt phrase accents, as these are perceived as prominences within phrases. Also, lack of appropriate boundaries will increase listening effort, firstly because it can also lead to a "[...] lack of pause which, for the listener, creates a false sense of speed [...] and reduces the time available for the processing of information" [Jenk00, p. 45], and secondly, because hints that are normally available to ease parsing are lost: "The absence of word-grouping is likely to result in non-fluent speech, with pauses occurring in unnatural places to facilitate the solving of linguistic problems [of the speaker] rather than to serve the purpose of signalling information structure [to the listener]." [Jenk00, p. 45]

Given the relative ease with which phrase boundaries can be realized, it seems definitely to be worthwhile to train non-native speakers in that respect. For example, learners with a tendency towards hesitations can be trained to 'portion' their speech into smallest acceptable phrases, separated by generous pauses. Thus, learners are given the time they need to produce the speech, but the pauses are placed at appropriate syntactic boundaries.

2.2.3 Rhythm

Of the phenomena treated here, producing the appropriate L2 rhythm is probably most difficult, as rhythm is emerging as an 'epiphenomenon' from the phonological structure, the way syllables are accented or lengthened, whether unstressed syllables are weakened, and other factors. There are plenty of chances for learners to fail on one or multiple aspects, also through segmental pronunciation mistakes, and more trivially, through hesitations, resulting in speech rhythm inappropriate for the target language. Often, the produced rhythm shares properties with the native rhythm. This is especially evident when L1 is syllable-timed (e. g. Spanish) and L2 stress timed (e. g.English): the produced speech is then sometimes described exhibiting a 'machine-gun' rhythm.

Non-native rhythm can result in problems for the listener, as basic assumptions about duration and prominence used in decoding are violated: "Effective, recognizable rhythm is essential for the listener. If he is unable to perceive a rhythm which he can recognize by using his native speaker's competence, which he can respond to empathetically [...], and which corresponds to his kinesthetic memories [...], then he lacks the means to break up the message into its coherent parts. He cannot recognize the natural divisions and groups which are essential cues to meaning, and considerable impairment of understanding may result." [Tayl81] Thus, intelligibility as well as listening effort can be affected.

It is not straightforward how appropriate rhythm should be taught. Although measures have been proposed that are more or less established for discriminating language rhythm classes, these are not suitable for instruction: Suggesting to the learner to de- or increase the standard deviation of the duration of his or her consonantal segments will not help. Rather, it seems that rhythm can only be improved indirectly, by training the underlying aspects diligently, in consideration of both L1 and L2. For example, training the production of clear word accents, appropriate lengthening, and pauses, weakening of unstressed syllables and function words [Gims 01, p. 255], clear production of phrase accents, and isolation of small phrases can help. Also training segmental production can considerably improve the rhythmic impression.

2.2.4 Paralinguistic aspects

The interference of the linguistic and paralinguistic functions of prosody has implications for how non-native speakers perceive paralinguistic phenomena, as well as how non-native speakers are perceived by native listeners. First, it is to be noted that non-natives are considerably less able to identify emotions in speech than natives [Grah 01, Naka 02]. Similarly, producing emotional prosody is more difficult in L2 [Zhu 13, p. 128]. Surprisingly, Graham et al. found advanced L2 learners to perform no better in perception than beginning level learners [Grah 01]. This could mean that the difficulties of non-natives are caused by language-specific prosodic cues used for conveying emotion, rather than by interference between linguistic and paralinguistic functions of prosody (because such interference would be handled better by the more advanced learner). On the other hand, a pronounced difference between advanced learners and novice listeners (without any experience in the target language) has been reported for the case of Mandarin vs. Dutch [Zhu 13, p. 127], so both effects could play a role. A pronounced interference effect has been reported for Chinese as a tonal language, where pitch has a lexical function (lexical tone): Chinese novice listeners were unable to identify emotions in Dutch above chance level, while vice versa, Dutch listeners were as good as native Chinese listeners [Zhu 13]. Apparently, "[...] listeners of a tonal language will be less proficient in the paralinguistic use of prosody than listeners of a non-tonal language." [Zhu 13, p. 128] (In that language pair, the effect is so strong that Chinese natives were actually *worse* in discriminating emotions in Chinese than advanced (Dutch) learners of Chinese as L2 [Zhu 13, p. 127].) As a cautionary note, it should be mentioned that these studies were based on acted, i. e. prototypical displays of emotion; this might lead to some distortion in the results.

The double function of prosody also means that non-native prosodic traits can be misinterpreted as emotional signals by the listener. For example, the French continuation rise before phrase boundaries, when transferred to L2 German, might seem affective, 'sexy', or 'cute' to native German listeners. In principle, the same paralinguistic impressions that can be attributed to foreign languages (cf. Section 2.1.4) are eligible to L2 accented speech due to L1 transfer.

This chapter covered the linguistic background of the present work—the phenomenon of prosody. We will now move on to the automatic assessment of the same, which is a necessary precondition for dealing with prosody in computer assisted language learning. In order to help understand, classify and appraise the approaches presented later on, the following chapter commences by detailling previous work in the area.

3

Automatic assessment of prosody: state of the art

This chapter will lay out some relevant prior work in automatic analysis of prosody. For brevity, we will refrain from covering work in speech synthesis: Although concepts and methods are related, and although there is definitely a potential for synergies, the use and role of prosody is still quite different in analysis and synthesis [Batl 05].

We will first cover concrete prosodic events, from approaches primarily aimed at classifying prosodic events in L1 speech (Section 3.1.1) to the detection of actual learner errors in L2 (Section 3.1.2). Section 3.2 will review approaches for assessing the general quality of L2 prosody, in particular rhythm.

3.1 Analysis of prosodic events

3.1.1 Classification of prosodic events in a first language

The first interest in automatically analysing and classifying prosodic phenomena began in the context of enhancing automatic speech recognition (ASR) and understanding (ASU) [Lea 73c, Medr 78, Nöt 91, Komp 96, Batl 00, Gall 02]. Given the importance of prosodic cues for the human listeners, the general idea was to put automatic systems in a position to exploit prosodic parameters, too. Prosody is an obvious candidate for helping segmentation into sentences or dialogue acts [Batl 00]; Compared to using only the recognized word sequence, adding prosodic information was reported to decrease error rates by 4 % relative both in studies from Nöth et al. [Nöt 00, German data] and Shriberg and Stolcke [Shri 04, English data]. At the lower levels of ASR processing, prosodic constraints such as accents and boundaries can be used to restrict the (in general immense) search space in ASR, reducing memory and computational requirements. With the increasing capabilities of computers, these motivations receded however. The incorporation of prosodic information such as accents and boundaries can also improve word recognition accuracy. The reported improvement varies strongly, e.g. between a relative reduction of word error rate by 0.3 % [Anan 07, English data], 4 % [Gall 01, German data], 10 % [Chen 04a, English data], and 15.2 % [Chen 12, Mandarin data]. Despite the improvements apparently attainable, current state-of-the-art recognition systems such as the *Kaldi* toolkit [Pove 11] practically ignore prosody[1], which is probably related to the considerable effort involved in accounting for prosody (e. g. missing standards for prosodic classes, annotation of training material, language dependency). For higher-level processing and speech understanding, the use of linguistically related prosodic information seems even more important [Komp 94b, Shri 98]. Indeed, the gains seem to be higher than for pure word recognition. For example, in the work of Guinaudeau and Hirschberg [Guin 11, French data], prosody improved the F1-measure (harmonic mean of precision and recall) for topic tracking from 35.1 % to 48.1 %, a relative reduction of error rate by 21 %. Nevertheless, up to date, few end-to-end systems seem to be using prosody in that sense [Batl 05], but things may change as systems get more complex and semantically deep.

The methods for classifying prosodic events that were developed in the context of improving ASR were designed for native speech; however, they should be useful templates for processing non-native speech as well; therefore we will review some relevant studies in the following.

Word accent has been classified automatically as early as 1960. Feeding five features derived from loudness, pitch and duration into a decision tree for classification, the perceived (reference) stress in read sentences such as

"I bought a new *re*cord" vs. "Let's re*cord* this"

was successfully identified in 99.1 % of the cases according to Lieberman [Lieb 60, English data]. Note however that speech material was selected very carefully: The perceived stress was annotated twice by two labellers; only the cases where all four votes coincided were taken for evaluation. That means, all the difficult cases were omitted—and they amounted to 11 % of the originally recorded data. Furthermore, the performance was not strictly evaluated on unseen test data; instead, the method was devised on all the data, which probably leads to some overestimate of performance. Similar problems seem to hold for the studies by Aull and Zue [Aull 85, English data] (1 % error rate; text independent, but apparently not evaluated on unseen speakers) and Freij and Fallside [Frei 88, English data] (1 % error rate; not evaluated on unseen speakers). To features derived from loudness, pitch and duration, Aull and Zue [Aull 85] add the average spectral change, to reflect that stressed syllables (except diphthongs) seem to be more spectrally stable than unstressed syllables.

A more realistic performance was reported by Waibel [Waib 86, English data]: On sentences and speakers independent of the training set, 8.91 % of stresses were missed, and 15.71 % of stress label were erroneously inserted. However, the reported errors also include syllable segmentation errors, plus cases where the speaker deviated from canonical word accent positions; also, the training set contained only five speakers. Thus, these error rates seem a rather conservative estimate of the performance that should be attainable for word stress detection.

---

[1][Ghah 14] integrates pitch into Kaldi for the sake of lexical tone; the integration happens at the segmental level by enhancing the standard short-time features with pitch features, leading to a relative decrease error rates for tone languages by about 8 %, but also for some non-tonal languages (but not English), by around 3 %; see also [Wang 01] and [Zoln 03].

Sluijter and Van Heuven [Slui 96] add spectral balance to the acoustic features for classifying word accent: Stressed syllables are "[...] produced with more vocal effort. It is known that, if a speaker produces more vocal effort, higher frequencies increase more than lower frequencies." [Slui 96] At least for Dutch, spectral balance seems to be a reliable cue [Slui 96].

Phrase Accent is very similar to word accent, therefore the means for its automatic detection are similar to those mentioned for word accents. Some authors do not discriminate between phrase and word accents, but just globally assign to each syllable a stress label, either discrete (stressed vs. unstressed [Koch 05], stressed vs. unstressed vs. reduced [Lea 73b], or primary vs. secondary vs. unstressed [Jenk 96]), or continuous [Nöt 88]. Since this conceptualization ignores word boundaries, these approaches are listed here under phrase accents. Lea [Lea 73a, English data] uses local increase of pitch and the integrated intensity within syllable nuclei to identify stressed vs. the union of unstressed and reduced [Lea 73b] syllables. Lea reports 1 % misses and 21 % false alarms; errors include wrong syllable segmentations (the method is not evaluated on unseen speakers or texts). Nöth et al. [Nöt 88, German data] additionally uses duration, and information from different frequency bands: if there is a local maximum in the 100–300 Hz range, and none in the 300–2300 Hz range, a reduction to a syllabic nasal is assumed, i. e. no stress. Coarse errors (perceived stress (range 0–15): ≤ 2 and automatically predicted stress (range 0–1): ≥ 0.8) are reported to occur in 14 % of the cases. Jenkin and Scordilis [Jenk 96, English data] use five loudness, pitch and duration features derived from the syllables and their associated nuclei. Context is included by adding features from up to three preceding syllables (using just one preceding syllable was found optimal, however). For the three-class problem primary vs. secondary vs. no stress, a speaker- and text-independent (i. e. evaluated on unseen speakers and texts) recall of 88.31 %, 71.41 %, and 86.91 %, respectively, is reported (to be compared to a chance level of 33 % on average). Overall recall is 84.51 % (to be compared to a chance level > 31 % since 'no stress' is most frequent); this is better than pairwise labeller agreement (82.1 %).

Kochanski et al. [Koch 05] present a comprehensive study on accent detection, again without attempting to disentangle word and phrase accent. Multiple British and Irish dialects and different styles of speech (isolated sentences, read story, retold story) are covered. To the acoustic parameters loudness, duration, pitch, spectral slope, a voicing measure (aperiodicity) is added; "[...] it is sensitive to some prosodic changes (e. g., pressed versus modal versus breathy speech) and so might plausibly be correlated with prominence." [Koch 05] Local duration information is obtained "[...] by finding regions with relatively stable acoustic properties and measuring their length." The evolution over time of the used acoustic parameters is modelled by fitting Legendre polynomials over a window centred on the current syllable; suitable weighing is used to bias the fit towards regions where the parameters are relevant (e. g. during unvoiced regions, pitch is ignored). A window size of 452 ms was found optimal. The results of automatic classification show that "[c]ontrary to textbooks and common assumption", loudness is by far the most important predictor of accent; the second most important is duration (except for isolated sentences, where pitch is slightly better). On average, loudness alone achieves 76.6 % correct classification, and all acoustic parameters combined yield 78.6 % (to be compared with a chance level of 59 %, the recognition rate of always deciding for the most likely class, i. e. unstressed). By that, the authors corroborate the findings of Batliner et al. [Batl 99, Batl 01].

Actual phrase accents are classified by Batliner and Nöth [Batl 89, German data]. Ten features derived from duration, pitch, and intensity are extracted from each sub-phrase, including sophisticated normalization steps. In a speaker-independent (and text-dependent) evaluation, 84 % of the phrases with the main prominence are classified correctly (since the two classes are balanced, to be compared with a chance level of 50 %). It is also shown that focus is realized with slightly different means (or conversely, the means are employed differently) depending on sentence mood (question vs. non-questions). Consequently, separate modelling improves results (81 % for questions, 91 % for non-questions). Automatic classification is used by Batliner et al. [Batl 91, German data] to study "[. . .] whether more special structures like double focus vs. single focus or narrow focus vs. broad focus (focus projection)" are actually marked by prosodic means or have to be inferred from linguistic content. The authors conclude that these structures are indeed marked by prosodic means, but not always and not very clearly, e. g. for narrow vs. broad focus, a speaker-independent recognition rate of 61 % was observed (again to be compared with a chance level of 50 %). Wightman and Ostendorf [Wigh 92, English data] classify phrase accents (and boundaries) in English speech; in a speaker independent and text-dependent evaluation, 81 % of the accented syllables are detected, 11 % are missed. Ren et al. [Ren 04, English data] add spectral features to pitch, intensity, and duration, and use a time-delay recursive neural network for capturing context. The authors report a recall of 78.1 % for accented and 86.1 % for non-accented syllables.

Kießling [Kies 97, German data] studies phrase accent (and boundary) recognition on comprehensive read and spontaneous (non-prompted) material. Evaluation is speaker- and text-independent. For read speech, binary classification of accent/no accent achieved 95.1 % average recall (average recall of all classes, i. e. to be compared with a chance level of 50 %). For spontaneous material (Verbmobil [Kohl 94]: non-prompted; elicited in a Wizard-of-Oz scenario), 82.1 % are reported (again to be compared with a chance level of 50 %). Kießling employs a comprehensive feature set of 143 features computed from a context of up to six neighbouring syllables, which lead to a pronounced improvement compared to earlier results with fewer features and smaller context (e. g. read material: from 88.1 % to 95.1 % [Kies 97, p. 188]). Adding information from the word level to information from the syllable level also proved beneficial for recognition. A similar finding is reported in [Rose 09, English data].

Chen et al. [Chen 04b, English data] compare the automatic recognition of phrase accents from text and acoustics. Using semantic features derived from text, a recognition rate of 82.67 % results, using prosodic features yields 77.34 %. The combination improves results to 84.21 % (all rates to be compared to a chance level of 55 %). Rosenberg [Rose 10a, English data] performs a cross-corpus evaluation, giving a more realistic estimate of the general performance attainable. For the binary problem, Rosenberg reports a recall of 73.1 % (to be compared with a chance level of roughly 50 %), substantially lower than within-corpus performance (82.9 %; also to be compared with 50 %). Zhao et al. [Zhao 12, English data] present a method for automatically including a suitable amount of context. Articulatory features for accent detection [Zhao 13, English data] are reported to yield an improvement from 79.11 % recall to 81.20 % recall, i. e. a relative reduction of error rate by 11 % (chance level: 70 %).

Phrase boundaries Lea [Lea 72, English data] uses the fall-rise pattern in pitch for automatic boundary detection, reporting 80 % recall for boundaries (false alarm rate is apparently not stated, but seems to be reasonable: "[...] few false alarms will occur"; evaluation not speaker or text-independent). Bear and Price [Bear 90, English data] study phrase boundaries on an (ordinal) six-point scale. Combining pause duration with the normalized phone duration of the syllable coda (or the nucleus vowel if the syllable ends in a vowel), a continuous automatic break index is computed that correlates to hand-labelled indices with 0.85 (presumably Pearson's correlation coefficient; might be slightly optimistic since the automatic index is normalized per sentence, assuming known sentence boundaries). The duration of the nucleus is omitted because that seems to be more confounded by phrase accents [Bear 90]. That is in line with the detailed study of the effects of accents and boundaries on duration in [Camp 93, English data]: Accents tend to lengthen onset consonants more than coda consonants, and vice versa for boundaries.

Wang and Hirschberg [Wang 92, English data] use textual and durational cues for automatic boundary classification. Speaker-independent recognition rate is 79.5 % for boundaries and 92.7 % for non-boundaries. Wightman and Ostendorf [Wigh 92, English data], using pitch and duration, report a recall of 76,6 % for boundaries and 94.4 % for non-boundaries. Kompe et al. [Komp 94a, German data] seem to be the first to study the problem on a large corpus. In the binary problem, boundaries were recognized with 73 % recall, non-boundaries with 82 %. Combination with textual information increased results to 91 % and 89 %, respectively.

Kießling [Kies 97, German data] studies boundary recognition on read and spontaneous (non-prompted) material. For read speech, a three-way classification of B0, B2, and B3 (cf. Section 2.1.2) with an average recall of 90.9 is presented (to be compared with a chance level of 33 %). For spontaneous material [Kohl 94], 86.8 % average recall is reported for the binary problem B0/B2 vs. B3 (to be compared with a chance level of 50 %). Similarly to phrase accents above, the comprehensive feature set employed (143 features from a context of up to six neighbouring syllables) leads to a pronounced improvement compared to earlier approaches using fewer features and smaller context (e.g. read material: from 74.5 % to 95.1 %, [Kies 97, p. 188]).

Shriberg et al. [Shri 00, English data] and Liu et al. [Liu 06, English data] investigate the recognition of boundaries and the spoken word sequence at the same time; this is a more difficult task than working on a known word sequence. Shriberg et al. [Shri 00] use text (language models) and prosody (durations and stylized pitch contours). On broadcast news, i.e. planned speech, the authors achieve an error rate for the binary problem boundary/non-boundary of 3.6 % when using only prosody, and 4.1 % when using only text; combination improves to 3.3%. These figures assume the spoken words as known, and are to be compared to a chance level 6.2. When using ASR (with an word error rate of 46.7 %) for estimating the spoken word sequence, prosody yields 10.9 %, text 11.8 % and the combination 10.8 % (to be compared with a chance level of 13.3 %). For telephone conversations, the results are 6.7 %, 4.3 %, 4.0 %, respectively, when assuming the transcribed word sequence (chance level: 11 %). When using the recognized word sequence (ASR error rate: 30.5 %), results are 22.9 %, 22.8 %, and 22.5 %, respectively (chance level: 25.8 %). Liu et al. [Liu 06] reports results for the NIST Fall 2004 Rich Transcription Task [Nati 04]. Again, conversational telephone speech, and broadcast news are studied. Both prosodic and textual features are used for boundary detection. The equal error rate (the operating point where false alarm rate equals miss rate) for conversational speech is about 10 % if ASR (14.9 % word error rate) is used, while using the reference transcription would give about 7 %. For the broadcast news data, equal error rate is about 13 % with ASR (11.7 % word error rate) and 9 % when using reference transcriptions. Thus, the errors introduced by ASR deteriorate detection of boundaries more than may be expected from the error rate of ASR.

Rosenberg [Rose 10a] performs within- and cross-corpus evaluation also for boundary classification. For example, for major phrase boundaries, the accuracy decreases slightly from 93.13 % to 90.8 % (to be compared with a chance level > 50 % since average length of phrases is given as 5.32 for the training corpus and 3.57 words on the test corpus).

3.1.2   Detection of learner errors

This section will review studies detecting concrete prosodic events in non-native speech, for the aim of detecting prosodic pronunciation errors in CAPT.

Word accent in non-native speech has probably been studied first by Minematsu et al. [Mine 97, L2 English, L1 Japanese]. Accented and unaccented syllables are modelled by a Hidden Markov Model (HMM), using spectral features, pitch, and intensity, plus the respective derivatives, as features. Taking into account the position of syllables in the word (separate HMM for each position) seemed to help. Enforcing syllable boundaries obtained from phoneme alignment (rather than leaving it up to the syllable HMMs) was beneficial. Models were trained with native English speech only; on the native test data, 93 % of the words are

assigned a correct accent position. On L2 data (Japanese speakers), performance was 90 %. No chance levels are given; for the native data, that should be
the frequency of initial stress, i. e. about 80 %. However, it is not clear whether
that imbalance is exploited (possibly via the syllable position in word, or implicitly by spectral cues; a priori probabilities are not mentioned). Thus, the
performance seems quite high. Unfortunately, it is not evaluated in how many
cases pronunciation errors (deviations from canonical word accent position) are
detected or missed (cf. Section 8.2.4 for an explanation why this is important).
Fujisawa et al. [Fuji 98, same data] additionally study how to weight the features
to improve performance on non-native data (e. g. emphasizing pitch, which is
the sole means for realizing Japanese word accent).

Menzel et al. [Menz 01] present one of the few studies that actually evaluate
the proposed methods in terms of how well word accent *errors* are detected.
Identification of the accented syllable is "[...] based on a Gaussian classifier
using phone segment length, energy and some spectral features of the vocalic
region as input." [Menz 01] On non-native English from Italian and German
speakers (the ISLE database, [Menz 00]), 26 % of the errors in word accent
position are detected (hit rate), and 8 % of correct words are hypothesized as
mispronounced (false alarm rate). This performance is a start; it is, however,
far below the reported human performance (75 % hit rate, 3 % false alarms).

Delmonte et al. [Delm 97, Delm 00, Delm 02] presents a software module for
practising prosody including the evaluation of word accent. The focus is on
pedagogical issues; details about implementation and performance seem to be
missing.

Hönig et al. [Hön 09, L2 English, different L1s] also study the detection of word
accent error. Information from both the word level and syllable level is used;
probabilistic modelling is used to estimate the conditional probability of the
canonical word accent position. If this probability is below a given threshold,
an error is assumed; varying the threshold can be used to change the operating
point of the system (trading false alarms for misses). Accordingly, a receiver
operating characteristic (ROC) analysis is performed. At the hit rate of a
human labeller on the data (35 %), the system generates 6 % false alarms—twice
as many as a human labeller, who shows a false alarm rate of 3 %. When using
a priori information about likely mispronounced words, the system is roughly
en par with human performance. Training separate models for each syllable
count yielded a slight improvement. Another aspect covered is training data:
Does it suffice to train with speech from native speakers (assuming canonical
word stress positions), or is it necessary to collect and hand-label non-native
speech? As expected, non-native data yields better performance but native
data is nearly as good. (A similar result was achieved by Ferrer et al. [Ferr 15],
see below.) This is good news because it indicates that the system can be
transferred to new domains or languages with relatively little effort.

Shi et al. [Shi 10, L2 English, L1 Chinese] also present a method for the identification of word accent in non-native speech; 79 % accuracy are achieved; no
chance level is given, no evaluation of error detection is done.

Arias et al. [Aria 10, L2 English, L1 Spanish] present an interesting approach for classifying whether word accent is correct. Instead of modelling stress on the syllable level, the energy and pitch contours of a word are directly compared with a reference realization. If similarity is below a given threshold, a wrong word accent position is assumed. The authors evaluate performance with a ROC analysis; an equal error rate (EER) of 21.5 % is reported for detection whether the word accent position differs from the reference. This is higher than in [Hön 09] (about 29 % EER for the system not exploiting a priori information about word difficulty); however, the evaluation seems to be rather optimistic: only selected words are taken (without secondary phrase accent), and the authors did not annotate real learner attempts, but instead work with simulated data: "Each word was uttered with all the possible stress variants" [Aria 10]. Thus, the data will contain much fewer difficult and ambiguous cases than can realistically be expected in CAPT.

Tepperman and Narayanan [Tepp 05] study word accent recognition in the ISLE corpus [Menz 00]. Non-native data is used for training; the accuracy on word level is around 88 %. There is no ROC or other evaluation that tells how well learner errors were detected.

Chen and He [Chen 07b] study non-linear features based on the Teager energy operator. On the ISLE database, they report an improvement from 81.5 % accuracy to 83.3 % compared to using only traditional features. Evaluation conditions are unclear; error detection is not evaluated.

Chen and Wang [Chen 10, L2 English, different L1s] train separate models for each syllable count as Hönig et al. [Hön 09]. The models are trained on native data. On native test data, 89.78 % of all words are classified correctly, on non-native data 77.37 % (chance level not specified, but should be around 80 % for native data). There is no report how well the system detects errors.

Kim and Beutnagel [Kim 11, L2 English, different L1s] also cover secondary stress; the correct stress pattern is recognized for 3-syllabic words in 83 % of the cases in a cross-validation on the training set (no chance level given). However, the training set contains only a single female speaker; on a different database, containing native and non-native speakers, 71.6 % accuracy are obtained on the native data, and only 49.8 % on the non-native data. It is not evaluated how well errors are detected, and it is not clear whether the actually produced accent pattern was annotated in the non-native data or whether just the canonical accent position was assumed.

Zhao et al. [Zhao 11, L2 English, L1 Taiwanese] study the binary problem using matched non-native data for training. An accuracy of 88.6 % is reported; there is no evaluation on how well errors are recognized.

Li et al. [Li 11, L2 English, L1 Mandarin/Cantonese] suggest using psycho-physical loudness instead of intensity, and propose a prominence model that takes into account syllabic context. Both measures are reported to have beneficial effects on the recognition rate (e. g. for primary vs. secondary/unstressed: 80.50 % with intensity $\rightarrow$ 83.50 % with loudness, 86.99 % $\rightarrow$ 89.80 % through the use of the prominence model; chance level: 74 %). There is no evaluation of error detection.

Li and Meng [Li 12, L2 English, L1 Mandarin/Cantonese] discuss different levels of strictness when evaluating a learner's production regarding primary and secondary stresses. Based on human as well as automatic performance, they conclude that it is most useful just to require the learner to place the primary accent correctly ('P-N'), or to even allow swapping primary and secondary accents ('A-P-N'). Training is done with matched non-native data; on syllable level, the three-class accuracy is 78.6 %; primary vs. secondary/unstressed is classified correctly in 89.9 % of the cases. Error detection is evaluated for different strictness strategies: For P-N, hit rate is 86 % at a false alarm rate of 25 %. For the more relaxed A-P-N strategy, hit rate is 81 %, false alarms occur in 21 %.

Li et al. [Li 13, L2 English, L1 Mandarin/Cantonese] study the use of deep neural networks for word accent recognition. Non-native data is used for training the networks; native data is used for unsupervised pre-training (initialization), which seems to help. A recognition rate of 80.1 % is reported for the three-class problem (chance level: 62 %); primary vs. secondary/unstressed is recognized with 87.1 % (chance level: 77 %). There is no evaluation on how well errors are recognized.

Ferrer et al. [Ferr 15, L2 English, L1 Japanese] present a comprehensive evaluation, considering native and non-native training data, prior probabilities, secondary or just primary stress, agreement of labellers, contribution of feature groups, and evaluation of error detection. For error evaluation, false alarm rate was adjusted to 5 %. At this operating point, a hit rate of 34.1 % is obtained when using only native data for training. When using non-native data to estimate a priori stress probabilities and adapt the acoustic models, a hit rate of 51.6 % resulted. It is to be noted, however, that these results were obtained on the cases with unanimous annotator decisions which was the case only in 70 %. Thus, the performance might be comparable to the one in [Hön 09] (similar hit rates at 5 % false alarm: 32 % and 48 % when using a priori information; task is easier because disregarding secondary accents but more difficult because all data, also the ambiguous cases, are considered).

Vakil and Trouvain [Vaki 15, L2 German, L1 French] present another study on non-native word accent classification. From the results, which are given in terms of precision and recall of 'correct pronunciation', and the involved frequencies (63.8 % 'correct pronunciation'), one can compute the more informative measures [Davi 06] of ROC analysis: hit rate is 40 % and false alarm rate is 8 % for conventional cross-validation across all data. In speaker-independent evaluation, hit rate is 25 %, and false alarm rate 10 %. This performance seems below the ones reported in [Hön 09, Ferr 15].

Phrase accents: Bagshaw [Bags 94] considers the automatic detection of phrase accents for the aim of CAPT. Using a large number of features and normalization techniques, an accuracy of 79.1 % is reported for a three-class problem (chance

level: 61 %). For the two-class problem phrase accent vs. rest, a hit rate of
69 % and a false alarm rate of 9 % is reported [Bags 94, p. 182]. These results
are obtained on a single native (bilingual) speaker; there is no evaluation of
pronunciation error detection.

Imono et al. [Imot 02, L2 English, L1 Japanese] use a method very similar
to [Mine 97] (cf. above). For the three class problem primary vs. secondary
vs. unstressed (on syllable level), a recognition accuracy of 95.1 % on native data
and 84.1 % on non-native data is reported (chance level: 58 %, the frequency of
unstressed syllables). It is not evaluated how well errors are recognized.

Rosenberg and Hirschberg [Rose 10b, L2 English, L1 Mandarin] classify and
evaluate phrase accent on the word level. When training with matched non-
native data, speaker-independent accuracy is 87.23 % (chance level: 61.9 %).
When using only native data for training, 74.77 % accuracy result (chance level
51.3 %). There is no evaluation of how well errors are recognized.

In contrast to the results obtained by Imono et al. [Imot 02] and Rosenberg
and Hirschberg [Rose 10b], binary classification of phrase accent in non-native
speech did not benefit from matched training data in a study of Levow [Levo 09,
L2 English, L1 German]: matched non-native accuracy: 81.2 %; mismatched:
81.6 % (chance level not given).

Li et al. [Li 11] evaluate their suggestions (psychophysical loudness instead of
intensity and prominence model for context, see above) also for the detection
of phrase accent. Loudness instead of intensity is reported to improve accuracy
from 75.02 % to 78.25 %; the prominence model improves accuracy from 80.61 %
to 83.30 % (chance level: 71 %). There is no evaluation how well errors are
detected.

Zechner et al. [Zech 11, L2 English, (presumably) different L1s] also classify
phrase accents. For the binary problem, an accuracy of 84.4 % is achieved
(chance level is 71.9).

Phrase boundaries: Kolář et al. [Kola 06, L2 English, L1 German, Spanish and
others] study the detection of dialogue act boundaries. The target application
is not CAPT but automatic processing of multi-party meetings; however, the
study is of interest here because performance is analysed separately for native
and non-native speakers. Error measure is the boundary error rate (insertions
plus deletions, divided by number of words). Training is done with both native
and non-native data; average speaker-independent performance is 8.1 ± 1.1 %
on native speakers, and 8.7 ± 1.0 % on non-native speakers (chance level is about
16 %). It is also studied how speaker-dependent models improve performance,
and in doing so, feature importance is evaluated per speaker. An interesting
finding is that feature importance is pretty similar within native speakers, but
differs strongly between individual non-native speakers: Uniformly for native
speakers, duration is most important, followed by pitch and pause at roughly
equal levels. For non-native speakers, the picture is diverse: some follow the
native pattern, but for others, pause is most important, followed by either pitch
or duration.

Shi et al. [Shi 10] study the automatic detection of phrase boundaries for the purpose of rhythm assessment in CAPT. Reference boundary probabilities are obtained from a classifier using syntactic features. Boundary classification is done by thresholding inter-word silences. Evaluation is done indirectly:

1. If a boundary is detected but the reference probability for boundary is below 0.2, a rhythm error is assumed for the whole utterance.

2. Compared with manual labels for 'rhythm problems', the automatic ones show a precision of 97 %, and recall (alias hit rate) of 74 %.

From that and the provided counts (75 utterances with rhythm problems, 283 without), one can compute the false alarm rate, which is more informative [Davi 06] than precision: A false alarm rate of 7 % results, which seems to be an excellent performance. Given that just pause duration is used as a feature, a possible explanation might be that the task that was evaluated was quite straightforward (just 283 sentences, details on evaluation missing).

Chen and Yoon [Chen 11a, L2 English, (presumably) different L1s] study recognition of clause boundaries (CBs) in non-native speech. The aim is not rhythm assessment but detection of syntactic clause boundaries in order to assess grammatical language proficiency. An interesting finding is, however, that long pauses (> 0.15 sec) are not a good predictor of syntactic phrase boundaries if speaker proficiency is low (only 15 % of long pauses are CBs in the group of least proficient speakers, while for the most proficient group, 35 % indicate a CB).

3.2 Assessment of rhythm in a second language

This section reviews approaches for *overall, gradual* assessment of the appropriateness of the rhythm of non-native speech. That means assessment is mid-term, and not aimed at identifying local or concrete errors.

Weakening. A relatively early approach for assessing rhythm in non-native speech is presented by Hiller et al. [Hill 94]. The authors see the main point of rhythm analysis in checking the presence or absence of weakening, depending on the L2. Decision is based on a phoneme classifier; there is no evaluation about performance. In the same vein, Asakawa et al. [Asak 05, L2 English, L1 Japanese] show that an automatic measure of the contrast between full and reduced vowels correlates highly with teacher's pronunciation scores for Japanese English learners: The reported Pearson correlation (r) is 0.89. These pronunciation scores seem to reflect general proficiency, not specifically rhythm, however.

Rhythm indices. White and Mattys [Whit 07a, L2/L1 Spanish/English/Dutch] study the distribution of rhythm indices for native and non-native speakers. Although not aimed for CAPT, the study is of some interest in this context. The variation coefficient for vowels VarcoV [Dell 03] and ratio of vocalic segments %V [Ramu 02] are not influenced by speech rate, and showed the most discrimination power for nativeness [Whit 07a, Fig. 3]. VarcoV was also shown by White and Mattys [Whit 07b] to be a strong predictor of ratings of non-native accent.

Jang [Jang 09, L2 English, L1 Korean] studies the automatic assessment of rhythm for Korean Learners of English. For each of the read sentences, reference scores are obtained from two human raters, on a scale from 1 (lower quality) to 5 (native). A number of pertinent rhythm measures are calculated automatically (%V, VarcoV, VarcoC, nPVI-V, rPVI-C); together with the number of pauses and the speaking rate, and the number of function words in the sentence, they are converted into an automatic rhythm quality score by multiple linear regression. The automatic score correlates with the average of the human labellers with r=0.625, which is slightly higher than the inter-rater correlation of 0.584.

Chen and Zechner [Chen 11b, L2 English, L1 Mandarin] compare rhythm indices with features describing fluency and segmental pronunciation (read English by L1 Mandarin speakers). The single most predictive measure for rhythm scores is word accuracy (r=0.50); each fluency measure is more predictive (|r| between 0.36 and 0.44) than the rhythm indices (|r| between 0.08 and 0.34). Nevertheless, in combination, rhythm measures do seem to add some useful information (r=0.539 vs. r=0.522; human-human correlation: r=0.673).

Lai et al. [Lai 13, L2 English, different L1s] study the correlation of rhythm metrics with rhythm scores for spontaneous speech. Speech rate (r=0.41) and a measure of the local variability of syllable duration (r=-0.40; a variant of Grabe's and Low's raw PVI, [Grab 02]) performs best.

Fluency measures. A number of works focus on fluency, which is not the same as rhythm: fluency is mainly related to speech rate, but rhythm is independent of speech rate to some extent. Nevertheless, there is some overlap between the concepts; therefore, automatic assessment of fluency is briefly covered here. Cucchiarini et al. [Cucc 98, L2 Dutch, different L1s] score fluency of non-native speech with a number of measures such as speech rate, articulation rate, length of pauses, or number of disfluencies. Indeed speech rate, i.e. number of segments per total duration of speech including silence, correlates best with perceived fluency ratings (r=0.93). This correlation was obtained for a group of both native and non-native speakers, i.e. with highly diverse fluency ratings; but also within non-natives, correlation to rate of speech is high (r=0.88, [Cucc 00]). Cucchiarini et al. [Cucc 02, L2 Dutch, different L1s] study the difference between rating read and spontaneous speech. Inter-rater reliability was slightly lower for spontaneous speech (r about 0.85 vs. 0.90). All automatic measures correlate much less with fluency on spontaneous speech compared to read speech (e. g. rate of speech: r=0.57 for beginner level learners, r=0.39 for intermediate level learners vs. r=0.92 for read speech). The best automatic measure on spontaneous speech was mean length of runs ("average number of phonemes occurring between unfilled pauses of no less than 0.2 s"): r=0.65 for intermediate learners. This could be interpreted like this: "[...] pauses are tolerated, provided that sufficiently long uninterrupted stretches of speech are produced [...] the speaker has to present his/her arguments in a coherent and organized manner" [Cucc 02].

Zechner et al. [Zech 07, L2 English, difference L1s] include fluency measures for scoring (general) speaking proficiency of spontaneous speech. A correlation of 0.51 is reported for single items (inter-human correlation: 0.37-0.51); on Speaker level (combining 6 tasks), 0.67 is reported (inter-human correlation: 0.94).

Modelling phrasing. Shi et al. [Shi 10, L2 English, L1 Chinese] approach rhythm assessment by checking appropriate pausing according to a phrase structure prediction model (cf. 3.1.2). Zechner et al. [Zech 11] derives features from automatically recognized prosodic events such as phrase accents. These are partly based on comparison with a 'gold standard' for these events. The features are then tested for their ability to predict human pronunciation scores; these scores reflect general proficiency ("[...] accuracy and appropriateness in pronunciation, intonation, stress and pacing." [Zech 11]) The F1 measure of stress prediction (relative to the gold standard) yielded a correlation to the pronunciation scores of r=0.42; another good feature was the mean deviation of time intervals between stressed syllables with r=-0.38.

Montacié and Caraty [Mont 15, L2 English, difference L1s] present features related to boundaries of acceptable phrasing, plus likelihoods of canonical phrase accents (manually annotated for the target text). The features are combined with the baseline features provided by the organizers of the 2015 INTERSPEECH Computational Paralinguistics Challenge on Nativeness, Parkinson's & Eating Condition [Schu 15], and seem to improve results slightly (ρ=0.462 vs. ρ=0.457; cross-corpus correlation on the official test set). Separate performance is not reported.

Comparison to reference utterances. Chen et al. [Chen 07a, L2 Mandarin, (presumably) different L1s] compare syllable intensities and durations with those of native reference utterances. The results of these comparisons are combined with segmental measures to classify the learner's pronunciation as good vs. medium vs. bad. For the three-class problem, an accuracy of 75 % is reported (chance level: 37.5 %). The individual contribution of the scores derived from intensities and durations is not reported. Also Tepperman et al. [Tepp 10, L2 English, L1 Japanese] evaluate non-native prosody by comparing segment durations and pitch contour with reference utterances. Cast as a classification problem between native vs. non-native, the proposed system achieves an accuracy of 89.9 % (chance level: 52 %). There is no evaluation in how far this can be used to predict the general or rhythmic proficiency level of a learner. Arias et al. [Aria 10] assess intonation by correlating the processed pitch curves of the learner and a reference speaker. A correlation of r=0.88 to a 'subjective' score is reported; however, this score is computed by comparing manual annotations of intonation patterns (high rise, high falling, low rise, low falling) of the learner's utterance and reference recordings. Thus, the score does not necessarily represent perceived pronunciation proficiency.

General modelling. Teixeira et al. [Teix 00, L2 English, L1 Japanese] study the use of several prosodic features for predicting general pronunciation scores (5-point scale, average inter-rater correlation: 0.8). For computation of the features, segmentation of the utterance is achieved by aligning the known target text with the help of a speech recognizer. Features used were rate of speech, normalized phoneme durations (by native phoneme-specific durations and rate of speech), durations and distances of stressed syllables, average distance between pitch maximum and longest vowel in words (and similar features), amplitude of pitch, transition frequencies for rising/falling pitch (and similar features from the pitch signal), the durations of the two longest words, vowels and pauses in the utterance. A continuous automatic score derived from these prosodic features correlates to the reference pronunciation scores with r=0.434. Automatic segmental scores correlate with r=0.680; the combination with the proposed prosodic features improves the result to r=0.707.

Bernstein and Cheng [Bern 07, Bern 10, L2 English, Dutch, Arabic; different L1s] assess fluency as part of an overall language proficiency test, where fluency comprises "rhythm, phrasing and timing, as evident in constructing, reading and repeating sentences". (For earlier related work, cf. [Town 98, Jong 01].) Fluency is evaluated on different tasks: 'Read aloud', 'Repeat sentence', 'Sentence build', and 'Open response'. The automatic score is based on "[...] durations of events, (e.g. response latency, words per time, segments per articulation time, inter-word times) and combinations of theses durations." [Bern 10] The methods [Rose 03] are not described in much detail, and it is difficult to assess in how far the resulting fluency score represents rhythm. The automatic fluency score correlates highly to human scores: r=0.89 (L2 English). Note that this builds upon intelligent aggregation of information from a sizeable amount of data (12 minute telephone interview).

Tepperman and Narayanan [Tepp 08, L2 English, L1 German/Italian] present an interesting generic approach for scoring prosody by modelling speech as a sequence of different intonation units, e. g. high and low pitch accents, boundaries, and silence. A finite-state grammar models allowed sequences. Each intonation unit is modelled by an HMM; frame-wise observations (features) are pitch and intensity plus their first and second derivatives. The posterior probability is used as an automatic measure. Context-independent HMMs yielded a correlation (to overall pronunciation scores) of r=0.318; introducing context-dependent models improves results to r=0.398.

Hönig et al. [Hön 10a, L2 English, different L1s] study several measures for predicting the rhythm of non-native speech. Besides application of traditional rhythm indices, a comprehensive prosodic feature set is designed by aggregating over syllable-based pause, duration, pitch and intensity measures. Additional measures are derived from a larger context ($\pm$ 2 syllables) around all syllables that should bear an accent (based on word accent, and prototypic phrase accents for monosyllabic words). These features are shown to outperform traditional rhythm class measures for the prediction of non-native rhythm scores (r=0.83 vs. 0.56 for Grabe's and Low's PVI measures [Grab 02], for instance). Using all features (including word accuracy of a speech recognizer with respect to the target text), a correlation of 0.85 is obtained (features computed over 5 sentences; read non-native English). Maier et al. [Maie 09a, L1/L2 German/Japanese] show for a subset of these generic prosodic features that they are useful for predicting prosody scores even without sophisticated segmentation by a speech recognizer, and in so far language-independent. For non-native German, performance with word segmentation (r=0.89) is similar when using a simple segmentation into voiced regions (r=0.88); for non-native Japanese with voiced regions, the obtained correlation is r=0.76. Hönig et al. [Hön 10b] study performance as a function of the number of the human labellers employed; as a rule of thumb, at least

5–10 labellers should be employed where possible. German as L2 with (different L1 backgrounds) is studied in [Hön 11]. Hönig et al. [Hön 12b, L2 English, different L1s] combine prosodic features with short-time acoustic modelling, namely Gaussian mixture models (GMM) with a universal background model (UBM) approach as used in speaker or accent identification [Camp 06]. This should be useful in order to capture weakening aspects and general segmental proficiency which correlates highly with suprasegmental proficiency. Prosodic features alone yield r=0.793 for rhythm assessment, acoustic modelling r=0.639, and the combination improves results to r=0.822 (prediction and evaluation is based on single utterances). Hönig et al. [Hön 12a] treat further relevant issues such as text independent performance, the combination of local estimates, predictive power orthogonal to speech rate, and evaluate on material that contains less reading-related phenomena (practised dialogues). Hönig et al. [Hön 15] study speaker- and text-independent performance as a function of the number of speakers and diversity of text material used for training, and estimate upper baselines of the performance attainable with speaker adaptation techniques.

Lopez et al. [Lope 11, L2 English, different L1s] do not assess gradual proficiency but just classify native vs. non-native. Nevertheless, the methods are interesting enough to be briefly described here. As done in speaker identification, the authors use the GMM-UBM approach [Camp 06] to model deviations from the general distribution of short-time spectral features, i.e. segmental aspects of pronunciation. Additionally, they adapt the approach to generically model the distribution of prosodic features. To this end, syllable-like regions are automatically identified (voiced regions delimited by local minima in energy, $\geq 60\,\text{ms}$); energy and pitch contour within these regions are modelled by a 5th-order Legendre polynomial. The resulting coefficients plus the length of the syllable form 13 prosodic short-time features that are then processed according to the GMM-UBM approach. Equal error rates for classifying native vs. non-native are 13.1 % for the segmental approach, 30.1 % for the prosodic approach, and 10.6 % when combined.

Black et al. [Blac 15, L2 English, different L1s] present a recent, comprehensive approach to automatically scoring prosodic proficiency. The method shows a remarkable performance in the cross-corpus test set of the 2015 INTERSPEECH Computational Paralinguistics Challenge [Schu 15]: ρ=0.745 vs. the organizer's baseline of ρ=0.425 (which did not use particularly specialized features). First, generic (i.e. non-specialized) features are computed from the baseline descriptors of openSMILE (intensity, loudness, pitch, spectral features, voice quality, and others [Eybe 13]). Functionals are applied onto these descriptors across the utterance, and additionally first within short windows, and then across these windows. By this 'functionals-of-functionals' technique [Schu 08], an improvement to ρ=0.454 on the development set (dev) is achieved (organizer's result on dev: ρ=0.415). Specialized feature sets are pausing features (ρ on dev: 0.613), speaking rate features (ρ on dev: 0.627), rhythm index features (ρ on dev: 0.411), template features (correlations with time-aligned productions of the same sentence spoken by different speakers, relating to phone and word duration, pitch, and intensity; ρ on dev: 0.455), and segmental pronunciation features (ρ on dev: 0.444). All specialized features yield ρ=0.690 on dev; fusion with the generic features yields ρ=0.707 on dev. Since scores are similar within a speaker, smoothing the scores within speakers can be used to improve overall correlation, although this method is not particularly useful in a CAPT context [Hön 15]. Speaker identities are estimated via clustering; smoothing yields a further improvement to $\rho=0.744$ on dev.

This chapter covered the state of the art in automatic assessment of prosody. Before we can proceed to describe the approaches proposed in the present work, we first give some mathematical and technological background. Without trying to be exhaustive, the next chapter will introduce important existing concepts, models and techniques, which will help understanding and classifying the approaches presented later on.

4

Mathematical and technological foundations

The approaches considered here for automatic assessment are based on *pattern recognition* methods [Niem 83, Duda 01, Bish 06]. In general, pattern recognition aims to automatically obtain statements from observations; in other words, pattern recognition is the automation of perception, and as such, can be considered a sub-field of artificial intelligence. Although actual pattern recognition systems vary strongly depending on domain and purpose, many aspects are shared, and prototypical steps can be identified (cf. Figure 4.1): First, the phenomenon at hand is measured and digitized into a *signal* or *pattern*, enabling further automatic processing. Then, signal processing algorithms are applied to extract parameters relevant to the problem; this process is called *feature extraction*. The aims of that step, which typically implies a strong reduction of dimensionality (number of measurements/parameters), are speeding up further processing, facilitating subsequent steps, and improving reliability of the results. If the task involves processing a single isolated, fixed-size pattern (e. g. recognizing handwritten digits in pre-defined slots of a paper form), the features are available as a single *feature vector*, which is directly mapped to the *target class*, or in the case of continuous targets, to the *target score*, using classification or regression techniques. In more complex patterns (e. g. a visual scene with multiple objects; or a speech recording containing multiple words), in general a set of feature vectors is obtained. Special analysis methods are then applied to obtain a symbolic description: for instance, a visual scene is described by a set of objects plus their location; a speech recording is described by the spoken words and their timing.

A pivotal aspect of pattern recognition is that the majority of the free parameters of a given system are estimated *automatically* from data. The engineer implementing a system must still design the overall approach, the feature extraction process, and select the classification methods; but the construction of the actual mapping between feature vectors and targets is completely automatic, given a suitable set of example patterns. This process is called *learning phase* or *training* of the classifier; the field is called *machine learning*. For the example of classifying isolated handwritten digits, all that is needed is a suitable (and suitably large) set of *labelled or annotated* example patterns; modern classification methods can then learn the—quite complex—mapping from pattern (pixel intensities) to classes (digits) with high reliability, even if feature

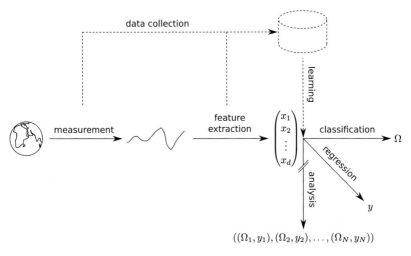

Figure 4.1: Prototypical layout of a pattern recognition system (after [Niem 83]). A selected aspect of the world is measured and digitized to obtain a pattern. Next, features are extracted that compactly represent the relevant information. A classification or regression method is used to convert a feature vector into a target class Ω or target score y; for analysis of more complex patterns, multiple feature vectors are transformed into a symbolic description. In the learning phase, the free parameters of the recognition methods are estimated automatically from annotated data.

extraction as a simplifying intermediate step is left out. Constructing a classifier in a data-driven way has two important advantages: firstly, it saves engineering effort, and secondly, a certain optimality can often be guaranteed. Together, these aspects have led to a huge success of pattern recognition methods in both research and industry.

This chapter will detail pattern recognition methods relevant to this thesis, namely computation of relevant acoustic features (Section 4.1), classification and regression methods for fixed-size, isolated patterns (Sections 4.2, 4.3, and 4.4), and sequence classification (Section 4.5). Note that the methods described here are state-of-the art and generic; methods that have been developed within the scope of this thesis, with the specific aim of non-native prosody assessment, are described in Chapter 7.

4.1 Acoustic short-time features

Speech is a very complex pattern. A common strategy to handle this complexity is to break up the speech signal and analyze the properties of short snippets. This is easier because at small time scales, speech is much less complex; for instance, it is nearly stationary. The process of calculating features for each of many short speech snippets is called *short-time analysis*; each snipped is called an *analysis window* or *frame*. Usually, frames of constant duration are used, and the frames are distributed over time—often with some overlap—with a fixed frequency, resulting in a sequence of feature vectors whose length depends on the duration of the recording. The sequence of short-time features can be the direct input of pattern recognition methods (cf. Section 4.5), or it can serve as a basis for extracting higher-level features from larger time scales (cf. Chapter 7).

4.1.1 Short-time frequency analysis

Many properties of speech can best be analysed in the frequency domain. For example, the amplitude of different frequencies will be influenced by the shape of the vocal tract, and thus provide hints about the speaker's identity. On short term, the frequencies will mainly be influenced by the current position of the articulators, and thus contain information about the phoneme being pronounced. All vowels and all consonants except plosives have a steady-state phase during which the signal is approximately stationary; and even during transition phases, the inertia of articulators usually leads to a smooth change of frequency characteristics. Thus, there is some justification for the simplifying assumption of short-term stationarity [Rabi 07, p. 35] [Schu 95, p. 48]. It turns out that even though there are clear violations of the stationarity assumption (e. g. plosives), it still leads to useful results.

Short-term frequency analysis aims at keeping a balance between approximate stationarity (shorter windows) and a good resolution and coverage of frequencies analysed (longer windows). A typical compromise is to use frames with $T = 25\,\mathrm{ms}$

duration, which results, depending on the sampling rate f_s, in $N = T \cdot f_s$ samples[1]
$s_0, s_1, \ldots, s_{N-1}$. A window function such as the Hann window

$$w_n = 0.5 \left(1 - \cos \left(\frac{2\pi n}{N-1} \right) \right) \tag{4.1}$$

is used to minimize spectral leakage [Huan 01, p. 277] [Schu 95, p. 49], i. e. the smearing
of frequencies that results from extracting a finite analysis window.

Then, a discrete Fourier transform (DFT) is performed on the windowed frame
$s'_n = s_n \cdot w_n$:

$$F_k = \sum_{n=0}^{N-1} s'_n e^{-2\pi i k n / N}, \qquad 0 \leq k < N. \tag{4.2}$$

Since the input is real, the resulting Fourier spectrum is symmetric up to complex
conjugation:

$$F_k = \overline{F_{N-k}}, \qquad 1 \leq k \leq N - M \tag{4.3}$$

where $M = \lceil (N+1)/2 \rceil$, i. e. $M = N/2 + 1$ if N is even, and $M = (N+1)/2$ if
N is odd. The *power spectrum*, i. e. the energy of spectral amplitudes, $P_k = |F_k|^2$ is
symmetric; its non-redundant part runs from P_0 to P_{M-1}. The k-th power spectral
coefficient corresponds to the energy sampled at the frequency $f = k/M \cdot f_{\text{nyquist}}$
where $f_{\text{nyquist}} = f_s/2$ is the Nyquist frequency. The DFT can be computed efficiently
with the fast Fourier transform (FFT); in its original form [Cool 65], N needs to be a
power of two. Generalized versions require N to be composed of few prime factors to
be efficient, but there is also an efficient algorithm for N prime [Rade 68]. In practice,
the analysis window is usually padded with $N' - N$ zeros such that $N' \geq N$ is a power
of two; this has the positive side effect of increasing frequency resolution. In fact, for
low sampling rates, it is useful to apply more padding than would be needed to get
a power of two; typically, it is advisable to use $N' = 2^k$ with $\mathbb{N} \ni k \geq 9$. Figure 4.2
illustrates the whole process of short-time frequency analysis. The spectra nicely
reflect the properties of the spoken phones, for example:

- fricatives show more energy in the high frequencies;

- plosives appear usually in a single frame, as burst of energy across a wider
  frequency range;

- voiced sounds display more energy in the lower frequencies, with the harmonics
  showing up in the fine structure of the spectrum, and formants in the coarse
  structure.

4.1.2   Mel-frequency cepstral coefficients

Short-time spectral analysis yields a detailed, insightful representation of the speech
signal; however, for the purpose of speech recognition, we need a more compact representation. *Mel-Frequency cepstral coefficients* (MFCC) are the most popular choice

---

[1] As common practice in signal processing, indices start with zero in this section.

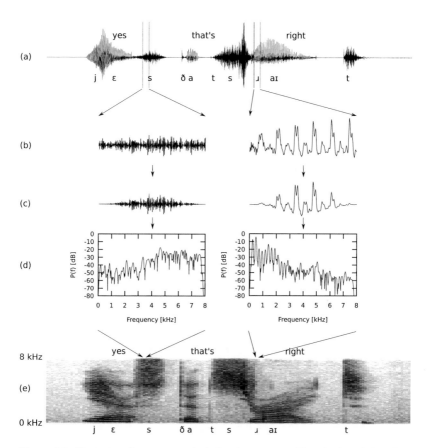

Figure 4.2: Short-time frequency analysis for the sentence 'Yes, that's right' spoken by a female speaker. In (a), the whole signal is shown (duration 1.5 sec). Then, the extraction (b), windowing (c) and frequency analysis (d; in logarithmic scale) of two frames is exemplified: the left one is part of the fricative /s/, with higher energies above 4 kHz; the right frame is taken from the alveolar approximant /ɹ/, with most energy concentrated in the frequencies below 2 kHz. The sequence of power spectra over time is visualized in (e) in a so-called *spectrogram*: the power spectrum of each frame makes up one column of the image (darker = higher energy; in logarithmic scale). One frame = 25 ms; distance between frames = 10 ms; zero padding to 1024 input values → 513 non-redundant frequency bins.

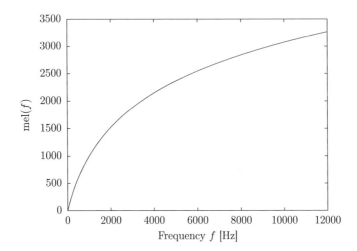

Figure 4.3: Mapping of physical frequency to perceived magnitude of pitch according to the mel scale as in (4.4).

for this purpose [Davi 80]. They are based on the *mel* scale [Stev 37], which relates physical frequency to perceived magnitude of pitch. A commonly used approximation is given by [OSha 87, p. 150]

$$\text{mel}(f) = 1127 \cdot \ln(1 + \frac{f}{700\,\text{Hz}}), \qquad (4.4)$$

cf. Figure 4.3. The mel scale reflects the non-linear frequency resolution capability of human hearing based on the coding of frequencies by the "location of the resonant areas of the basilar membrane" [Stev 37]. This is not to be confused with the mechanisms used for identifying musical intervals ("finely tuned neurons throughout the auditory system" [Tram 01]), which work nearly linearly in physical frequency over a wide frequency range, at least for musical listeners [Thom 14, p. 1152]. The mel scale has been criticised as biased by the experimental flaws [Gree 97], and different scales have been suggested [Moor 83]; however, that does not compromise its usefulness as a non-linear frequency warping for our purposes.

For computation of MFCC, the information contained in the power spectrum is compressed by the *mel filter bank*: the power spectrum, weighted by triangular filters, is integrated; these triangular filters have equal width in the mel scale, and are uniformly distributed on the mel scale with an overlap of 50 %, cf. Figure 4.4[2]. The resulting mel filter spectrum is a coarse representation of the power spectrum, with a higher resolution at low frequencies. As the filters are distributed over the available frequency range from 0 to $f_s/2$, and a certain amount of smoothing ($=$ width

---

[2]In the original formulation by Davis and Mermelstein [Davi 80], a linear mapping was used for the frequencies below 1000 Hz, and the weights were not normalized to sum up to one.

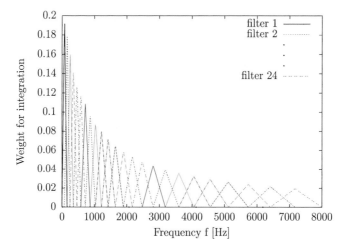

Figure 4.4: Mel filter bank used for weighted integration of the power spectrum in MFCC (24 filters).

of filters in mel frequency) is desired, the number of filters (or their overlap) needs to be adapted according to the sampling rate [Hön 05]. For f_s=16 kHz, 24 filters are commonly used, corresponding to filter triangles with a width of 227 mel (8000 Hz $\rightarrow$ 2840 mel; width of 24 triangles with 50 % overlap: $2840/(24+1) \cdot 2 = 227$). As frequencies above 12 kHz do not contribute much phoneme-related information, it makes sense to limit the range of the filter-bank accordingly for $f_s > 24$ kHz.

Then, the cepstrum of the mel filter spectrum is computed: the logarithm is taken[3], and the discrete cosine transform (DCT), in the version DCT-II [Huan 01, p. 228], is applied. The first 13 coefficients[4] are usually taken as the final MFCC[5]. The effect of the logarithm is that multiplicative changes to the spectrum are converted into additive changes; simple mean normalization (called cepstral mean subtraction, CMS) will thus remove constant influences from the recording channel and the speaker. (Note that the situation is complicated by additive noise, the mel filter bank, and the words spoken.) Applying the DCT and retaining only the lower coefficients results in a smooth, dimension-reduced representation of (the logarithms of) the mel filter spectrum. Further, the resulting coefficients tend to be less correlated [Schu 95,

---

[3]Zero energies are substituted by a small positive constant

[4]For sampling rates > 16 kHz, it makes sense to retain some more coefficients. In practice, however adapting the number coefficients (and filters) to the sampling frequency is most often avoided by just downsampling the signal to 16 kHz, even though some useful information between 8 and 12 kHz is lost.

[5]Traditionally, the first coefficient, which is just the sum of the (logarithms of the) mel filter spectrum, i. e. an energy measure, is substituted by a more direct energy measure, namely the logarithm of total energy in the (windowed) frame, cf. (4.5). However, often this substitution does not have a clear advantage; it seems to get out of fashion.

p. 59f, referring to [Ahme 74, Pols 77]], which can be beneficial for later modelling
(e. g. by diagonal Gaussian densities). The steps for computing MFCC are visualized
in Figure 4.5. Together, MFCC are a compact representation of the coarse structure
of the power spectrum with two main properties:

Auditive adequacy: The approximation of the spectrum is more precise where human hearing has a greater frequency resolution; arguably, this should be beneficial for speech recognition. Just as well, one can explain the usefulness
of increased precision at lower frequencies phonetically: Formants are packed
relatively densely in the lower frequency range, while fricatives in the upper
frequencies extend over larger ranges.

Upper envelope: Seen from the perspective of logarithmic magnitude, MFCC approximate an upper envelope of the spectrum (cf. upper graph of Figure 4.5).
This is because the smoothing by the mel filter bank is done before taking
the logarithm. The upper envelope is beneficial for speech recognition as the
location of the harmonic peaks is determined by the vocal tract transfer function, while the valleys in between are dominated by noise and spectral analysis
artefacts.

4.1.3   Intensity

Intensity is a basic prosodic parameter. One could compute psychophysically adequate loudness measures as in [Li 11]; we contend ourselves here with the short-term
energy of the (windowed) frame on a logarithmic scale:

$$\ln \sum_{n=0}^{N-1} (s'_n)^2. \tag{4.5}$$

Mean-subtraction readily removes the gain of the channel. If more information about
loudness at different frequencies is required, e. g. to discriminate between the intensity
of vowels and fricatives, one can always take MFCC parameters as additional features:
As we have seen above, they represent the coarse structure of the spectrum and thus
the loudness at different frequencies.

4.1.4   Pitch

Pitch is the subjectively perceived frequency of a voiced sound. Most of the time,
pitch is a function of the *fundamental frequency* (F0), i. e. the physical oscillation
frequency of the glottis; but sometimes, the "most reasonable objective F0 is clearly
at odds with the auditory percept." [Talk 95]; see also [Chev 02]. Nevertheless, the
usual (and usually successful) strategy to estimate the pitch contour of a speech
signal is to estimate its smooth F0 contour.

   The perceived magnitude of pitch can be approximated by the mel scale or ERB
scale [Moor 83], if one wants to account for the non-linear frequency resolution of
human hearing due to different critical bandwiths (cf. Section 4.1.2). If musical
interval hearing is targeted, linear F0 is more appropriate (doubling of F0 = one

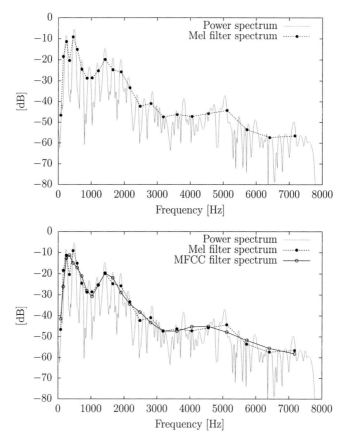

Figure 4.5: Steps of MFCC computation: application of mel filter bank (top) and further smoothing/compression with DCT (bottom; visualized by re-transforming the (zero-padded) MFCC with inverse DCT). The analysis window is the same as in the right hand side of Figure 4.2.

octave up). For our purposes, we use the logarithm of (linear) F0, which maps musical intervals to equal distances irrespective of absolute F0; mean subtraction readily removes person-specific differences (absolute F0 level due to glottis size).

Estimating F0 is difficult due to a number of reasons: oscillation of the glottis is sometimes irregular, voice can be breathy, F0 can be highly variable over time, F0 has a wide amplitude and frequency range (at least between 50 and 500 Hz), vocal-tract resonances impede estimation, estimation is inherently ambiguous due to the harmonic structure, and voiced periods can be as short as a few oscillation cycles [Talk 95]. The RAPT algorithm (robust algorithm for pitch tracking) by Talkin [Talk 95] has the "best combination of wide distribution and very careful testing and benchmarking" [Slan 03], and an open-source implementation is available under the BSD licence. Although better F0 extraction algorithms may have been developed, RAPT has an excellent performance and is the standard baseline. Therefore, we will shortly describe it here.

As many F0 trackers, RAPT first generates local (short-time) F0 candidates, and then searches globally for a consistent F0 contour within the sequence of local candidates. For identifying local F0 candidates, the normalized cross-correlation (NCC) is used to find periodicities via local *self-similarities* in the signal. NCC compares two frames of the signal, with length N and offset by the lag k, by their correlation, normalized with the energies of the frames, resulting in a value in $[-1; 1]$:

$$\phi_k = \frac{\sum_{i=0}^{N-1} s_i s_{i+k}}{\sqrt{\sum_{i=0}^{N-1} s_i^2 \sum_{i=0}^{N-1} s_{i+k}^2}}. \tag{4.6}$$

The lags of interest are determined by the assumed minimum and maximum F0 values $F_{\min}$ and $F_{\max}$: $\lfloor 1/F_{\max} \rfloor \leq k \leq \lceil 1/F_{\min} \rceil =: L$; the superordinate analysis window is $s_0, s_1, \ldots, s_{N-1+L}$.

In RAPT, a surprisingly small value of N corresponding to 7.5 ms is used, which deserves some explanation. First it is important to note that methods based on auto-correlation or the short-time spectrum/cepstrum need quite a large analysis window to account for lower F0 values. Usually, one would want to include at least two glottal cycles, which corresponds to $2/50$ Hz = 40 ms. However, such a large window cannot resolve rapid F0 changes, especially for higher F0 values, precluding the detection of periodicity in some cases [Talk 95]. Using NCC with a short window solves this problem because (a) that window is short enough to cope with high, rapidly changing F0, and (b) even though the window covers less than a glottal cycle for F0 $< 1/7.5$ ms=133 Hz, there is still enough structure in the signal to detect periodicity, cf. Figure 4.6. Further, the normalization of NCC allows the detection of periodicity even during extreme amplitude changes as observed at on- and offset. In the original version of Talkin [Talk 95], computation of the NCC is sped up by first downsampling the signal, identifying candidates by local maxima of the NCC, and then refining candidates with the original signal. A more straightforward alternative to this is computing the cross correlation with the help of the FFT.

After acquiring the 20 best pitch candidates (peaks with highest NCC value) for each frame, RAPT uses dynamic programming to search for that sequence of candidates (always including one 'unvoiced' hypothesis per frame) that is optimal

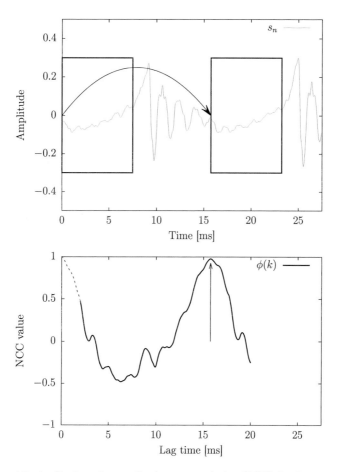

Figure 4.6: Application of normalized cross correlation (NCC) for detecting glottal periodicity. The top graph shows the signal, the 7.5 ms analysis window, and its shifted version (rectangles). The window does not cover a whole glottal period; nevertheless, the structure within the window suffices for detecting the correct period (15.6 ms → F0=64 Hz) as a clear local maximum in the NCC function (bottom; maximum indicated by arrow). Minimum lag: 1/500 Hz = 2 ms, maximum lag: 1/50 Hz = 20 ms; male speaker; sustained /aː/.

across the whole signal according to a certain cost function. This cost function depends on [Talk 95]

- the NCC value (higher NCC: lower cost for voiced candidates and higher cost for the unvoiced hypothesis),

- the lag (favouring lower lags to discourage octave errors),

- the ratio of neighbouring pitch values (favouring smooth pitch contours),

- the energy ratio of neighbouring frames (favouring onsets when energy increases, and favouring offsets when energy decreases),

- the similarity of neighbouring short-time spectra (favouring both on- and offsets at stronger spectrum changes),

- and the number of on- and offsets (favouring few transitions between voiced and unvoiced in general),

cf. Figure 4.7. In effect, the resulting F0 contour (and segmentation into voiced and unvoiced) correlates highly with perceived pitch and voicing states, and the extraction is very robust to noise and invariant to microphone gain. The NCC values corresponding to the estimated pitch contour can serve as estimates of harmonicity (lower NCC: more breathiness/noise).

4.2 Classification by parametric density estimation

Training a classifier is the process of estimating a function

$$f : \boldsymbol{x} \to y \tag{4.7}$$

that maps a feature $\boldsymbol{x}$ vector to an associated class y, by means of a training database. In supervised learning, each feature vector or *instance* of the training database $\boldsymbol{x}_1, \boldsymbol{x}_2, \ldots, \boldsymbol{x}_N$ has an attached label indicating its class $y_1, y_2, \ldots, y_N$, with $y_i \in \{\Omega_1, \Omega_2, \ldots, \Omega_K\}$.

A very successful method to analysing and constructing classifiers is the statistical approach: classes and feature vectors are regarded as random variables, and the densities of the feature vectors are conditioned by the associated class. If the *a posteriori* probability $P(y|\boldsymbol{x})$ is known, a decision rule with *minimum misclassification probability* can be constructed:

$$f(\boldsymbol{x}) = \operatorname*{argmax}_{y} P(y|\boldsymbol{x}), \tag{4.8}$$

i.e. decide for the class that is most likely given the observed feature vector. The set $\{\boldsymbol{x} : P(y|\boldsymbol{x}) = P(z|\boldsymbol{x})\}$ is called the *decision boundary* between class y and z; for classification, it just matters on which side of the decision boundary the feature vector is located. The values of the densities can be used for estimating the confidence of a decision. This classifier is known as the maximum *a posteriori* or Bayes (optimal) classifier. If misclassification costs are not uniform, a related rule can be used to

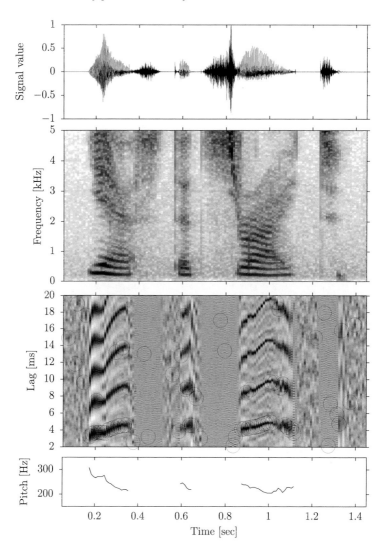

Figure 4.7: Pitch extraction with RAPT: signal (top), spectrogram (second from top), NCC (third from top), and pitch contour resulting from the search (bottom). In the NCC plot, each column shows the NCC for one frame (higher value = darker). The best local candidate per frame is shown by a circle (only if above 0.5). Minimum lag: $1/500\,\text{Hz} = 2\,\text{ms}$, maximum lag: $1/50\,\text{Hz} = 20\,\text{ms}$; speech signal as in Figure 4.2.

minimize the *expected cost* of a decision given the costs r_{yz} for (mis)recognizing class y as class z:

$$f(\boldsymbol{x}) = \operatorname*{argmin}_{z} \sum_{y} r_{y,z} \cdot P(y|\boldsymbol{x}). \qquad (4.9)$$

This has been referred to as 'der optimale Klassifikator' (the optimal classifier) in the German literature [Niem 83, p. 161], [Schu 95, p. 77]; it is also known under the name cost sensitive classification.

For implementing (4.8) or (4.9) it can be useful to reformulate $P(y|\boldsymbol{x})$. Applying the formula for conditional probability $P(A|B) = P(A, B)/P(B)$ twice, we get Bayes' rule

$$\begin{aligned} P(y|\boldsymbol{x}) &= \frac{p(y, \boldsymbol{x})}{p(\boldsymbol{x})} \\ &= \frac{p(\boldsymbol{x}, y)}{p(\boldsymbol{x})} \\ &= \frac{p(\boldsymbol{x}|y) \cdot P(y)}{p(\boldsymbol{x})}. \end{aligned} \qquad (4.10)$$

This form is easier to handle as we can now use one parametric density function $p(\boldsymbol{x}|y)$ for each discrete value of y. Note that $p(\boldsymbol{x}) = \sum_{y} P(y) \cdot p(\boldsymbol{x}|y)$ does not depend on y and is thus irrelevant for the maximization in (4.8) and (4.9). $P(y)$ is called the *a priori* probability of class y.

If we know or can reasonably assume that $\boldsymbol{x}$ is distributed according to a certain probability distribution, such as the multivariate Gaussian density with mean $\boldsymbol{\mu}_y$ and covariance matrix $\boldsymbol{\Sigma}_y$,

$$\mathcal{N}(\boldsymbol{x}|\boldsymbol{\mu}_y, \boldsymbol{\Sigma}_y) = \frac{1}{\sqrt{|2\pi\boldsymbol{\Sigma}_y|}} \exp\left(\frac{1}{2}(\boldsymbol{x} - \boldsymbol{\mu})^{\mathsf{T}} \boldsymbol{\Sigma}_y^{-1}(\boldsymbol{x} - \boldsymbol{\mu})\right), \qquad (4.11)$$

we can estimate the free parameters with maximum likelihood methods from the training data. In the case of the Gaussian density there is a closed-form solution [Niem 83] (δ_{ij} is the Kronecker delta):

$$\hat{\boldsymbol{\mu}}_y = \frac{1}{\sum_{i=1}^{N} \delta_{y_i y}} \sum_{i=1}^{N} \delta_{y_i y} \boldsymbol{x}_i, \qquad (4.12)$$

$$\hat{\boldsymbol{\Sigma}}_y = \frac{1}{\sum_{i=1}^{N} \delta_{y_i y}} \sum_{i=1}^{N} \delta_{y_i y} (\boldsymbol{x}_i - \hat{\boldsymbol{\mu}}_y)(\boldsymbol{x}_i - \hat{\boldsymbol{\mu}}_y)^{\mathsf{T}}. \qquad (4.13)$$

Maximum likelihood estimates for $P(y) =: p_y$ are obtained by computing the relative frequencies $\sum_{i=1}^{N} \delta_{y_i y}/N$ of the labels in the training database; the resulting decision boundaries are quadratic functions. This special case is called the Gaussian classifier; Figure 4.8 illustrates the estimation process on the basis of two classes with the true distribution

$$p_{\Omega_1} = 0.8, \boldsymbol{\mu}_{\Omega_1} = \begin{pmatrix} 1 \\ 1 \end{pmatrix}, \boldsymbol{\Sigma}_{\Omega_1} = \begin{pmatrix} 1 & 0 \\ 0 & 1 \end{pmatrix} \qquad (4.14)$$

$$p_{\Omega_2} = 0.2, \boldsymbol{\mu}_{\Omega_2} = \begin{pmatrix} -1 \\ -1 \end{pmatrix}, \boldsymbol{\Sigma}_{\Omega_2} = \begin{pmatrix} 2 & 1 \\ 1 & 1 \end{pmatrix} \qquad (4.15)$$

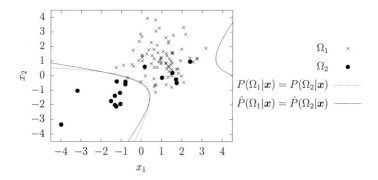

Figure 4.8: Estimation of a Gaussian classifier: The training database are samples drawn from the true distribution (see text), shown as points in the graph. Both the ideal decision boundary with $P(y|\boldsymbol{x}) \propto p_y \cdot \mathcal{N}(\boldsymbol{x}|\boldsymbol{\mu}_y, \boldsymbol{\Sigma}_y)$ and the estimated decision boundary with $\hat{P}(y|\boldsymbol{x}) \propto \hat{p}_y \cdot \mathcal{N}(\boldsymbol{x}|\hat{\boldsymbol{\mu}}_y, \hat{\boldsymbol{\Sigma}}_y)$ are shown. Error rate on the training set is 7.0 % and 6.0 % for the true and estimated parameters, respectively. On an independent and larger test set, the true and estimated parameters have an error rate of 7.6 % and 7.8 %, respectively.

and the distribution estimated from 100 samples drawn from the true distribution:

$$\hat{p}_{\Omega_1} = 0.83, \hat{\boldsymbol{\mu}}_{\Omega_1} = \begin{pmatrix} 1.0 \\ 1.1 \end{pmatrix}, \hat{\boldsymbol{\Sigma}}_{\Omega_1} = \begin{pmatrix} 0.7 & 0.0 \\ 0.0 & 1.1 \end{pmatrix} \tag{4.16}$$

$$\hat{p}_{\Omega_2} = 0.17, \hat{\boldsymbol{\mu}}_{\Omega_2} = \begin{pmatrix} -0.5 \\ -0.9 \end{pmatrix}, \hat{\boldsymbol{\Sigma}}_{\Omega_2} = \begin{pmatrix} 2.9 & 1.4 \\ 1.4 & 1.2 \end{pmatrix}. \tag{4.17}$$

The approaches based on estimating densities are not necessarily optimal for real applications, however. This is because even if distribution assumptions are met, estimating their free parameters from data is inherently error-prone, especially for high-dimensional feature vectors. That will impact performance on data not seen in the training set: the classifier will *overfit* to the training data. In many cases, however, already the assumption about the probability distributions is unjustified. Gaussian mixture models (GMM) [Schu 95], i. e. weighted sums of multivariate Gaussian densities, are in principle able to approximate arbitrary densities, given enough mixture components, so they can be a solution if feature vectors are not Gaussian. Yet, their practical usefulness depends on how well the GMMs estimated with the—always limited—training data perform for the specific task at hand.

4.3 Support vector machines

A more fundamental approach to the problem with densities estimation is to avoid it in the first place. After all, the only thing that matters for classification according to (4.8) is on which side of the decision boundary the feature vectors are located. So instead of taking the detour of estimating densities, we can apply "Vapnik's principle never to solve a problem which is more general than the one we actually need to solve" [Scho 99], and directly model how decision boundaries partition the input space into classes. An (affine) hyperplane

$$\{ \boldsymbol{x} : \boldsymbol{\beta}^{\mathsf{T}} \boldsymbol{x} + \beta_0 = \langle \boldsymbol{\beta}, \boldsymbol{x} \rangle + \beta_0 = 0 \} \tag{4.18}$$

with norm vector $\boldsymbol{\beta}$ and intercept β_0 can be used as a decision boundary; the sign of the (scaled) signed distance from the hyperplane

$$\boldsymbol{\beta}^{\mathsf{T}} \boldsymbol{x} + \beta_0 \tag{4.19}$$

can be used for a class decision.

At first, linear decision boundaries seem to be a drastic limitation; note, however, that a non-linear transformation of the input

$$\boldsymbol{\varphi}(\boldsymbol{x}) \quad : \quad \mathbb{R}^d \to \mathbb{R}^D \tag{4.20}$$
$$\boldsymbol{\varphi}(\boldsymbol{x}) \quad = \quad (\varphi_1(\boldsymbol{x}), \varphi_2(\boldsymbol{x}), \dots, \varphi_D(\boldsymbol{x})), \tag{4.21}$$

e. g. polynomials[6] of x_i of degree p,

$$\boldsymbol{\varphi}_p^{\mathrm{poly}}(\boldsymbol{x}) = \left(x_1^p, x_1^{p-1} x_2, \dots, x_1^{p-2} x_2 x_1, \dots, x_1^{p-2} x_2^2, x_1^{p-2} x_2 x_3, \dots, x_d^p \right), \tag{4.22}$$

or polynomials up to degree p,

$$\begin{aligned}
\boldsymbol{\varphi}_p^{\mathrm{poly}+}(\boldsymbol{x}) \quad = \quad & (1,\ x_1, x_2, \dots, x_d, \\
& x_1^2, x_1 x_2, \dots, x_1 x_d,\ x_2 x_1, x_2 x_2, \dots, x_2 x_d, \dots x_d x_1, x_d x_2, \dots, x_d^2, \\
& \vdots \\
& x_1^p, x_1^{p-1} x_2, \dots, x_1^{p-2} x_2 x_1, \dots, x_1^{p-2} x_2^2, x_1^{p-2} x_2 x_3, \dots, x_d^p) \tag{4.23} \\
= \quad & \boldsymbol{\varphi}_p^{\mathrm{poly}} \left((1, x_1, x_2, \dots, x_d)^{\mathsf{T}} \right), \tag{4.24}
\end{aligned}$$

can overcome this limitation: The *generalized linear* model $\boldsymbol{\beta}^{\mathsf{T}} \boldsymbol{\varphi}(\boldsymbol{x}) + \beta_0$ is able to model non-linear boundaries in the original input space—with linear methods in the transformed space, cf. Figure 4.9 for an illustration.

4.3.1   The kernel trick

For practical problems, the dimension of the transformed vectors $\boldsymbol{\varphi}(\boldsymbol{x})$ quickly gets too large to handle (for example $D = d^p$ for product terms of degree p). If the linear method can be expressed such that feature vectors $\boldsymbol{x}_i$ only occur in *scalar products*, there is a cure, however: For specific transforms, the scalar product of the transformed vectors can be computed from the scalar product of the original vectors. For polynomials of degree p, and two feature vectors $\boldsymbol{x}, \boldsymbol{y}$,

$$\left\langle \boldsymbol{\varphi}_p^{\mathrm{poly}}(\boldsymbol{x}), \boldsymbol{\varphi}_p^{\mathrm{poly}}(\boldsymbol{y}) \right\rangle = \langle \boldsymbol{x}, \boldsymbol{y} \rangle^p, \tag{4.25}$$

---

[6]The multiple occurrence of mixed terms such as $x_1^{p-2} x_2 x_1 = x_1^{p-1} x_2$ is intentional, as will become clear later.

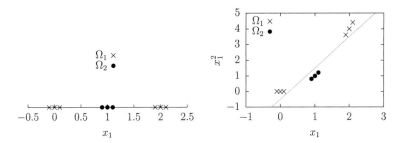

Figure 4.9: Classes that are not linearly separable (left). A non-linear transformation $(x_1) \to (x_1, x_1^2)^\mathsf{T}$, however, makes the classes separable by a hyperplane (right).

which we illustrate for the example of $d = p = 2$:

$$
\begin{aligned}
\left\langle \varphi_2^{\mathrm{poly}}(\boldsymbol{x}), \varphi_2^{\mathrm{poly}}(\boldsymbol{y}) \right\rangle &= \left\langle \left(x_1^2, x_1 x_2, x_2 x_1, x_2^2\right)^\mathsf{T}, \left(y_1^2, y_1 y_2, y_2 y_1, y_2^2\right)^\mathsf{T} \right\rangle && (4.26) \\
&= x_1^2 y_1^2 + 2 x_1 x_2 y_1 y_2 + x_2^2 y_2^2 && (4.27) \\
&= \left(x_1 y_1 + x_2 y_2\right)^2 && (4.28) \\
&= \langle \boldsymbol{x}, \boldsymbol{y} \rangle^2. && (4.29)
\end{aligned}
$$

Note that we do need the mixed products such as $x_1 x_2, x_2 x_1$ to appear more than once (or once, but scaled, e. g. $\sqrt{2} x_1 x_2$) for this to work; thus, they get more weight than the 'pure' products x_i^p, but that does not compromise usefulness.

This is the so-called *kernel trick* [Scho 00]; $k(\boldsymbol{x}, \boldsymbol{y}) := \langle \varphi(\boldsymbol{x}), \varphi(\boldsymbol{y}) \rangle$ is called the *kernel function*. The domain of φ (the space of the original feature vectors) is called *input space*, the image of φ (the space of the transformed feature vectors) is called implicit feature space or just *feature space*[7]. It turns out that there is no need to explicitly define the mapping φ; one can use an arbitrary kernel function as long as it is a *positive semidefinite kernel* [Scho 00] or *mercer kernel* [Merc 09, cited in [Scho 00]] which requires

$$
\sum_{i=1}^{N} k(\boldsymbol{x}_i, \boldsymbol{x}_j) c_i c_j \geq 0 \tag{4.30}
$$

for all real numbers $c_1, c_2, \dots, c_d$ and sets of points $\mathbb{R}^d \ni \boldsymbol{x}_1, \boldsymbol{x}_2, \dots, \boldsymbol{x}_N$; i. e. the so-called *kernel matrix* $K = (k(\boldsymbol{x}_i, \boldsymbol{x}_j))$ must be positive semidefinite. A widely used kernel function is the *radial basis function* (RBF) kernel

$$
k^{\mathrm{rbf}}(\boldsymbol{x}, \boldsymbol{y}) = \exp\left(-\gamma \|\boldsymbol{x} - \boldsymbol{y}\|^2\right), \tag{4.31}
$$

---

[7]That denomination originates from a situation where the input vectors $\boldsymbol{x}_i$ are formed directly from the observed pattern (e. g. pixel intensities in digit recognition), without any feature extraction taking place. Thus, the non-linear transformation can be viewed as the feature extraction step, explaining the name 'feature space'.

which has a feature space of infinite dimension, as one may see in its expansion (shown for $\gamma = 1/2$)

$$
k_{\frac{1}{2}}^{\text{rbf}}(\boldsymbol{x}, \boldsymbol{y}) = \exp\left(-\frac{1}{2}(\boldsymbol{x} - \boldsymbol{y})^{\top}(\boldsymbol{x} - \boldsymbol{y})\right) \tag{4.32}
$$

$$
= \exp\left(-\frac{1}{2}\boldsymbol{x}^{\top}\boldsymbol{x}\right) \exp\left(\boldsymbol{x}^{\top}\boldsymbol{y}\right) \exp\left(-\frac{1}{2}\boldsymbol{y}^{\top}\boldsymbol{y}\right) \tag{4.33}
$$

$$
= \frac{1}{\exp\left(\frac{1}{2}||\boldsymbol{x}||^2\right)\exp\left(\frac{1}{2}||\boldsymbol{y}||^2\right)} \sum_{i=0}^{\infty} \frac{(\boldsymbol{x}^{\top}\boldsymbol{y})^i}{i!} \tag{4.34}
$$

$$
= \frac{1}{\exp\left(\frac{1}{2}||\boldsymbol{x}||^2\right)\exp\left(\frac{1}{2}||\boldsymbol{y}||^2\right)}
$$
$$
\cdot \left(1 + \sum_{j=1}^{d} x_j y_j + \frac{1}{2!}\left(\sum_{j=1}^{d} x_j y_j\right)^2 + \frac{1}{3!}\left(\sum_{j=1}^{d} x_j y_j\right)^3 + \ldots\right); \tag{4.35}
$$

with notating concatenation of vectors $\boldsymbol{a} \in \mathbb{R}^L, \boldsymbol{b} \in \mathbb{R}^M$ as

$$
(\boldsymbol{a}; \boldsymbol{b}) := (a_1, a_2, \ldots, a_L, b_1, b_2, \ldots, b_M)^{\top}, \tag{4.36}
$$

this may be written as

$$
k_{\frac{1}{2}}^{\text{rbf}}(\boldsymbol{x}, \boldsymbol{y}) = \left\langle \frac{1}{\exp\left(\frac{1}{2}||\boldsymbol{x}||^2\right)}\left((1); (\boldsymbol{x}); \frac{1}{\sqrt{2!}}\boldsymbol{\varphi}_2^{\text{poly}}(\boldsymbol{x}); \frac{1}{\sqrt{3!}}\boldsymbol{\varphi}_3^{\text{poly}}(\boldsymbol{x}); \ldots\right), \right.
$$
$$
\left. \frac{1}{\exp\left(\frac{1}{2}||\boldsymbol{y}||^2\right)}\left((1); (\boldsymbol{y}); \frac{1}{\sqrt{2!}}\boldsymbol{\varphi}_2^{\text{poly}}(\boldsymbol{y}); \frac{1}{\sqrt{3!}}\boldsymbol{\varphi}_3^{\text{poly}}(\boldsymbol{y}); \ldots\right)\right\rangle. \tag{4.37}
$$

This means (with γ reintroduced)

$$
\boldsymbol{\varphi}_{\gamma}^{\text{rbf}}(\boldsymbol{x}) = \frac{1}{\exp\left(\gamma||\boldsymbol{x}||^2\right)}\left((1); \sqrt{2\gamma}(\boldsymbol{x}); \sqrt{\frac{(2\gamma)^2}{2!}}\boldsymbol{\varphi}_2^{\text{poly}}(\boldsymbol{x}); \sqrt{\frac{(2\gamma)^3}{3!}}\boldsymbol{\varphi}_3^{\text{poly}}(\boldsymbol{x}); \ldots\right) \tag{4.38}
$$

is a polynomial of infinite degree, with weights approaching zero as the order of the products $p \to \infty$, as $\sqrt{\frac{(2\gamma)^p}{p!}} \to_{p\to\infty} 0$. The transformed vectors have unit length as may be seen from

$$
1 = \exp(0) = \exp\left(-\gamma||\boldsymbol{x} - \boldsymbol{x}||^2\right) = k^{\text{rbf}}(\boldsymbol{x}, \boldsymbol{x}) = \left\langle \boldsymbol{\varphi}_{\gamma}^{\text{rbf}}(\boldsymbol{x}), \boldsymbol{\varphi}_{\gamma}^{\text{rbf}}(\boldsymbol{x})\right\rangle. \tag{4.39}
$$

4.3.2   Optimal separating hyperplanes

If the classes are linearly separable, there are infinitely many possibilities for defining a separating hyperplane. Which should we take? A very successful answer is given by Vapnik's so-called *optimal separating hyperplanes* [Vapn 74, Vapn 82]. These maximize the *margin*, i.e. the minimum distance of the points in the training data to the separating hyperplane, cf. Figure 4.10. They are 'optimal' in the sense that they maximize the margin; intuitively, this is a good idea. Assume that noise is added

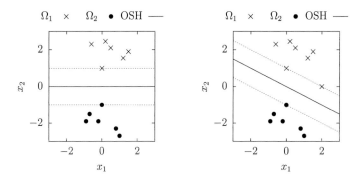

Figure 4.10: Optimal separating hyperplanes (OSH) for two data sets. The margin is visualized with dotted lines. In the right plot, a single observation has been added for Ω_1 at $(2,0)^{\mathsf{T}}$; this changes the OSH and shrinks the margin as shown.

to the points in the training data: The maximum margin will give the points as much space as possible without transgressing the decision boundary. To make this explicit: It means that the training could move by up to a distance equal to the margin M without being misclassified by the hyperplane, cf. Figure 4.11. This is a discriminative criterion, paying most attention to outliers.

For formulating this criterion mathematically, we first make a simplification: we assume that the class y associated to the feature vector $\boldsymbol{x}$ is either -1 or 1. The classification rule, cf. Equation (4.7), is then $f(\boldsymbol{x}) = \text{sgn}(\boldsymbol{\beta}^{\mathsf{T}}\boldsymbol{x} + \beta_0)$. Thus, we can use y easily in calculations and only have to treat a single decision boundary. This restriction to binary classification problems is less severe than it may seem: Any K-class classification problem may be approached by combining the output of K binary classifiers ('one-versus-rest' scheme), or the output of $K \cdot (K-1)/2$ binary classifiers ('one-versus-one' scheme).

We further note that the unscaled signed distance to the hyperplane is

$$\frac{1}{||\beta||}\left(\boldsymbol{\beta}^{\mathsf{T}}\boldsymbol{x} + \beta_0\right). \tag{4.40}$$

Finding a hyperplane that separates the training data with maximum margin can now be expressed as the following optimization problem:

$$\max_{\boldsymbol{\beta},\beta_0} M$$
$$\text{subject to } y_i \cdot \left(\frac{1}{||\beta||}\left(\boldsymbol{\beta}^{\mathsf{T}}\boldsymbol{x}_i + \beta_0\right)\right) \geq M \qquad \forall i = 1, 2, \ldots, N. \tag{4.41}$$

However, this determines the parameters $\boldsymbol{\beta}, \beta_0$ of the hyperplane only up to an arbitrary scaling factor. Thus, we may restrict ourselves to the particular solution where

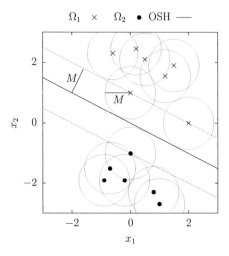

Figure 4.11: Circles of radius M around the training vectors; inside the circles, the training vectors could move without being misclassified. The illustration relates to the data used in right hand side of Figure 4.10.

$||\boldsymbol{\beta}|| = 1/M$, which determines the scale and leads to a simpler form [Hast 08, p. 132]. Additionally, to get a convex objective function, we minimize $\frac{1}{2}||\boldsymbol{\beta}||^2$ instead of $||\boldsymbol{\beta}||$:

$$\min_{\boldsymbol{\beta},\beta_0} \frac{1}{2}||\boldsymbol{\beta}||^2$$

$$\text{subject to } y_i\left(\boldsymbol{\beta}^\mathsf{T}\boldsymbol{x}_i + \beta_0\right) \geq 1 \qquad \forall i = 1, 2, \ldots, N. \tag{4.42}$$

This is a quadratic objective function with affine constraints; thus the problem is convex [Boyd 04, p. 152] and can be solved with quadratic programming methods. The optimization problem can be expressed in a different form, the so-called Wolfe dual problem [Hast 08, p. 133]:

$$\max \sum_{i=1}^{N} \alpha_i - \frac{1}{2} \sum_{i=1}^{N} \sum_{j=1}^{N} \alpha_i \alpha_j y_i y_j \boldsymbol{x}_i^\mathsf{T} \boldsymbol{x}_j$$

$$\text{subject to } \left\{ \begin{array}{c} \alpha_i \geq 0 \\ \alpha_i\left(y_i(\boldsymbol{\beta}^\mathsf{T}\boldsymbol{x}_i + \beta_0) - 1\right) = 0 \end{array} \right\} \ \forall i = 1, 2, \ldots, N \tag{4.43}$$

where the hyperplane is given by $\boldsymbol{\beta} = \sum_{j=j}^{N} \alpha_j y_j \boldsymbol{x}_j$. In this form, one can see that $\boldsymbol{\beta}$ is a linear combination only of the *support vectors*, i.e. those vectors which have exactly a distance M to the separating hyperplane: In order to satisfy

$$\alpha_i\left(y_i(\boldsymbol{\beta}^\mathsf{T}\boldsymbol{x}_i + \beta_0) - 1\right) = 0, \tag{4.44}$$

α_i has to be zero for the non-support-vectors with

$$\left(y_i(\boldsymbol{\beta}^\mathsf{T}\boldsymbol{x}_i + \beta_0) - 1\right) \neq 0. \tag{4.45}$$

That corroborates our notion from above that the separating hyperplane is primarily determined by *outliers*, cf. also Figure 4.10. Further, the formulation allows the application of the kernel trick, as the $\boldsymbol{x}_i$ only occur in scalar products when solving the optimization problem. Also when evaluating the (scaled) signed distance of a test vector $\boldsymbol{x}$ to the hyperplane, $\boldsymbol{x}$ only occurs in scalar products with the $\boldsymbol{x}_i$:

$$\boldsymbol{\beta}^{\mathsf{T}}\boldsymbol{x} + \beta_0 = \sum_{j=1}^{N} \alpha_j y_j \boldsymbol{x}_j^{\mathsf{T}} \boldsymbol{x} + \beta_0. \tag{4.46}$$

For evaluation of that distance, only scalar products with the support vectors need to be calculated: $\boldsymbol{\beta}^{\mathsf{T}}\boldsymbol{x} + \beta_0 = \sum_{\alpha_j \neq 0} \alpha_j y_j \boldsymbol{x}_j^{\mathsf{T}} \boldsymbol{x} + \beta_0$. It should be noted that even if the kernel implies an infinite dimensional feature space, the vector $\boldsymbol{\beta}$ defining the hyperplane lies in an $N-1$ dimensional subspace.

4.3.3 Soft margin

So far we assumed separability, and the margin criterion was strict; this is referred to as the *hard margin* case. In practice, however, the classes are rarely separable; in these cases, no solution will be found. Even if a solution can be found, the solution might be influenced too much by outliers. This problem is approached by allowing some violations of the original constraints, up to misclassification for some training vectors. For this, *slack variables* $\xi_1, \xi_2, \ldots, \xi_N > 0$ are introduced [Cort 95], which specify by how far each training vector may be on the wrong side of the margin tube, relative to the size of the margin. Thus, the original constraints of (4.41) change to [Hast 08, p. 419]:

$$y_i \cdot \left(\frac{1}{||\beta||} \left(\boldsymbol{\beta}^{\mathsf{T}}\boldsymbol{x}_i + \beta_0 \right) \right) \geq M \cdot (1 - \xi_i); \tag{4.47}$$

additionally, the total sum of these violations is limited: $\sum \xi_i \leq$ const. As $\xi_i > 1$ means misclassifying $\boldsymbol{x}_i$, this sum is roughly proportional to the number of misclassifications one allows in the training data. Fixing the scaling of the hyperplane parameters as above, one arrives at [Hast 08, p. 419]:

$$\min_{\boldsymbol{\beta},\beta_0} ||\boldsymbol{\beta}||$$
$$\text{subject to } y_i \left(\boldsymbol{\beta}^{\mathsf{T}}\boldsymbol{x}_i + \beta_0 \right) \geq 1 - \xi_i, \ \xi_i \geq 0 \ \forall i; \ \sum \xi_i \leq \text{const.} \tag{4.48}$$

A computationally more convenient equivalent problem is [Hast 08, p. 420]

$$\min_{\boldsymbol{\beta},\beta_0} \frac{1}{2}||\boldsymbol{\beta}||^2 + C \sum_{i=1}^{N} \xi_i$$
$$\text{subject to } \xi_i \geq 0, \ y_i \left(\boldsymbol{\beta}^{\mathsf{T}}\boldsymbol{x}_i + \beta_0 \right) \geq 1 - \xi_i \ \forall i. \tag{4.49}$$

Here, C has the role of penalizing misclassifications of the training data. The resulting classifier is called a *Support Vector Machine* (SVM) [Vapn 95, Burg 98]. Equation

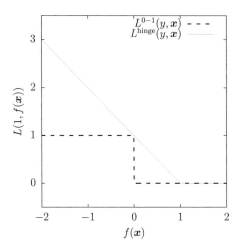

Figure 4.12: Loss functions for $y = 1$. For for $y = -1$, the graph would be mirrored horizontally.

(4.49) is a convex problem, too, and is solvable with quadratic programming; specialized algorithms with better performance have been developed [Plat 98]. Again, the Wolfe dual can be used to apply the kernel trick [Hast 08, p. 420].

Additionally to the support vectors of the hard margin case with $y_i(\boldsymbol{\beta}^\mathsf{T}\boldsymbol{x}_i + \beta_0) = 1$, i. e. with distance M to the separating hyperplane (and $\xi_i = 0$), the x_j with $\xi_j > 0$ are also support vectors, i. e. those vectors that are allowed to be on the wrong side of the margin tube.

It is enlightening to view (4.49) in a different form. As in Section 4.2, we use $f(\boldsymbol{x})$ to denote the classifier that we want to learn; however, this time we allow $f(\boldsymbol{x})$ to output a real number and are satisfied if the sign of $f(\boldsymbol{x})$ corresponds to the associated class -1 or 1. Thus, we can directly use the (scaled) signed distance to the hyperplane:

$$f(\boldsymbol{x}) = \boldsymbol{\beta}^\mathsf{T}\boldsymbol{x} + \beta_0; \qquad (4.50)$$

the classifier is correct if $y \cdot \mathrm{sgn}(f(\boldsymbol{x})) = 1$. A *loss function* that captures the cost of $f(\boldsymbol{x})$ accordingly is the so-called zero-one loss function

$$L^{0-1}(y, f(\boldsymbol{x})) = \frac{1}{2}\left(1 - y \cdot \mathrm{sgn}(f(\boldsymbol{x}))\right), \qquad (4.51)$$

cf. figure 4.12. Let us substitute this by a related, but mathematically more tractable *loss function*, namely the *hinge loss*

$$L^{\mathrm{hinge}}(y, f(\boldsymbol{x})) = \max(0, (1 - yf(\boldsymbol{x}))). \qquad (4.52)$$

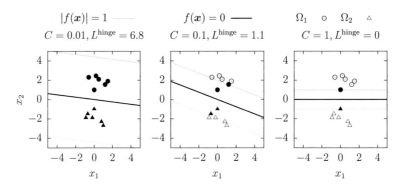

Figure 4.13: Linear SVM for different values of C. Support vectors are drawn as filled dots/triangles. For this example, $C = 1$ results in the solution of the hard-margin case. A lower C causes more training vectors to determine the position of the hyperplane, even though the data is perfectly separable. Data is the same as in the left hand side of Figure 4.10.

As Figure 4.12 visualizes, the hinge loss gets higher the more $y \cdot f(\boldsymbol{x})$ is below 1. It may intuitively be seen how this relates to (4.49); in fact, an optimization problem that leads to the same solution [Hast 08, p. 426] is

$$\min_{\boldsymbol{\beta},\beta_0} \sum_{i=1}^{N} L^{\text{hinge}}(y_i, f(\boldsymbol{x}_i)) + \frac{\lambda}{2}||\boldsymbol{\beta}||^2, \tag{4.53}$$

with $\lambda = 1/C$. That means that the SVM minimizes the hinge loss under a penalization of $||\boldsymbol{\beta}||^2$. The penalization relaxes the minimization of the loss in favour of a larger margin tube $|f(\boldsymbol{x})| = 1$; the higher λ (and the lower C), the more training vectors are allowed to have $y_i f(\boldsymbol{x}_i) < 1$, allowing less 'outlierish' training vectors to have an influence on the hyperplane (and increasing the number of support vectors). This is visualized in Figure 4.13.

When more training vectors determine the position of the hyperplane, the resulting model is in effect limited in complexity. Thus, C is called the *complexity parameter*; the complexity of the model rises with increasing C. Figure 4.14 and 4.15 visualize this for different kernel functions. The figures also show that complexity can alternatively, or complementarily, be adjusted by the parameters of the kernel function: For the polynomial kernel k_p^{poly}, complexity rises with the degree p of the polynomials, and for the RBF kernel, complexity rises with γ.

The SVM turns out to be a classifier with excellent performance even in very high dimensional feature spaces. What makes it especially attractive is that it is a non-linear method that has a unique, optimal solution due to its convexity. The usual price for applying the kernel trick is that the whole training data set has to be used (and kept in memory); for SVM, this is alleviated by the fact that only the support vectors are required. A downside of SVM is that training does not scale well for databases with many instances, as the cost of solving the optimization problem grows at least

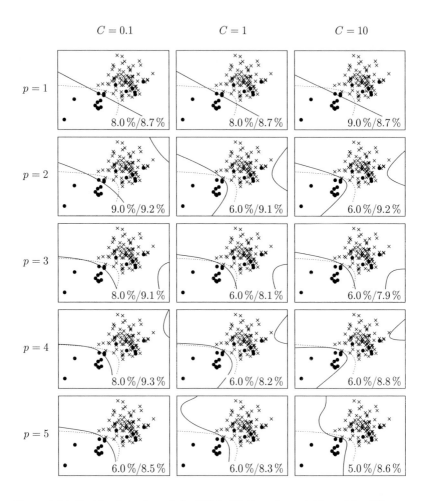

Figure 4.14: Decision boundary of the SVM with the polynomial kernel for different degrees p and complexities C. The two percentages in the graphs give the training and test error rate, respectively. The test error rate does not decrease further than 7.9 % (p=3, C=10) for any $p \in \{1, 2, \ldots, 10\}$ and $C \in \{10^{-3}, 10^{-2}, \ldots, 10^4\}$. The Bayes optimal decision boundary (training error 7.0 %, test error 7.6 %) is drawn as a dotted line; data and axes are the same as in Figure 4.8.

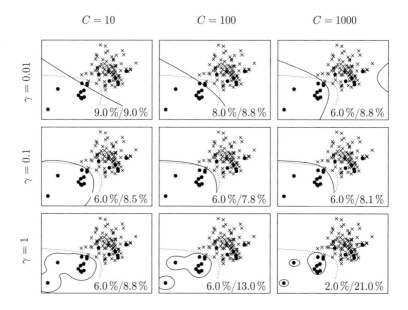

Figure 4.15: Decision boundary of the SVM with the radial basis function kernel for different values of γ and complexities C. The two percentages in the graphs give the training and test error rate, respectively. The test error rate does not decrease further than 7.8 % (γ=0.1, C=100) for any $\gamma \in \{10^{-3}, 10^{-2}, \ldots, 10^1\}$ and $C \in \{10^{-3}, 10^{-2}, \ldots, 10^4\}$. The Bayes optimal decision boundary (training error 7.0 %, test error 7.6 %) is drawn as a dotted line; data and axes are the same as in Figure 4.8.

with N^2 if C is small, and with N^3 when C is large [Bord 05]. Further, SVM does not provide class probabilities for the purpose of estimating confidences; however, pseudo-probabilities can be estimated by transforming $f(\boldsymbol{x})$ [Plat 00]. Although the formulation for binary classification is more straightforward, there are formulations of true multi-class SVMs [Cram 02]. In practice, nevertheless the usage of the binary form with one-versus-one or one-versus-rest schemes prevails, cf. e. g.. [Pedr 11].

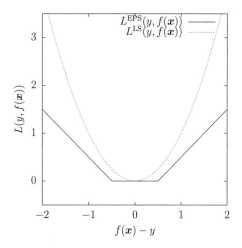

Figure 4.16: Loss functions for regression. $L^{\text{EPS}}(y, f(\boldsymbol{x}))$ is shown for $\epsilon = 1/2$.

4.4 Support vector regression

In regression, we want to estimate a function $f(\boldsymbol{x})$ with a continuous output $y \in \mathbb{R}$. The *linear regression* approach assumes that f is an affine linear function of the features, i. e.

$$f(\boldsymbol{x}) = \boldsymbol{\beta}^{\mathsf{T}} \boldsymbol{x} + \beta_0. \tag{4.54}$$

When using a loss function that minimizes the squared prediction error,

$$L^{\text{SE}}(y, f(\boldsymbol{x})) = ||y - f(\boldsymbol{x})||^2, \tag{4.55}$$

the parameters $\boldsymbol{\beta}, \beta_0$ can be estimated from the training data by solving a system of linear equations. As in the case of linear decision boundaries for classifiers, using a non-linear transformation of the feature vectors $\boldsymbol{\varphi}(\boldsymbol{x})$ can be used to construct a generalized linear model—linear in the parameters to be estimated but non-linear in the original features.

If the dimension of the feature vector is large, or the features are noisy, the solution $\hat{\boldsymbol{\beta}}, \hat{\beta}_0$ estimated from the least squared error on the training data can exhibit a large error on unseen data. *Support vector regression* (SVR) [Druc 96] is an approach to linear regression that is especially robust in such situations and has further advantages that we will discuss later. SVR uses the so-called ϵ-insensitive loss function

$$L^{\text{EPS}}(y, f(\boldsymbol{x})) = \max(0, |f(\boldsymbol{x}) - y| - \epsilon) \tag{4.56}$$

regression, which ignores errors up to ϵ and then increases linearly with absolute error, cf. Figure 4.16. SVR minimizes the norm of $\boldsymbol{\beta}$ while constraining $L^{\text{EPS}}(y_i, f(\boldsymbol{x}_i))$ to

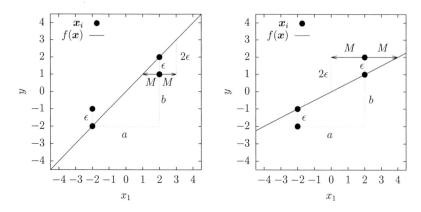

Figure 4.17: Two solutions satisfying zero ϵ-insensitive loss for a regression data set with one-dimensional input vectors. The SVR solution on the right-hand side additionally minimizes $||\boldsymbol{\beta}||$, which results in the maximum margin M (see text).

zero for the training data:

$$\min_{\boldsymbol{\beta},\beta_0} \frac{1}{2}||\boldsymbol{\beta}||^2$$

$$\text{subject to} \begin{cases} y_i - \boldsymbol{\beta}^{\mathsf{T}} x_i - \beta_0 \leq \epsilon \\ \boldsymbol{\beta}^{\mathsf{T}} x_i + \beta_0 - y_i \leq \epsilon \end{cases} \forall i = 1, 2, \ldots, N. \tag{4.57}$$

Minimization of the length of $\boldsymbol{\beta}$ has been motivated as a penalization, promoting "flatness" [Smol 04]; we will give a more direct interpretation here that is very similar to the margin interpretation of SVM. First, we have a look at a simple one-dimensional example data set with $N/2 - 1$ points at $(-2, -2)$, $N/2 - 1$ points at $(2, 2)$, and two more points at $(-2, 1)$ and $(2, 1)$. Figure 4.17 shows two solutions satisfying zero ϵ-insensitive loss. As the data set is centred, $\beta_0 = 0$, and as $\boldsymbol{x} \in \mathbb{R}^1$, the regression has the form $f(\boldsymbol{x}) = \beta_1 x_1$.

The left solution uses $\beta_1 = (b+\epsilon)/a$; it would result as the least-squares solution for $N \rightarrow \infty$. The right side shows the SVR solution minimizing $||\boldsymbol{\beta}||$, with $\beta_1 = (b-\epsilon)/a$. Why should that be a good idea? Let the *margin* M denote the distance up to which each training point may move while still having an absolute error $|y_i - f(\boldsymbol{x}_i)| \leq 2\epsilon$ (or equivalently, having $L^{\mathrm{EPS}}(y_i, f(\boldsymbol{x}_i)) \leq \epsilon$). For the left solution, $M = \epsilon/\beta_1 = \epsilon a/(b+\epsilon)$, cf. Figure 4.17. The right solution has a larger $M = \epsilon/\beta_1 = \epsilon a/(b - \epsilon)$. That means minimizing $||\boldsymbol{\beta}||$, leading to smaller, 'less courageous' predictions, can have an advantage in terms of maximum absolute error if one wants to allow for uniform noise added to the features[8].

---

[8]The example might seem a bit artificial; but also in the balanced case of $N = 4$, least squares with $\beta_1 = b/a$ can have a smaller margin $M = \frac{3}{2}\epsilon a/b$, depending on the value of ϵ. In the case at hand with $a = 4, b = 3, \epsilon = 1$, there is a tie: $\frac{3}{2}\epsilon a/b = 2 = \epsilon a/(b-\epsilon)$.

Minimization of $||\boldsymbol{\beta}||$ further selects the *direction* of the hyperplane $y = \boldsymbol{\beta}^\mathsf{T}\boldsymbol{x} + \beta_0$ such that the margin $M = \epsilon/||\boldsymbol{\beta}||$ is maximum. This is visualized in Figure 4.18 by means of a two-dimensional data set with two points, $(\boldsymbol{x}^+, y^+) = ((1,0)^\mathsf{T}, 1)$ and $(\boldsymbol{x}^-, y^-) = (((-1,0)^\mathsf{T}, -1)$.

For many real world problems, there is no solution that satisfies (4.57). To address this, slack variables ξ_i, ξ_i^* are used to relax the zero loss restriction [Vapn 95, Smol 04]:

$$\min_{\boldsymbol{\beta},\beta_0} \frac{1}{2}||\boldsymbol{\beta}||^2 + C\sum_{i=1}^{N}(\xi_i + \xi_i^*)$$

$$\text{subject to } \left\{ \begin{array}{l} y_i - \boldsymbol{\beta}^\mathsf{T}x_i - \beta_0 \leq \epsilon + \xi_i \\ \boldsymbol{\beta}^\mathsf{T}x_i + \beta_0 - y_i \leq \epsilon + \xi_i^* \\ \xi_i, \xi_i^* \geq 0 \end{array} \right\} \ \forall i = 1, 2, \ldots, N. \tag{4.58}$$

The constant C penalizes errors on the training data; the lower C, the more $\xi_i, \xi_i^* \geq$ are allowed, leading to a larger margin tube $|f(\boldsymbol{x}) - y| = \epsilon$, and a model that is in effect limited in complexity. As in the case of SVM, the optimization criterion of SVR can also be written as a minimization of a loss function under a penalization of $||\boldsymbol{\beta}||$ [Hast 08, p. 436]:

$$\min_{\boldsymbol{\beta},\beta_0} \sum_{i=1}^{N} L^{\mathrm{EPS}}(y_i, f(\boldsymbol{x}_i)) + \frac{\lambda}{2}||\boldsymbol{\beta}||^2. \tag{4.59}$$

Equation (4.58) is a convex problem with affine constraints, solvable with quadratic programming. As in the case of SVM, the dual form [Smol 04] allows the application of the kernel trick, and only the support vectors with $\boldsymbol{x}_i$ with $|f(\boldsymbol{x}_i) - y_i| = \epsilon$ or either $\xi_i \neq 0$ or $\xi_i^* \neq 0$ are needed to evaluate $f(\boldsymbol{x})$. Analogously to SVM, the outcome of the procedure is primarily determined by outliers. A lower ϵ and/or a lower C will result in more support vectors, allowing less 'outlierish' training vectors to have an influence on the regression. Figure 4.19 illustrates the interplay between ϵ and C. Figures 4.20 and 4.21 illustrate non-linear SVR using the polynomial and RBF, respectively.

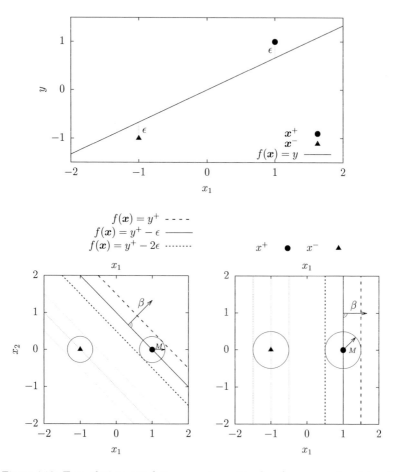

Figure 4.18: Two solutions satisfying zero ϵ-insensitive loss for a regression data set with two two-dimensional input vectors $\boldsymbol{x}^-$ and $\boldsymbol{x}^+$. The graphs at the bottom show the solutions from a bird's eye view, hiding y. The top graph is a side view showing x_1 and y; here, the two solutions look identical. Both solutions are flat in the sense that $f(\boldsymbol{x}^-) = -1 + \epsilon$ and $f(\boldsymbol{x}^+) = 1 - \epsilon$. In the graphs in the bottom, it can be seen that the left solution has a smaller margin $M = \epsilon/||\boldsymbol{\beta}||$ than the SVR solution with maximum margin at the right.

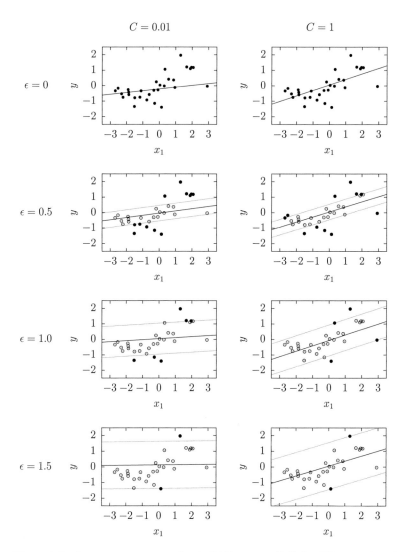

Figure 4.19: Support vector regression (solid line: $y = f(\boldsymbol{x})$) for different values for C and ϵ. Support vectors are drawn as filled dots; the epsilon-tube $|f(\boldsymbol{x}) - y| = \epsilon$ is drawn as a dotted line.

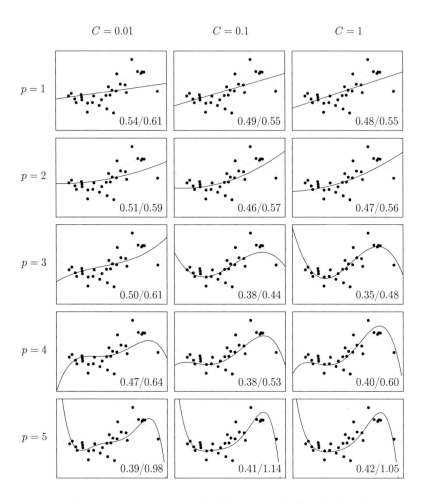

Figure 4.20: Support vector regression (solid line: $y = f(\boldsymbol{x})$) with the polynomial kernel for different degrees p and complexities C. A fixed $\epsilon = 0.5$ is used. The two percentages in the graphs give average absolute error for training and test, respectively. The ideal regression function $y = \sin(x_1)$, drawn as a dotted line, has an error of 0.39 and 0.40 on training and test, respectively. Data and axes are the same as in Figure 4.19.

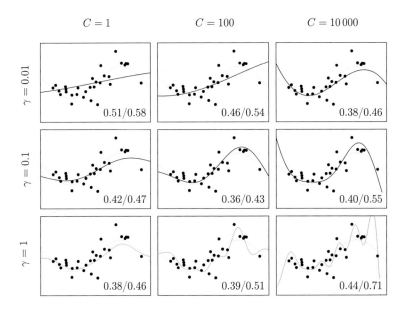

Figure 4.21: Support vector regression (solid line: $y = f(\boldsymbol{x})$) with the radial basis function kernel for different values of γ and complexities C. A fixed $\epsilon = 0.5$ is used. The two percentages in the graphs give average absolute error for training and test, respectively. The ideal regression function $y = \sin(x_1)$, drawn as a dotted line, has an error of 0.39 and 0.40 on training and test, respectively. Data and axes are the same as in Figure 4.19.

4.5   Hidden markov models

The analysis of complex patterns can usually not be cast as a direct mapping between features and classes. For recognizing the sequence of spoken words in a recording, for instance, the number of possible outputs is huge; additionally, the duration of a given word sequence is highly variable, so standard pattern classification techniques which require a fixed-length feature vector are not suitable. Thus, one needs a method that analyses parts of the recording and yields a set of recognized units. For speech, suitable units are words, syllables or phonemes; again, the duration of these units is variable, which prevents the straightforward application of standard classification methods. An additional complication is the fact that the units cannot be segmented easily, which means that recognizing the sequence of spoken units requires solving the combinatorial problem of finding out the durations and locations of the units.

The Hidden Markov Model (HMM) represents a very elegant and efficient (both in terms of parameters to be estimated and computational effort) solution to these problems [Levi 83]. First, we describe its use for classifying *single, isolated patterns of variable length* into discrete classes.

An HMM is a generative model for a sequence of observations with variable length. In a two-stage random process, the model first adopts a certain *state* at each discrete point in time, according to a certain probability distribution. Then, an observation is generated at each point in time, conditioned on the adopted state at that time. Thus, the HMM models a probability density for *sequences* of observations; this is very suitable to describe the evolution or trajectory of short-time feature vectors calculated across the pattern we wish to classify.

The states are drawn from a finite set $\{s_1, s_2, \ldots, s_N\}$; the adopted state at time index t with $1 \leq t \leq T$ is denoted q_t. In our case the model is *causal*, i.e. the distribution of q_t depends only on past states; and the model is *stationary*, i.e. the distribution does not depend on absolute time [Schu 95, p. 126]. We further take the *first-order* Markov assumption, i.e. q_t depends solely on the preceding state q_{t-1}. Thus, the distribution of the state sequence is characterized by the *start probabilities* $\boldsymbol{\pi}$ with

$$\pi_i = P(q_1 = s_i), \quad 1 \leq i \leq N, \quad \sum_{i=1}^{N} \pi_i = 1 \qquad (4.60)$$

and the *transition probabilities* $\boldsymbol{A} = (a_{ij})$ with

$$a_{ij} = P(q_t = s_j | q_{t-1} = s_i), \quad \sum_{j=1}^{N} a_{ij} = 1 \; \forall i = 1, 2, \ldots, N. \qquad (4.61)$$

If $\pi_1 = 1$ and transitions are non-zero only for $j \geq i$, the model is called a left-right HMM [Rabi 89]; a special case of that is the linear HMM where only the probabilities for recurrence $(i = j)$ and transitioning to the next state $(j = i + 1)$ are non-zero. A model topology where all a_{ij} may be non-zero is called ergodic.

The distribution of the observation O_t is solely conditioned on the emitting state q_t; that means the observations do not directly dependent on each other (only indirectly through the interdependence of the states). In case of discrete observations

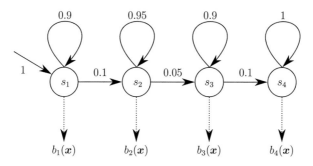

Figure 4.22: Illustration of a linear HMM.

with a finite inventory $v_1, v_2, \ldots, v_K$, the observations are governed by discrete probabilities

$$b_j(O_t) = b_j(v_k) = P(O_t = v_k | q_t = s_j). \tag{4.62}$$

For continuous observations such as our feature vectors, the observations are distributed according to continuous density functions

$$b_j(O_t) = b_j(\boldsymbol{x}) = p(O_t = \boldsymbol{x} | q_t = s_j); \tag{4.63}$$

a typical choice for a distribution are GMMs.

Figure 4.22 illustrates an example for a linear HMM; Figure 4.23 shows samples generated by that HMM. The observations are continuous, one-dimensional, and follow a (unimodal) Gaussian distribution; the parameters are

$$(\pi_i) = (1, 0, 0, 0)^{\mathsf{T}} \tag{4.64}$$

$$(a_{ij}) = \begin{pmatrix} 0.9 & 0.1 & 0 & 0 \\ 0 & 0.95 & 0.05 & 0 \\ 0 & 0 & 0.9 & 0.1 \\ 0 & 0 & 0 & 1 \end{pmatrix} \tag{4.65}$$

$$b_i(\boldsymbol{x}) = b_i(x_1) = \mathcal{N}(x_1 | \mu_i, \sigma_i^2), \tag{4.66}$$

$$(\mu_i) = (5, 10, 15, 10)^{\mathsf{T}}, \tag{4.67}$$

$$\sigma_i = 1. \tag{4.68}$$

Note how variable the timing of the state transitions is in Figure 4.23; this is an illustration of the fact that HMMs are not very strong in duration modelling; taken to extremes, it might be said that HMMs mainly care about the *order* of observations. This deficiency of HMMs is typically alleviated by putting more context information into the short-time feature vectors, e. g. by adding derivatives over time.

4.5.1 Production probability

In order to use HMMs for classification, we need to compute the likelihood that an HMM λ generated a given observation sequence $\boldsymbol{O} = O_1, O_2, \ldots, O_T$. If we assume

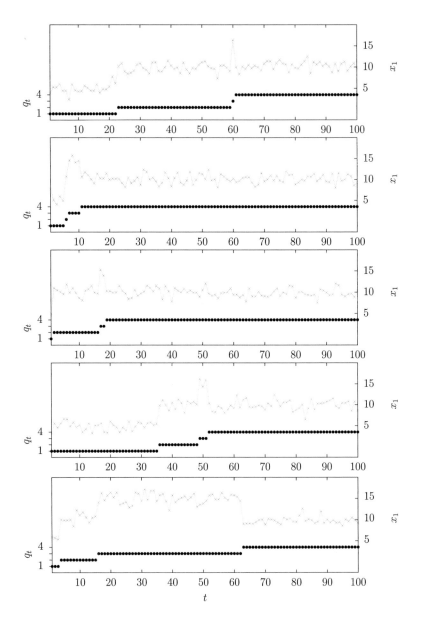

Figure 4.23: Samples generated from a linear HMM with one-dimensional, continuous observations. The states are shown as dots, the observations as crosses.

a certain state sequence $\boldsymbol{q} = q_1, q_2, \ldots, q_T$, the production probability is—thanks to the independence assumption—given by

$$P(\boldsymbol{O}|\boldsymbol{q}, \lambda) = \prod_{t=1}^{T} b_{q_t}(O_t). \tag{4.69}$$

However, we are only given the observations, not the state sequence; hence the 'hidden' in the name of the models. To deal with that missing information, we marginalize over all possible state sequences:

$$P(\boldsymbol{O}|\lambda) = \sum_{\boldsymbol{q}} P(\boldsymbol{O}, \boldsymbol{q}|\lambda) = \sum_{\boldsymbol{q}} P(\boldsymbol{O}|\boldsymbol{q}, \lambda) \cdot P(\boldsymbol{q}, \lambda). \tag{4.70}$$

Thereby, the probability of the state sequence is given by

$$P(\boldsymbol{q}, \lambda) = \pi_{q_1} \prod_{t=2}^{T} a_{q_{t-1}q_t}. \tag{4.71}$$

Together, we have

$$P(\boldsymbol{O}|\lambda) = \sum_{\boldsymbol{q}} \pi_{q_1} b_{q_1}(O_1) \prod_{t=2}^{T} a_{q_{t-1}q_t} b_{q_t}(O_t). \tag{4.72}$$

The number of all possible state sequences $\boldsymbol{q} = q_1, q_2, \ldots, q_T$ is N^T; thus, a direct evaluation of (4.72) is infeasible in many practical cases. A solution to this is exploiting the first-order assumption by dynamic programming; expanding the product and factoring out elements in (4.72) shows how this works:

$$\begin{aligned} P(\boldsymbol{O}|\lambda) &= \sum_{q_1} \sum_{q_2} \cdots \sum_{q_T} \pi_{q_1} b_{q_1}(O_1) \cdot a_{q_1 q_2} b_{q_2}(O_2) \cdot a_{q_2 q_3} b_{q_3}(O_3) \cdot \ldots \cdot \\ &\quad a_{q_{T-2} q_{T-1}} b_{q_{T-1}}(O_{T-1}) \cdot a_{q_{T-1} q_T} b_{q_T}(O_T) \end{aligned} \tag{4.73}$$

$$\begin{aligned} &= \sum_{q_1} \pi_{q_1} b_{q_1}(O_1) \sum_{q_2} a_{q_1 q_2} b_{q_2}(O_2) \sum_{q_3} a_{q_2 q_3} b_{q_3}(O_3) \cdot \ldots \cdot \\ &\quad \underbrace{\sum_{q_{T-1}} a_{q_{T-2} q_{T-1}} b_{q_{T-1}}(O_{T-1}) \cdot \underbrace{\sum_{q_T} a_{q_{T-1} q_T} b_{q_T}(O_T) \cdot \underbrace{1}_{\beta_T(q_T)}}_{\beta_{T-1}(q_{T-1})}} \end{aligned} \tag{4.74}$$

or

$$\begin{aligned} P(\boldsymbol{O}|\lambda) &= \sum_{q_T} \sum_{q_{T-1}} \cdots \sum_{q_1} b_{q_T}(O_T) \cdot a_{q_{T-1} q_T} b_{q_{T-1}}(O_{T-1}) \cdot a_{q_{T-2} q_{T-1}} b_{q_{T-2}}(O_{T-2}) \cdot \ldots \cdot \\ &\quad a_{q_2 q_3} b_{q_2}(O_2) \cdot a_{q_1 q_2} b_{q_1}(O_1) \cdot \pi_{q_1} \end{aligned} \tag{4.75}$$

$$\begin{aligned} &= \sum_{q_T} b_{q_T}(O_T) \sum_{q_{T-1}} a_{q_{T-1} q_T} b_{q_{T-1}}(O_{T-1}) \sum_{q_{T-2}} a_{q_{T-2} q_{T-1}} b_{q_{T-2}}(O_{T-2}) \cdot \ldots \cdot \\ &\quad \underbrace{\sum_{q_2} a_{q_2 q_3} b_{q_2}(O_2) \underbrace{\sum_{q_1} a_{q_1 q_2} \underbrace{b_{q_1}(O_1) \cdot \pi_{q_1}}_{\alpha_1(q_1)}}_{\alpha_2(q_2)}}. \end{aligned} \tag{4.76}$$

Evaluating (4.76) efficiently is called the *forward algorithm*. We introduce the auxiliary *forward* variables

$$\alpha_1(i) = \pi_i b_i(O_1), \quad 1 \leq i \leq N \tag{4.77}$$

and use the recursion

$$\alpha_{t+1}(j) = \left(\sum_{i=1}^{N} \alpha_t(i) a_{ij} \right) b_j(O_{t+1}), \quad 1 \leq t \leq T-1, \quad 1 \leq j \leq N. \tag{4.78}$$

Since everything after the first sum sign $\sum_{q_T}$ in (4.76) is $\alpha_T(q_T)$, the final probability is given as

$$P(\boldsymbol{O}|\lambda) = \sum_{i=1}^{N} \alpha_T(i). \tag{4.79}$$

The same result, but maybe more intuitively, is obtained when exploiting the first-order assumption together with the definition [Rabi 89]

$$\alpha_t(i) = P(O_1, O_2, \ldots, O_t, q_t = s_i | \lambda), \tag{4.80}$$

i. e. the probability of having observed the partial sequence $O_1, O_2, \ldots, O_t$ and being in state s_i at time t.

Similarly, evaluating (4.74) efficiently is called *backward* algorithm with the auxiliary *backward* variables

$$\beta_T(i) = 1, \quad 1 \leq i \leq N, \tag{4.81}$$

the recursion

$$\beta_t(i) = \sum_{j=1}^{N} a_{ij} b_j(O_{t+1}) \beta_{t+1}(j), \quad 1 \leq i \leq N, \quad 1 \leq t \leq T-1, \tag{4.82}$$

and the termination

$$P(\boldsymbol{O}|\lambda) = \sum_{i=1}^{N} \pi_i b_i(O_1) \beta_1(i), \tag{4.83}$$

since in (4.74), the sum $\sum_{q_2}$ and everything that follows equals $\beta_1(q_1)$.

The same result is obtained by defining [Rabi 89]

$$\beta_t(i) = P(O_{t+1}, O_{t+2}, \ldots, O_T | q_t = s_i, \lambda), \tag{4.84}$$

i. e. the probability of observing the partial sequence $O_{t+1}, O_{t+2}, \ldots, O_T$ when starting at time t in state s_i. Both forward and backward algorithm are linear in T and quadratic in N. For a numerically stable implementation, a time-dependent scaling factor [Rabi 89] has to be introduced, because the auxiliary variables typically decay quickly over the iterations.

4.5.2 Most likely state sequence

For a number of purposes, we might be interested in the *most likely state sequence*, given a sequence of observations. One such purpose is *segmentation*; note however that without further measures (cf. Section 4.5.4), the states are not necessarily a meaningful unit of segmentation *per se*.

We are looking for the state sequence $\boldsymbol{q}$ that is most likely when observing the observation sequence $\boldsymbol{O}$, i. e.

$$\boldsymbol{q}^* = \underset{\boldsymbol{q}}{\operatorname{argmax}} P(\boldsymbol{q}|\boldsymbol{O}, \lambda) \tag{4.85}$$

$$= \underset{\boldsymbol{q}}{\operatorname{argmax}} \frac{P(\boldsymbol{O}, \boldsymbol{q}|\lambda)}{P(\boldsymbol{O}|\lambda)} \tag{4.86}$$

$$= \underset{\boldsymbol{q}}{\operatorname{argmax}} P(\boldsymbol{O}, \boldsymbol{q}|\lambda) \tag{4.87}$$

$$= \underset{\boldsymbol{q}}{\operatorname{argmax}} P(\boldsymbol{O}|\boldsymbol{q}, \lambda) \cdot P(\boldsymbol{q}|\lambda). \tag{4.88}$$

Again, direct evaluation of (4.88) is typically infeasible due to the large number of possible state sequences, but similarly to the production probability above, we can exploit the first-order assumption. Let us switch from 'argmax' to 'max', i. e.

$$P^* = \max_{\boldsymbol{q}} P(\boldsymbol{O}, \boldsymbol{q}|\lambda) \tag{4.89}$$

$$= \max_{\boldsymbol{q}} \pi_{q_1} b_{q_1}(O_1) \prod_{t=2}^{T} a_{q_{t-1}q_t} b_{q_t}(O_t) \tag{4.90}$$

$$= \max_{q_T} \max_{q_{T-1}} \ldots \max_{q_1} b_{q_T}(O_T) \cdot$$
$$a_{q_{T-1}q_T} b_{q_{T-1}}(O_{T-1}) \cdot a_{q_{T-2}q_{T-1}} b_{q_{T-2}}(O_{T-2}) \cdot \ldots \cdot$$
$$a_{q_2q_3} b_{q_2}(O_2) \cdot a_{q_1q_2} b_{q_1}(O_1) \cdot \pi_{q_1} \tag{4.91}$$

$$= \max_{q_T} b_{q_T}(O_T) \cdot$$
$$\max_{q_{T-1}} a_{q_{T-1}q_T} b_{q_{T-1}}(O_{T-1}) \cdot \max_{q_{T-2}} a_{q_{T-2}q_{T-1}} b_{q_{T-2}}(O_{T-2}) \cdot \ldots \cdot$$
$$\max_{q_2} a_{q_2q_3} b_{q_2}(O_2) \cdot \max_{q_1} \underbrace{\underbrace{a_{q_1q_2} b_{q_1}(O_1) \cdot \pi_{q_1}}_{\delta_1(q_1)} \cdot}_{\delta_2(q_2)} \tag{4.92}$$

Efficient evaluation of (4.92), and additionally tracking the arguments of the maxima, is called the *Viterbi algorithm* [Vite 67]. We define the auxiliary variables

$$\delta_1(i) = \pi_i b_i(O_1), \quad 1 \le i \le N \tag{4.93}$$

with the recursion

$$\delta_{t+1}(j) = \max_{1 \le i \le N} \delta_t(i) a_{ij} b_j(O_{t+1}), \quad 1 \le t \le T-1, \quad 1 \le j \le N, \tag{4.94}$$

and the termination

$$P^* = \max_{1 \le i \le N} \delta_T(i), \tag{4.95}$$

since everything after $\max_{q_T}$ in (4.92) is $\delta_T(q_T)$. The actual state sequence can be obtained by tracking the arguments of the maxima through time with the variable $\psi_t(i)$:

$$\psi_1(i) = 0, \quad 1 \leq i \leq N, \tag{4.96}$$

$$\psi_{t+1}(j) = \operatorname*{argmax}_{1 \leq i \leq N} \delta_t(i) a_{ij}, \quad 1 \leq t \leq T-1, \quad 1 \leq j \leq N, \tag{4.97}$$

$$q_T^* = \operatorname*{argmax}_{1 \leq i \leq N} \delta_T(i), \tag{4.98}$$

$$q_{t-1}^* = \psi_t(q_t^*), \quad 2 \leq t \leq T. \tag{4.99}$$

The Viterbi algorithm is maybe more intuitively obtained when exploiting the first-order assumption through defining [Rabi 89]

$$\delta_t(i) = \max_{q_1, q_2, \ldots, q_{t-1}} P(q_1, q_2, \ldots, q_{t-1}, q_t = s_i, O_1, O_2, \ldots, O_t | \lambda), \tag{4.100}$$

i.e. the probability of observing the partial sequence $O_1, O_2, \ldots, O_t$ and arriving in state s_i at time t when taking the optimal (most likely) partial state sequence $q_1, q_2, \ldots, q_{t-1}$.

The scores $P^* = \max_q P(\boldsymbol{O}, \boldsymbol{q} | \lambda)$ are highly correlated to the true production probabilities $P(\boldsymbol{O} | \lambda) = \sum_q P(\boldsymbol{O}, \boldsymbol{q} | \lambda)$, and P^* is often taken as a substitute in practice [Schu 95, p. 133]. A further reduction in effort can be achieved by *beam search*, i.e. approximating P^* by retaining only few of the highest δ_{t+1} in (4.94) in each iteration.

4.5.3   Estimation

How can we estimate the parameters of an HMM from observations? We are looking for a set of parameters λ that maximize the probability $P(\boldsymbol{O} | \lambda)$. Due to the marginalization over the hidden state sequence, there is no close-form solution; therefore, one resorts to some suitable initialization and iterative improvement to a local maximum using gradient descent [Levi 83] or the expectation maximization (EM) algorithm [Demp 77]. The application of EM to HMM parameter estimation is called *Baum-Welch algorithm* [Levi 83] in recognition of Baum [Baum 68] and Welch who first derived the algorithm (using an approach different from EM) [Schu 95, p. 137]. A derivation using EM can be found for instance in [Schu 95, p. 138]; here we give a less rigorous but more intuitive derivation along the lines of Rabiner [Rabi 89].

We introduce a new auxiliary variable

$$\gamma_t(i) = P(q_t = s_i | \boldsymbol{O}, \lambda), \tag{4.101}$$

i.e. the probability being in state s_i at time t for the given observations. That probability can be calculated from the forward and backward variables. Consider

$$\alpha_t(i) \cdot \beta_t(i) = P(O_1, O_2, \ldots, O_t, q_t = s_i | \lambda) \tag{4.102}$$
$$\cdot P(O_{t+1}, O_{t+2}, \ldots, O_T | q_t = s_i, \lambda)$$
$$= P(\boldsymbol{O}, q_t = s_i | \lambda) \tag{4.103}$$
$$= P(q_t = s_i | \boldsymbol{O}, \lambda) \cdot P(\boldsymbol{O} | \lambda). \tag{4.104}$$

Dividing by $P(\boldsymbol{O}|\lambda)$ we get

$$\gamma_t(i) \;=\; \frac{\alpha_t(i)\beta_t(i)}{P(\boldsymbol{O},\lambda)}. \tag{4.105}$$

By definition, $\sum_{j=1}^{N}\gamma_t(j)=1$; therefore $\sum_{j=1}^{N}\alpha_t(j)\beta_t(j)=P(\boldsymbol{O},\lambda)$ and

$$\gamma_t(i) \;=\; \frac{\alpha_t(i)\beta_t(i)}{\sum_{j=1}^{N}\alpha_t(j)\beta_t(j)}. \tag{4.106}$$

Another auxiliary variable is

$$\xi_t(i,j) = P(q_t = s_i, q_{t+1} = s_j | O, \lambda), \tag{4.107}$$

i. e. the probability of transitioning at time t from s_i to s_j. This quantity can be calculated from the forward and backward variables, too:

$$\xi_t(i,j) \;=\; \frac{\alpha_t(i)a_{ij}b_j(O_{t+1})\beta_{t+1}(j)}{P(\boldsymbol{O},\lambda)} \tag{4.108}$$

$$\;=\; \frac{\alpha_t(i)a_{ij}b_j(O_{t+1})\beta_{t+1}(j)}{\sum_{j=1}^{N}\alpha_t(j)\beta_t(j)}. \tag{4.109}$$

When summing up $\gamma_t(i)$ over $1 \le t \le T$, we get a quantity that can be interpreted as the expected number of visits to state s_i; if we just sum until $t = T - 1$, we can interpret that as the expected *number of transitions* originating from s_i. Similarly, summing up $\xi_t(i,j)$ over $1 \le t \le T - 1$, we get a measure of the *expected number of transitions* from s_i to s_j. With these interpretations, the update formulas for the Baum-Welch algorithm, here given for the case of discrete observations, can be interpreted directly as the most likely parameter update (given forward and backward variables calculated from previous parameters):

$$\pi_i' \;=\; \text{``probability of being in state } s_i \text{ at } t = 1\text{''} \tag{4.110}$$

$$\;=\; \gamma_1(i) = \frac{\alpha_1(i)\beta_1(i)}{\sum_{j=1}^{N}\alpha_1(j)\beta_1(j)}, \tag{4.111}$$

$$a_{ij}' \;=\; \frac{\text{``expected number of transitions from } s_i \text{ to } s_j\text{''}}{\text{``expected number of transitions from } s_i\text{''}} \tag{4.112}$$

$$\;=\; \frac{\sum_{t=1}^{T-1}\xi_t(i,j)}{\sum_{t=1}^{T-1}\gamma_t(i)} \tag{4.113}$$

$$\;=\; \frac{\sum_{t=1}^{T-1}\alpha_t(i)a_{ij}b_j(O_{t+1})\beta_{t+1}(j)}{\sum_{t=1}^{T-1}\alpha_t(i)\beta_t(i)} \tag{4.114}$$

$$b_i'(v_k) \;=\; \frac{\text{``expected visits to } s_i \text{ while observing } v_k\text{''}}{\text{``expected visits to } s_i\text{''}} \tag{4.115}$$

$$\;=\; \frac{\sum_{t=1}^{T}\gamma_t(i)\delta_{O_t v_k}}{\sum_{t=1}^{T}\gamma_t(i)} \tag{4.116}$$

$$\;=\; \frac{\sum_{t=1}^{T}\alpha_t(i)\beta_t(i)\delta_{O_t v_k}}{\sum_{t=1}^{T}\alpha_t(i)\beta_t(i)}; \tag{4.117}$$

hereby, normalizations by $P(\boldsymbol{O}, \lambda)$ cancelled each other out, and δ_{ij} is the Kronecker delta. Note that there is no need to explicitly enforce a model topology: initializing a certain transition a_{ij} to zero makes sure it will stay zero forever, cf. the occurrence of a_{ij} in (4.114) and (4.109). Figure 4.24 illustrates the iterative estimation process by means of an observation generated by the example HMM of Section 4.5; it may be observed how the training learns the states' distributions 'outside to inside' (relating to the order they appear in the training data).

The update formulae for continuous outputs with GMMs, and how to estimate parameter updates from multiple observation sequences simultaneously, can be found for instance in [Rabi 89] or [Schu 95]. A simpler algorithm for estimating parameter updates is obtained when computing the most likely state sequence with the Viterbi algorithm and updating the parameters by counting the observed observations, visits and transitions in the obtained state sequence. This is called Viterbi training or segmental k-means [Rabi 89]; a further simplification is given by applying beam search in the training.

HMMs in the classic definition as reproduced here describe processes of infinite duration. They do not choose the length of the generated sequence; rather, the length is enforced during application to a finite sequence of given length. For purposes such as speech recognition with the ordered 'left-to-right' notion associated with the states, this is not perfectly suitable, and an *explicit final state* is usually introduced [Stem 05, p. 69]. The final state does not output an observation but rather ends the sequence; the forward/backward, Viterbi and Baum-Welch algorithms are adapted accordingly to enforce fully traversing of all states at the end of sequences. For example, $\beta_T(N) = 1$ for the final state s_N and $\beta_T(i) = 0$ for all 'normal' states s_i with $1 \leq i \leq N - 1$. This speeds up and stabilizes the training of left-right HMMs; consider how the classic HMM might leave states unassigned (cf. top of Figure 4.24) and how the explicit final state prevents this.

4.5.4 Modelling multiple events

Up to now, we have described the use of HMMs for modelling single, isolated patterns of variable length, so we could use them e. g. for speaker recognition (ergodic HMMs without explicit end state; training an individual HMM for each speaker), or for recognizing isolated words (left-right HMMs with explicit end state; training an individual HMM for each word). How can we use HMMs to model a *sequence of variable-length* patterns, which is necessary e. g. to recognize sentences containing more than one word?

The details depend on the specific application, but in principle this can be done by

1. segmenting the training patterns (manually) into the desired units

2. training a left-right HMM (with explicit end state) for each unit (on the respective sub-sequences of our observations), and

3. *concatenating* the HMMs for recognition.

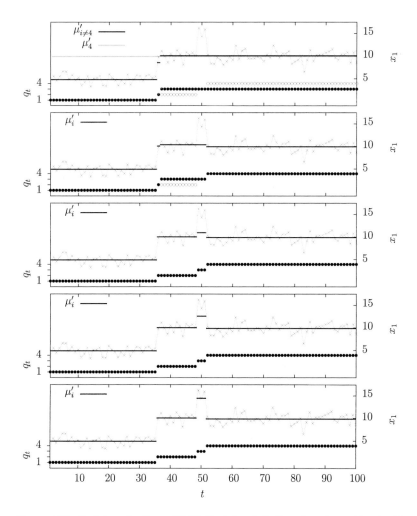

Figure 4.24: Training of a linear HMM (4 states, 1-D Gaussian observations) with a single observation sequence (crosses). The current estimate is visualized by the most likely state sequence (filled circles) and the mean of the respective Gaussian distribution. The model is initialized (top) by distributing the training sequence uniformly over the states. The graphs further below show the estimate after each Baum-Welch iteration. After the second iteration (third graph from top), the decoded states coincide with those that generated the observations (empty circles). After the fourth iteration (bottom), training has nearly converged; the estimated means of the Gaussians are close to those of the generating HMM with $(\mu_i) = (5, 10, 15, 10)^{\top}$.

Concatenation of left-right HMMs can (roughly) be achieved by arranging the original transition matrices, truncated before the end state, along the diagonal of the new transition matrix, and distributing the transition probabilities remaining from the final states such that all original start states can be reached[9]. The start probabilities can (for instance) be set to a uniform distribution, so that all units are equally likely to be visited first. The principle of this process is illustrated in Figure 4.25 and Figure 4.26.[10]

A sequence of units can now be recognized by calculating the most likely state sequence of the combined model for the given observation sequence; the recognized units can be identified by looking up which individual unit the states were originally associated with. A by-product is the *segmentation* of the observation in time in terms of the inventory of units. If the sequence of units is known, and just the segmentation is required, one can construct a suitable combined HMM that traverses each respective unit exactly once; an explicit final state is used to enforce fully traversing the model until the end. Segmentation can then be obtained by calculating the most likely state sequence of that combined HMM. That process if called *forced alignment* of the transliteration (known sequence of units) to the observation sequence.

Intriguingly, there is a way to construct the segmentation in step (1) above automatically, given the transliteration of the training patterns—in other words, given no other timing information than the order of occurring units. The process is iterative: First, segmentation is initialized *uniformly*, i. e. each observation sequence is divided into equally sized parts, which are assigned to the respective transliterated units. Then, iteratively, the HMMs are trained with the current segmentation, and the segmentation is updated from the HMMs via forced alignment. The process is very similar to Viterbi training; note that it implies a double loop as each HMM training means a number of Baum-Welch or Viterbi training iterations. This training procedure can learn both the HMM parameters of units and the segmentation of the training data; it will do so from 'outside to inside', just as individual HMM training (cf. Section 4.5.3 and Figure 4.24).

Note that this learning task of estimating the HMM parameters and the segmentation of the training data *at the same time* is ambiguous and can be ill-posed given unsuitable training data. In order to result in meaningful segmentations and models, the training procedure needs not only a data set large enough (to robustly estimate the free parameters) but also, it requires sufficient *variability* regarding order (to disambiguate the properties/locations of phonemes)[11]. To illustrate that, consider a recognizer that models each word with one HMM and a training set where all transliterations are identical:

<SILENCE> ONE TWO THREE <SILENCE>.

---

[9]Note that in a speech recognizer, things are more complex as the transition probabilities between words (language model) are modelled as a higher-order Markov process

[10]In modern speech recognizers, the combination of acoustic model and language model is achieved with the help of the uniform abstraction to *weighted finite state transducers* [Mohr 02, Alla 07, Pove 11].

[11]For speech, one typically requires at the very least one hour of transliterated speech containing several different sentences.

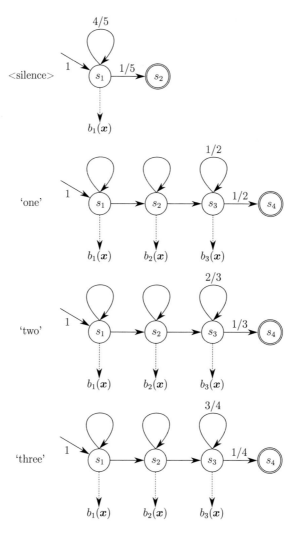

Figure 4.25: Individual HMMs for silence and three words.

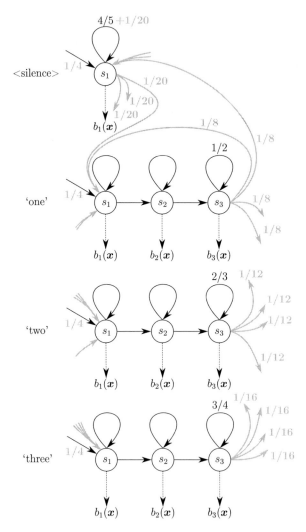

Figure 4.26:   Combination of the individual HMMs of Figure 4.25 into an ergodic HMM that can recognize any sequence of the words 'one', 'two', and 'three' with optional silence in between. Changes relative to the individual models are set in grey. For clarity, some transitions are just indicated, and the old state numbers are kept.

Here, the training procedure is not forced to learn the true words, however large the training set. For example, not only '<SILENCE>' but also 'ONE' and 'THREE' could be mapped to actual silence, and 'TWO' to the actual words sequence 'one two three', since the models are never observed in a different order that would encourage the correct disambiguation.

In this chapter, we have covered mathematical and technological background relevant for the approaches to automatic assessment in the present work. We will now continue by presenting the data collected because these have some implications on the approaches, and one also gets a clearer idea of what is being modelled.

5

Corpora

This chapter introduces the speech data used in this thesis. These data have two main functions: Firstly, they will be used for evaluating the reliability of the methods developed for automatic pronunciation assessment. Secondly, they will be used for constructing assessment procedures in a data-driven way, i.e. estimating free parameters such as β, β_0 of the SVM, and also choosing meta-parameters such as the SVM complexity C, cf. Section 4.3. Further, the material is useful for manual inspection when designing features appropriate for describing the different aspects of pronunciation (cf. Chapter 7). Note that the present chapter will only detail the material and methods used to elicit and record speech; the annotation of the data, i.e. manual assignment of pronunciation scores and labelling of errors, will be covered in Chapter 6.

5.1   C-AuDiT

This database was collected within the research project *Computer-assisted pronunciation and dialogue training*[1] (C-AuDiT) [Hön 09] jointly carried out by FAU (Friedrich-Alexander-Universität Erlangen-Nürnberg) and *digital publishing*[2], a supplier of computer-assisted language learning courses.

It contains dialogues on a hotel reservation scenario for developing a dialogue engine, and read speech for developing pronunciation assessment methods. Here, we will only relate to the latter. The database covers the two target languages English [Hön 09] and German [Hön 11]; here we will only refer to the English part.

Read material is less naturalistic than non-prompted speech, and it may contain artefacts that are more related to reading rather than pronunciation difficulties. However, "[...] it has two advantages: First, it is easier to process, and second, it allows incorporation into existing automatic training software which still builds upon written and read data. Thus, it is a relevant object of study, also from the point of view of [a] commercial applicant of CAPT." [Hön 12a]

---

[1]Funded by the German federal ministry of education, science, research and technology (BMBF) under grant 01IS07014B

[2]https://www.digitalpublishing.de, last visited September 8th, 2017

5.1.1   Text material

Each speaker read aloud 329 words and utterances; these were displayed one at a time by an automated recording software. The speakers were instructed to repeat their production in case of false starts etc. Where repetitions occurred, only the last one, i. e. the one assumed to be error-free (or at least as good as the speaker could do it) was later used for further processing. The material consists of two short stories broken down into individual sentences, isolated sentences featuring different phenomena such as accent shifts, tongue-twisters, and individual words/phrases, e. g.

> 'This is a *house*' vs. 'Is this *really* a house?' or
> 'A-*ra*-bic', 'A-*ra*-bia', 'The *A*-rab World'.

Additionally, pairs such as

> '*sub*-ject' vs. 'sub-*ject*'

had to be repeated after listening the pre-recorded production of a tutor. More details are given in Section A.1.

When designing the text material, we took 32 sentences from the ISLE database [Menz 00], which contains non-native English from 26 German and 26 Italian speakers. We did this to have the possibility to re-use existing material. Details are given in Table A.1.

For all utterances, an expert annotated a likely distribution of primary and secondary phrase accents and B2/B3 boundaries (cf. Section 2.1.2) of a prototypical, articulate realization, e. g.

> She *ate* a *bowl* of *porridge* || *checked herself* in the *mirror* || and
> *washed* her *face* | in a *hurry*.

5.1.2   Definition of subsets

To reduce the costs for some of the annotations, we retrospectively defined two smaller subsets of the data that contain those sentences "[...] prosodically most error-prone for L2 speakers of English" [Hön 10a]. The judgement relied on three experienced labellers and was given after extensive exposure to the actual recordings.

The first subset is the *reduced* set, which contains 24 sentences; the second subset is the *panel* set, which contains just 5 sentences. These 5 sentences are among those shared with the ISLE database; the name 'panel' relates to the fact that these recordings were submitted to a large panel of listeners in a perception experiment (cf. Section 6.1.2). Details are again given in Table A.1.

5.1.3   Speakers

The database comprises a total of 58 speakers; there are 26 German, 10 French, 10 Italian, 10 Spanish, and 2 Hindi native speakers. The age of the speakers varied between 17 and 51 years (mean: 32.4, standard deviation 7.2); 31 were female, 27 male. The distribution of proficiency levels according to the *Common*

CEFR level	Paraphrase	# Speakers
A1	I know some words and sentences.	1
A2	I can reply to easy questions.	8
B1	I know all basics for most situations.	12
B2	I can handle most situations.	23
C1	I can handle any complex situations.	12
C2	Near native speaker.	2

Table 5.1: CEFR skill levels of the non-native speakers in C-AuDiT. The paraphrase used in the self-assessment questionnaire is given in the second column.

European Framework of Reference for Languages (CEFR) [Coun 01], estimated by self-assessment, is given in Table 5.1.

Additionally, the material was read by 8 native US English and 3 native British English speakers. Their age varied between 24 and 49 years (35.8 ± 8.0); 5 were female, 6 male.

From the ISLE database, we used those 36 speakers that produced all 5 sentences in the panel set. These are 20 German, 16 Italian native speakers; 11 are female, 25 male.

5.1.4 Recordings

All recordings were performed in quiet offices (or similar rooms), using various inexpensive headsets/digitizers (analogue headset connected to PC sound card: 25 non-native speakers, 5 native speakers; connected to notebook sound card: 5 non-natives, 0 natives; USB headset: 28 non-natives, 6 natives). As far as possible, any manipulations by sound drivers that can deteriorate signal quality were switched off (such as 'noise' filters cutting frequencies above 4 kHz, or zeroing the signal during presumed silence). Sampling was done with a frequency of 44.1 kHz and a linear quantization with a resolution of 16 bit.

The speakers were allowed to operate the recording software at their own pace; specifically, as soon as they felt ready to speak the current prompt, they could start and stop the recording themselves. Without further provisions, that setup causes truncations: speakers often start speaking before they start the recording, and sometimes also stop the recording before they actually finished speaking. This is prevented by manipulating the recording interval chosen by the speaker: about two seconds are prepended, and about one second is appended. Technically, this is achieved by recording all the time and automatically cutting out the appropriate pieces later.

In total, $329 \times 58 = 19082$ non-native and $329 \times 11 = 3619$ native individual recordings are available, with a total duration of 29.4 h and 5.0 h, respectively. The duration of individual recordings varies from 1.0 to 28.8 seconds (5.6 ± 2.3) for the non-native data, and from 1.3 to 19.2 seconds (5.0 ± 1.8) for the native data.

For the panel set, we used 158 recordings from the ISLE database with a total duration of 0.3 h. The duration of the individual files ranges from 3.2 to 13.2 seconds (6.0 ± 1.6).

5.2 AUWL

"Reading leads to a special speaking style and can have a disruptive effect on speech, especially for learners with low L2 competence." [Hön 12a] We therefore changed the strategy for data collection in the research project *Automatic web-based learner-feedback system*[3] (AUWL) [Hön 12a] which was jointly carried out by FAU and digital publishing.

Specifically, the speakers practised pre-scripted dialogues, and a number of measures were taken to reduce reading-related problems:

- Before embarking on a given dialogue, the speakers were encouraged to make themselves familiar with the dialogue by listening to the whole dialogue spoken by reference speakers (*listening mode*). Three female and three male reference speakers were available; to take into account less proficient learners, one could choose between normal and slow realizations.

- By default, the speakers could read off their lines which were displayed as text when due (*karaoke mode*). Additionally, the speakers had the possibility to first listen to their lines spoken by a reference speaker and repeat afterwards (*listening & karaoke mode*).

- Another option was to speak simultaneously with a reference speaker (*shadowing mode*). To ease synchronization, recording and replay started after a countdown; additionally, there was the possibility to combine shadowing with first listening (*listening & shadowing mode*).

- For the sake of less proficient speakers, there was an option to subdivide down longer dialogue steps into smaller phrases, e.g. "I'm afraid | there are no more seats available | on the 8 o'clock train."

These measures were implemented by *dialogue of the day*, a web-based tool that also handled recording and storage of the data, cf. Figures 5.1 and 5.2.

5.2.1 Text material

The target language for AUWL was again English. Eighteen dialogues were available to the learner, on topics such as leisure activities, business negotiations or holidays. Six dialogues each were targeted for the CEFR skill levels A2 (elementary), B1 (pre-intermediate) and B2 (intermediate). In total, the material amounts to 159 dialogue lines; the option to subdivide the longer ones (applies to 98 out of the 159) adds 271 sub-phrases. More details about the dialogues are given in Section A.2.

For all turns, an expert annotated a likely distribution of primary and secondary phrase accents and B2/B3 boundaries (cf. Section 2.1.2) of a prototypical, articulate realization, e. g.

Hi | *welcome* to the ***company*** || *shall* I *show* you ***around***?

---

[3]Funded by the German ministry of economics (BMWi) under grant KF2027104ED0

Figure 5.1: The web-based dialogue training tool that was used for data collection in AUWL. Lines to be spoken by the learner are displayed in blue; the current one is set in bold face. There are displays for the current recording/replay loudness level, and whether loudspeakers or microphone are currently active. The buttons at the bottom allow the learner to navigate through the dialogue and manipulate settings (cf. Figure 5.2).

Figure 5.2: Settings of the AUWL dialogue training tool.

CEFR level	Paraphrase	# Speakers
A1	I know some words and sentences.	0
A2	I can reply to easy questions.	5
B1	I know all basics for most situations.	5
B2	I can handle most situations.	9
C1	I can handle any complex situations.	12
C2	Near native speaker.	0

Table 5.2: CEFR skill levels of the non-native speakers in AUWL. The paraphrase used in the self-assessment questionnaire is given in the second column.

5.2.2 Speakers

The database comprises speech from 31 speakers: 16 German, 4 Italian, 3 Chinese, 3 Japanese, 2 Arabic, 1 Brazilian Portuguese, 1 French, and 1 Hungarian native speaker. The age of the speakers varied between 17 and 69 (36.2 ± 15.4); 13 were female, 18 male. The distribution of CEFR skill levels, according to self-assessment, is given in Table 5.2.

The reference speakers were all native speakers of American English; as mentioned above, 3 were female and 3 male.

5.2.3 Recordings

The participants performed the recordings at home, using the web interface and their own hardware. Although we asked the speakers to use a headset, the precise recording conditions were outside our control. As a result of this, the audio quality is quite heterogeneous; on the other hand, this setup is quite realistic. According to a questionnaire, 14 USB headsets, 9 analogue connected headsets, 3 analogue connected table microphones and 5 other microphones were used. Sound level control was assisted by the dialogue training tool by issuing warnings when the sound level was either too low or too high (i. e. saturated). Sampling was done with a frequency of 32 kHz and a linear quantization with a resolution of 16 bits.

Through the possibility for pausing in between and navigating through the dialogue, the learners are able to train at their own pace. Several measures are taken by the tool to prevent cropped recordings: Where possible, recording starts half a second before the presumed start of the speaker's utterance; in case the learner interrupts the dialogue with the stop button, recording is only stopped half a second later. When the speaker starts the dialogue directly at a position where it is his or her turn to speak, and dialogue mode 'karaoke' or 'listening & karaoke' is chosen, there is an increased danger of cropping. This risk is mitigated by turning on the microphone display to 'active' only half a second after the user pressed the start button.

The learners were encouraged to try different dialogue modes; there were no measures to make sure all material was covered by each speaker. In total, 5145 non-native recordings were collected, corresponding to 7.8 h. According to manual inspection performed by a single listener, 3732 (5.5 h) of these were classified as clean (no word errors), 909 (1.7 h) as still usable (some word editing relative to target text; some louder noise), and 504 (0.6 h) as unusable (many word errors or dominant noise).

Of the $159 + 271 = 430$ possible dialogue lines and sub-phrases, 412 were actually realized. (That means that not all dialogues were covered completely with the subdivision option switched on.) The duration of clean recordings varies from 1.8 to 23.5 seconds (5.3 ± 2.2).

For the native reference data, all six speakers produced each dialogue line twice (normal and slow tempo), resulting in $159 \times 2 \times 6 = 1908$ recordings (1.8 h). Duration varied from 0.9 to 16.2 seconds (4.4 ± 2.4) for the slow version and from 1.0 to 15.3 seconds (4.0 ± 2.2) for the version in normal tempo. The corresponding $271 \times 2 \times 6 = 3252$ sub-phrases were automatically cut from the whole dialogue lines; for segmentation, forced alignment (cf. Section 4.5.4) of the target texts was used. The resulting files' duration ranges from 0.8 to 5.1 seconds (2.1 ± 0.7) for the slow version and from 0.8 to 5.1 seconds (2.0 ± 0.62) for the version in normal tempo; the total duration is 1.8 h.

After having laid out the nature of the recordings collected, we will now proceed to the annotation of the data, which is pivotal for our purposes, because this will provide us with a reference when inspecting the data during development, when evaluating the reliability of the approaches, and when applying supervised machine learning algorithms.

6

Annotation

This chapter will detail the manual annotation of the recordings presented in the previous chapter. Annotation comprises both the assignment of concrete pronunciation errors and the assessment of pronunciation quality on an ordinal scale, and is done according to the subjective perception of a human listener. Note that this chapter will only describe the actual collection of labels; the combination of multiple labellers to get an improved reference for machine learning will be treated in Chapter 8, as it is not clear a priori how to proceed best.

6.1 C-AuDiT

For C-AuDiT, two kinds of annotations were carried out: a detailed, costly annotation by relatively few labellers, and a global, quick annotation by many labellers.

6.1.1 Detailed annotation

Annotation scheme: A comprehensive annotation scheme was developed for supra-segmental and segmental aspects, covering different levels where applicable (global, phrase, word, syllable, and phoneme). An overview of the annotation scheme is given in Table 6.1; the software *Annotool* that was developed for this task is shown in Figure 6.1.

To speed up annotation of local aspects, the annotation tool provided the labellers with the possibility to automatically select individual words or phonemes in the recording. The segmentation necessary for this feature was created by forced alignment (cf. Section 4.5.4) of the target text.

When initially loading a recording, everything is assumed to be pronounced perfectly, i. e. no errors are selected and all scores are set to 'good'. To discriminate the state 'not yet annotated' from 'perfect', there were specific buttons to mark whether a certain group of aspects has been finished (supra-segmentals, segmentals on word, or segmentals on phoneme level).

Note that the different labels are not independent: For example, for a word marked as deleted, all annotations on word level or below do not apply. Labels are also not unique: For example, a syllable insertion can just as well be described by a syllable

Level	Criterion	Values
Global	Usable	yes/no (e. g. recording problems)
	Comment	arbitrary string
	General Prosody	good/middle/bad
	Rhythm	good/middle/bad
	Pitch Contour	good/middle/bad
	Sentence Mood	statement/question/command/exclamation
Phrase	Phrase Boundary	none/minor/full
	Phrase Accent	none/secondary/primary/emphatic
Word	Editing	none/substitution/deletion/insertion
	Pronunciation Quality	good/medium/bad
	Intelligibility	good/medium/bad
Syllable	Word Accent	none/secondary/primary
	Syllable editing	none/insertions/splitting (with accents)
Phoneme	Editing	variant/substitution/deletion/insertion

Table 6.1: Annotation scheme used in C-AuDiT. Insertion of phonemes just discriminates between vowels and consonants. Insertion and splits of syllables include specifying the accent structure (none/secondary/primary) per syllable.

split. These facts have to be kept in mind when comparing or merging the annotation of different labellers.

Annotated files: The first part of the annotations was carried out by three labellers (phoneticians experienced in annotation). As supra-segmental assessment was the more innovative aspect of C-AuDiT, we wanted to get data for according experiments quickly. We therefore skipped the annotation of the phoneme level at that time.

We obtained detailed annotations according to Table 6.1 (except phoneme level) for the full material of 24 speakers, i. e. $329 \times 24 = 7896$ recordings. Of the 24 speakers, 14 were annotated by all 3 labellers, 2 were annotated by 2 labellers, and 8 were annotated by one labeller.

During the course of the annotations, it became apparent that inter-labeller agreement was relatively low; to get more reliable data, we decided to engage more labellers in the task. Additionally, we now wanted to include the phoneme level. To use the funds available for annotation in the best way, we therefore decided to concentrate efforts on the reduced set of sentences (the prosodically most interesting subset, cf. Sections 5.1.2 and A.1).

We obtained detailed annotations according to Table 6.1 for the reduced material of all speakers, i. e. $24 \times 58 = 1392$ recordings. Of the 58 speakers, 6 were annotated by 10 labellers, 47 were annotated by 9 labellers, and 5 were annotated by 8 labellers.

6.1.2 Panel

That annotation scheme introduced above is very detailed; however, the global scores for prosody (general/rhythm/pitch) are quite coarse with just the three possible values good, middle, and bad. This may contribute to the relatively low correlation that

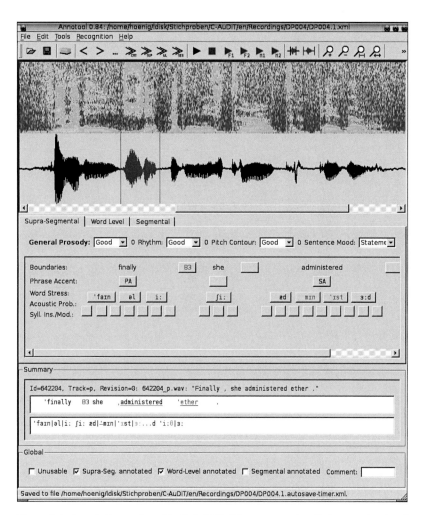

Figure 6.1: Annotation tool used in C-AuDiT. The user can visually inspect the signal and its spectrogram, zoom in or out, and listen to the whole or to selected parts of the recording. Annotated errors (or scores differing from 'good') are highlighted in red. The target text is displayed as well as a summary of the current annotation.

we observed between scores from different labellers. We therefore defined another annotation scheme for global scores; it was designed as a perception experiment with a *panel* of many listeners. To limit time for each listener, the panel annotation was just done with a very small subset of the C-AuDiT data comprising 5 sentences; however, we added speakers from the ISLE database cf. Sections 5.1.2 and A.1. We had the listeners rate intelligibility, general non-native accent, sentence melody, and rhythm on a 5-point Likert scale. Additionally, the listeners were asked to identify the presumable L1 of the speaker (among the given set of occurring L1s). The questions are given in Figure 6.2.

Annotations according to Figure 6.2 are available for 469 recordings (58 C-AuDiT speakers, 36 ISLE speakers; 5 sentences; minus one empty recording). For each file and criterion, labels from 22 native American English, 19 native British English, and 21 native Scottish English listeners are available. In total, this amounts to 124 285 individual labels. The PEAKS system [Maie 09b] was used for collecting the annotations over the internet.

6.2   AUWL

For the AUWL data, all clean and usable (cf. Section 5.2.3) recordings were annotated similarly to the panel scheme in C-AuDiT. However, as we observed only very small differences between the answers to the 'melody' and 'rhythm' questions [Hön 10a], we merged these two into a single prosody question:

> The English language has a characteristic prosody (sentence melody, and rhythm, i.e. timing of the syllables). This sentence's prosody sounds...
>
> (1) normal
>
> (2) acceptable, but not perfectly normal
>
> (3) slightly unusual
>
> (4) unusual
>
> (5) very unusual.

In total, 4641 recordings have been annotated accordingly by 5 native English (United Kingdom and Ireland) post-graduate phoneticians. This amounts to 92 820 individual labels.

6.3   Inter-rater agreement

All annotation criteria have been devised carefully in close cooperation with phonetic experts, and intuitively, they seem valid for their purpose, although a formal proof of validity—if possible at all—was considered beyond the scope of the thesis and was not attempted. A necessary condition for validity, however, is reliability, which we can measure by comparing the labels from different annotators.

We constrain ourselves here to measuring how well a *pair of labellers* is in agreement, on average. It would be more instructive to compare a labeller with hypothetical true labels, the so-called *ground truth*; but this is more difficult to estimate and

1. Did you understand what the speaker said?

   (1) yes, the sentence is completely understandable
   (2) yes, but some parts are not easy to understand
   (3) well, the sentence needs some effort to be understood
   (4) no, most parts of the sentence are not easy to understand
   (5) no, the sentence cannot be understood at all

2. Did you hear a foreign, non-English accent?

   (1) no
   (2) very slight
   (3) some accent
   (4) strong accent
   (5) extreme accent

3. What kind of accent do you think this speaker has?

   (1) American
   (2) British
   (3) French
   (4) Italian
   (5) German
   (6) Spanish
   (7) Russian
   (8) Japanese
   (9) Indian
   (10) I don't know

4. This sentence's melody sounds. . .

   (1) normal
   (2) acceptable, but not perfectly normal
   (3) slightly unusual
   (4) unusual
   (5) very unusual

5. The English language has a characteristic rhythm (timing of the syllables). How do you assess the rhythm of this sentence?

   (1) normal
   (2) acceptable, but not perfectly normal
   (3) slightly unusual
   (4) unusual
   (5) very unusual

Figure 6.2: Questions for the panel annotation in C-AuDiT.

Ground truth	1	0	1	0	1	0	1	0	0	1	0	1	0	1	0	1
Labeller 1	**0**	0	1	0	**0**	0	1	0	**1**	1	0	1	**1**	1	0	1
Labeller 2	**0**	1	**0**	1	1	0	1	0	0	1	0	1	0	1	0	1

Table 6.2: Pairwise disagreement vs. real error, illustrated for a hypothetical database with ground truth and human labels. Human errors are set in bold face. Interpreted as a binary classification task, each labeller's error rate is $4/12 = 0.25$, distinctly lower than the pairwise disagreement of $6/16 = 37.5\%$. Interpreted as a regression task, a labeller's Pearson correlation with the ground truth is 0.5, while the labeller's pairwise correlation is only 0.25.

needs a number of assumptions that may not be appropriate. We contend ourselves with noting that it has to be kept in mind that pair-wise comparisons will always be *pessimistic estimates* of the reliability of one labeller. We illustrate this for two idealized cases, a classification and a regression task.

The classification task is a binary classification task, assuming two balanced (i. e. equally likely) classes. Labellers have an equal probability $e < 0.5$ to assign an erroneous class label; errors are independent of the true class and of the errors of other labellers. The probability d for two labellers to disagree on an item is then

$$
\begin{aligned}
d \;&=\; P(\text{``Labeller 1 correct and labeller 2 wrong''}) \,+ \\
&\quad\;\; P(\text{``Labeller 1 wrong and labeller 2 correct''}) & (6.1)\\
&=\; (1-e)\cdot e + e\cdot(1-e) & (6.2)\\
&=\; 2e\cdot(1-e) & (6.3)
\end{aligned}
$$

which is larger than e as $1-e > 0.5$. To phrase this intuitively, one can say that pairwise disagreement is a pessimistic estimate of labeller errors because we are counting *both* labeller's errors ($2e$), although subtracting the (fewer) coinciding errors ($2e^2$). The situation is illustrated with a hypothetical database in Table 6.2.

For the regression task, we assume normally distributed labels $\boldsymbol{y}_i$ for labeller i with equal variance σ^2 and equal pairwise Pearson correlation $c > 0$ for any pair of labellers. The ground truth is defined as the mean of infinitely many labellers, i. e.

$$
\boldsymbol{y} = \lim_{N\to\infty} \frac{1}{N} \sum_{i=1}^{N} \boldsymbol{y}_i. \tag{6.4}
$$

The correlation r of one labeller $\boldsymbol{y}_1$ with the ground truth $\boldsymbol{y}$ is then

$$r = \frac{\mathrm{cov}(\boldsymbol{y}_1, \boldsymbol{y})}{\sigma \sigma_{\boldsymbol{y}}} \tag{6.5}$$

$$= \lim_{N \to \infty} \frac{\mathrm{cov}(\boldsymbol{y}_1, \frac{1}{N} \sum_{i=1}^{N} \boldsymbol{y}_i)}{\sigma \sqrt{\mathrm{cov}(\frac{1}{N} \sum_{i=1}^{N} \boldsymbol{y}_i, \frac{1}{N} \sum_{i=1}^{N} \boldsymbol{y}_i)}} \tag{6.6}$$

$$= \lim_{N \to \infty} \frac{\frac{1}{N} \mathrm{cov}(\boldsymbol{y}_1, \sum_{i=1}^{N} \boldsymbol{y}_i)}{\sigma \sqrt{\frac{1}{N^2} \mathrm{cov}(\sum_{i=1}^{N} \boldsymbol{y}_i, \sum_{i=1}^{N} \boldsymbol{y}_i)}} \tag{6.7}$$

$$= \lim_{N \to \infty} \frac{\sum_{i=1}^{N} \mathrm{cov}(\boldsymbol{y}_1, \boldsymbol{y}_i)}{\sigma \sqrt{\sum_{i=1}^{N} \sum_{j=1}^{N} \mathrm{cov}(\boldsymbol{y}_i, \boldsymbol{y}_j)}} \tag{6.8}$$

$$= \lim_{N \to \infty} \frac{\sigma^2 + (N-1) \cdot c\sigma^2}{\sigma \sqrt{N(\sigma^2 + (N-1)c\sigma^2)}} \tag{6.9}$$

$$= \lim_{N \to \infty} \frac{1 + (N-1) \cdot c}{\sqrt{N(1 + (N-1)c)}} \tag{6.10}$$

$$= \lim_{N \to \infty} \frac{Nc + 1 - c}{\sqrt{N^2 c + N - Nc}} \tag{6.11}$$

$$= \lim_{N \to \infty} \frac{c + \frac{1-c}{N}}{\sqrt{c + \frac{1-c}{N}}} \tag{6.12}$$

$$= \frac{c}{\sqrt{c}} \tag{6.13}$$

$$= \sqrt{c} \tag{6.14}$$

which is greater than the pairwise correlation c. Again, phrased intuitively, pairwise correlation is a pessimistic estimate of labeller performance because it compares a labeller with an imperfect reference. Table 6.2 serves as an example for the regression case, too.

This chapter detailed the annotation of the data, i. e. how we obtained a reference for the assessment we want to automatize. With that, we are now ready to present the approaches to automatic assessment proposed in this thesis.

7

Modelling of prosody

The pronunciation phenomena we aim to assess are properties of patterns with variable length. Two principle architectures are therefore conceivable:

Direct modelling as variable-length patterns. For global prosody scoring, the whole recording could be modelled as a single isolated, variable-length pattern, similar to isolated word modelling using an HMM, cf. Section 4.5. For assessing individual prosodic units (e. g. syllables), the recording would be modelled as a *sequence* of variable-length patterns, similar to a recognizer for word sequences built from multiple HMMs, cf. Section 4.5.4. In both cases, the observation sequences can be formed from acoustic short-time feature vectors, cf. Section 4.1.

A variant of this approach is supervising the segmentation process for prosodic units [Mine 97]: In order to take full advantage of phonetic knowledge and the target word sequence, a speech recognizer can be used to segment the target units. Then, each unit can be modelled as an isolated, variable-length pattern in the sense of Section 4.5.

Indirect modelling with higher-level features. Variable-length patterns are described by a *fixed-size* feature vector, which can then be processed by classification and regression methods for fixed-length patterns, cf. Sections 4.3 and 4.4. For individual prosodic units, each unit (as segmented by a speech recognizer) is processed separately; for global prosody scoring, only a single feature vector is computed and processed. In both cases, higher-level features can be obtained by describing the evolution of acoustic short-time feature vectors (cf. Section 4.1) within the patterns. For example, a feature describing a syllable could be the slope of the intensity during the respective interval. For global scoring, the slope could be computed over the whole recording; or the average slope of all syllables could be taken.

In general, direct modelling has the potential for superior accuracy—it skips the computation of heuristic higher-level features, which are lossy and may be based on doubtful segmentations, and leaves it to the model to learn in a data-driven way how to best accumulate information over time. However, a powerful model and a sufficiently large training database are necessary.

Indirect modelling has the advantage that the working of the model is potentially more easily accessible to inspection and interpretation. To reach that goal, however, typically a lot of expert knowledge and engineering is required.

In the specific case of prosody analysis, the traditional model for variable-length patterns, the HMM, may not be ideally suited. For example, durations are not modelled well, which are important in prosody. Also, it actually seems better to do segmentation with a speech recognizer (exploiting the knowledge of the spoken target words), rather than by the prosodic models themselves, as was shown by Minematsu [Mine 97]. These may be reasons why the vast majority of approaches for prosody analysis (cf. Chapter 3) are based on the indirect approach.

The development of the long short-term memory [Hoch 97], a powerful model for variable-length patterns, together with advances gained in the recent renaissance of neuronal networks (convolutional layers [LeCu 98], dropout and rectified linear units [Dahl 13], and improved initialization methods [He 15]; cf. [LeCu 15] for an overview), may change this in the future. Nevertheless, the traditional indirect approach was chosen here: First, methods based on neuronal networks typically require intensive tuning to reach the performance of traditional approaches [Mild 15] which is not well in line with the general focus of the thesis. Second, the better possibilities for inspection and interpretation were deemed very valuable in the given application context of language learning. Third, the traditional approach has advantages for integration in an end-to-end system [Komp 96] (e. g. re-usage of results from an utterance verification step).

This chapter will describe the design of suitable higher-level features (cf. Section 7.1) and details of the application of classification and regression algorithms (cf. Section 7.2). The features will be described separately, and first, because some of them will later be used for multiple purposes.

7.1 Features

Feature design can broadly be categorized into *specialized* and *exhaustive* approaches. In the specialized approach, a relatively small feature set is specifically crafted for the task and the target domain. The language rhythm metrics (cf. Sections 2.1.3 and 3.2) are examples of this approach. The advantage of the approach is that features can be designed such that they are well interpretable; however, as noted above, usually a lot of expert knowledge and engineering is required.

The exhaustive approach, on the other hand, will enumerate in a brute force manner every aspect of the signal that might possibly be relevant and leave it to the classifier to find out the actually relevant features, or the best weighting of them. In the extreme case, the whole signal is taken as feature vector without further processing. Through its exhaustiveness, the approach has the potential for superior classification and regression performance; however, that requires a sufficiently large and representative training database, and a powerful classification or regression method. (A very successful method in that context are convolutional neural networks [LeCu 98], which have built-in support for some translational invariance in the input space; thus, they can actually be viewed as a combination of automatic feature extraction and classification/regression.)

For our specific aim of constructing higher-level features for variable-length patterns (cf. above), a pure brute-force approach would be paradoxical: after all, one reason for indirect modelling was interpretability. Also, if we had aimed at purely data-driven methods, we would have chosen the direct modelling approach (cf. above), liberating us from the task of designing higher-level features in the first place. Nevertheless, we adopt one brute-force aspect in our feature extraction: we exhaustively include many features that might be relevant without manually checking their actual relevance. For instance, the same calculations that are carried out for short-time intensity are equally applied to the F0 contour. Similarly, calculations that are applied to syllables are equally applied to syllable nuclei. Thus, we reduce the chance of missing relevant information present in the speech signal; also we keep description and implementation concise. We are aware that this comes at the cost of some redundancy in the feature set, and also of a high dimensionality. With modern models such as SVM or SVR, however, that is not necessarily a problem. Interpretability suffers to some extent, too, but data-driven methods such as feature selection can be used to alleviate the problem.

In spite of the availability of a prosody module [Kies 97, Batl 00, Zeis 12], which implements a pertinent feature set that has been successfully applied to the tasks at hand [Hön 09, Hön 10a, Hön 10b, Hön 11, Hön 12b, Hön 12a, Hön 15], a new, more generic approach was taken here. The reasons were the following:

- A generic design allows a straightforward application to new tasks and domains, and thus has a higher potential impact;

- implementation and description can be kept more modular and concise; and

- the exhaustiveness has the potential for improved classification and regression performance.

Note that we do not attempt to replicate the quite complex scheme of phoneme specific (and syllable/word specific) normalizations featured by the prosody module. That might cost some performance for classification, as information about text-intrinsic properties is not exploited; however, some of this information can be substituted by other, easier measures: suitable selection of units to compute features from (e. g. syllables instead of whole words), or adding phoneme (or phoneme category) histograms. Also, phoneme-intrinsic normalizations are not necessarily well applicable to L2 speech, as the frequently occurring phoneme substitutions violate the underlying assumptions. A more promising strategy might be providing information about the *actually* produced phonemes, and leaving it to the classifier to perform suitable normalizations implicitly. This is easily possible with the taken approach, i. e. by adding MFCC to the other short-time features.

We now introduce a generic formulation for calculating higher-level features from short-time features within a given unit or *segment*. The actual application to the problems at hand (which short-time features, which segments) will be treated later on (cf. Section 7.1.2).

Note that our approach is less generic than the *Munich versatile and fast open-source audio feature extractor* (openSMILE, [Eybe 10, Eybe 13]), which also computes an acoustic-prosodic feature set: we exploit the knowledge of the spoken target sentence, and incorporate phonetic knowledge about the specific task when choosing the segments to compute features from, cf. Section 7.1.2 below.

7.1.1   Generic descriptors

The input, i. e. the sequence of short-time features within the segment is denoted[1] as $f_0, f_1, \ldots, f_{N-1} = \boldsymbol{f}$; in general, N is variable, and each of the f_i may be undefined (denoted as $f_i \notin \mathbb{R}$). This is to account for missing values in the data such as the F0 value where speech is unvoiced. The descriptors are primarily intended for describing short-time features spaced uniformly in time. They still can be applied to non-uniformly sampled data; however, some descriptors change their semantics then. The description here only relates to segments in one-dimensional data; note, however, that all features can be generalized to hypercubes in higher dimensional data in a straightforward manner. In the following, the functions used as segment descriptors are detailed; cf. Table 7.1 for an overview and a classification into different types. For conciseness, we assume all given functions to be well-defined for now (e. g. $N > 1$); special cases (such as $N \leq 1$, or $f_i \notin \mathbb{R}$ for all i) will be treated separately later on. Also the effects of the different normalizations will be treated later on.

Statistical descriptors: For brevity, $g_0, g_1, \ldots, g_{V-1} = \boldsymbol{g}$ denotes the vector composed of the $V \leq N$ *valid* (i. e. not undefined) inputs $f_i \in \mathbb{R}$. With that, the 14 statistical descriptors are comprised of the mean value

$$\mathrm{mean}(\boldsymbol{f}) = \frac{1}{V} \sum_{i=0}^{V-1} g_i =: \mu, \tag{7.1}$$

the standard deviation

$$\mathrm{sd}(\boldsymbol{f}) = \sqrt{\frac{1}{V} \sum_{i=0}^{V-1} (g_i - \mu)^2} =: \sigma, \tag{7.2}$$

Pearson's moment coefficient of skewness [Stan 70, p. 88]

$$\mathrm{skew}(\boldsymbol{f}) = \frac{1}{V} \sum_{i=0}^{V-1} \left(\frac{g_i - \mu}{\sigma} \right)^3, \tag{7.3}$$

the excess kurtosis [Stan 70, p. 89]

$$\mathrm{kurtosis}(\boldsymbol{f}) = \frac{1}{V} \sum_{i=0}^{V-1} \left(\frac{g_i - \mu}{\sigma} \right)^4 - 3, \tag{7.4}$$

and the minimum and maximum

$$\min(\boldsymbol{f}) = \min_{0 \leq i < V} g_i =: \alpha, \tag{7.5}$$

$$\max(\boldsymbol{f}) = \max_{0 \leq i < V} g_i =: \beta. \tag{7.6}$$

---

[1] As in Section 4.1, indices start with zero in this section.

Type	Feature(s)
Statistics	mean
	sd
	skewness
	kurtotis
	min
	max
	q0.0625, q0.125, q0.25, q0.5, q0.75, q0.875, q0.9375
	finite
Duration	length (∗)
	argmin
	argmax
	onsetpos
	offsetpos
	pausebeforeabs
	pauseafterabs
	pausebeforerel
	pauseafterrel
Shape	onset
	offset
	slope
	regerr
	masscenter (†)
	finitecenter
	dct0, dct1, ..., dct9
Frequency	pvi
	pvi2
	npvi (†)
	npvi2 (†)
	band0, band1, ..., band9

Table 7.1: Segment descriptors used for computing higher-level features from variable-length segments. Note that the type of a descriptor is sometimes ambiguous, and the given classification can only be viewed as an approximation: For example, 'min' or 'argmin' are also related to shape. Notations used: 'sd' is standard deviation; features prefixed with 'q' denote quantiles, prefix 'dct' denotes discrete cosine coefficients. 'pvi' is short for pairwise variability index (see text). Energies in frequency bands are prefixed with 'band'. (∗) only applies if N is not constant a priori; (†) only applies if input is positive a priori.

Seven quantiles ('q0.0625' for the 6.25 %-Quantile, 'q0.125' for the 12.5 %-Quantile, 'q0.25' for the 25 %-Quantile, 'q0.5' for the median, etc.) are similarly computed on $\boldsymbol{g}$. The proportion of valid inputs is also included as

$$\text{finite}(\boldsymbol{f}) = \frac{V}{N}. \tag{7.7}$$

Duration descriptors: There are 9 descriptors for duration, including the length of the segment

$$\text{length}(\boldsymbol{f}) = N, \tag{7.8}$$

which is only used in cases where the segments are known to be of variable length. The position of the minimum and maximum are normalized by dividing through the length N; in case of non-uniqueness, the average positions are used (δ_{ij} is the Kronecker delta):

$$\text{argmin}(\boldsymbol{f}) \quad = \quad \frac{1}{N} \cdot \frac{1}{\sum_{i=0}^{N-1} \delta_{\alpha f_i}} \sum_{i=0}^{N-1} \delta_{\alpha f_i} \cdot i \tag{7.9}$$

$$\text{argmax}(\boldsymbol{f}) \quad = \quad \frac{1}{N} \cdot \frac{1}{\sum_{i=0}^{N-1} \delta_{\beta f_i}} \sum_{i=0}^{N-1} \delta_{\beta f_i} \cdot i. \tag{7.10}$$

Further, the positions of the first and last valid input (relative to the length) are used:

$$\min_{f_i \in \mathbb{R}} i \quad =: \quad k, \tag{7.11}$$

$$\max_{f_i \in \mathbb{R}} i \quad =: \quad l, \tag{7.12}$$

$$\text{onsetpos}(\boldsymbol{f}) \quad = \quad \frac{k}{N}, \tag{7.13}$$

$$\text{offsetpos}(\boldsymbol{f}) \quad = \quad \frac{l}{N}. \tag{7.14}$$

The remaining duration descriptors are only relevant if the current segment is one of multiple segments in a row: 'pausebeforeabs' is the absolute difference between the last index of the previous segment and the first index of the current segment; 'pauseafterabs' is the absolute difference between the last index of the current segment and the first index of the next segment. 'pausebeforerel' and 'pauseafterrel' are variants which are normalized by dividing the absolute pauses by the length N of the current segment.

Shape descriptors: The 16 shape descriptors include the first and last valid input:

$$\text{onset}(\boldsymbol{f}) \quad = \quad f_k, \tag{7.15}$$
$$\text{offset}(\boldsymbol{f}) \quad = \quad f_l. \tag{7.16}$$

A further shape descriptor is the slope of the regression line through all valid inputs, normalized by multiplication with the length N of the segment. Using $\boldsymbol{h}$ to denote the indices of all valid inputs $f_i \in \mathbb{R}$ and $\mu_h = 1/V \sum_{i=0}^{V-1} h_i$ and $\sigma_h^2 = 1/V \sum_{i=0}^{V-1} (h_i - \mu_h)^2$ as the associated mean and variance, the slope is given by

$$\frac{\frac{1}{V} \sum_{i=0}^{V-1} g_i h_i - \mu \mu_h}{\sigma_h^2} =: \Delta, \tag{7.17}$$

and the normalized slope by

$$\text{slope}(\boldsymbol{f}) = N \cdot \Delta. \tag{7.18}$$

We also compute the mean squared error of the regression line,

$$\text{regerr}(\boldsymbol{f}) = \sqrt{\frac{1}{V} \sum_{i=0}^{V-1} \left(\Delta \cdot (h_i - \mu_h) + \mu - g_i \right)^2}. \tag{7.19}$$

(Adding the error of the regression line is redundant, since σ and Δ are already provided; however, the relationship is non-linear, so we prefer to add the value explicitly, also because we intend to (at least partly) use linear regression/classification approaches later.) A shape descriptor that is only used if the input is known to be positive a priori is the centre of mass of all valid inputs, normalized by dividing through the length N of the segment:

$$\text{masscenter}(\boldsymbol{f}) = \frac{1}{N} \frac{\sum_{i=0}^{V-1} g_i h_i}{\sum_{i=0}^{V-1} g_i}. \tag{7.20}$$

In all cases, the centre of mass of the binary feature "validity" (1 if value is valid; 0 if value is undefined) is used, normalized by dividing through the length N:

$$\text{finitecenter}(\boldsymbol{f}) \quad = \quad \frac{1}{N} \frac{\sum_{i=0}^{V-1} h_i}{V} \tag{7.21}$$

$$= \quad \frac{1}{N} \cdot \mu_h. \tag{7.22}$$

The final group of shape descriptors are the 10 lower coefficients of a DCT-II [Huan 01, p. 228] of the input, i.e. a representation of the coarse shape of the sequence of input values (cf. Section 4.1.2 where DCT-II is used for the same purpose). Undefined values are substituted by linear interpolation (at the tails, extrapolation with the nearest defined neighbour is used); the DCT coefficients are normalized by dividing through N. To avoid size-dependent changes in way the DCT coefficients represent shape, no zero-padding to the next power of two is applied[2]. Figure 7.1 illustrates interpolation and how the DCT coefficients represent shape.

---

[2]With the chosen DCT implementation (using the Python library scipy.fftpack, cf. https://docs.scipy.org/doc/scipy/reference/generated/scipy.fftpack.dct.html, last visited September 8th, 2017), the worst-case complexity (for N prime) is quadratic in N; however, since we apply the DCT not to the speech signal itself, but only to sequences of short-time features with a much lower sampling frequency, that does not present a problem.

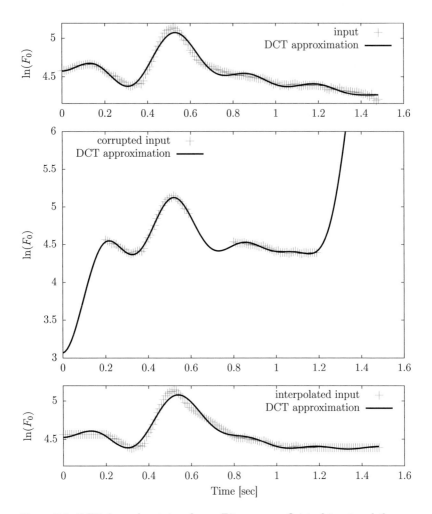

Figure 7.1: DCT shape descriptors for an F0 sequence: Original input and the approximation by 10 DCT coefficients, visualized by re-transforming the zero-padded DCT coefficients (top); corrupted input (undefined values before 0.2 sec, between 0.6 and 0.8 sec, and after 1.2 sec), with DCT coefficients minimizing the squared re-transformation error (middle); linear interpolation of the missing values (bottom). Linear interpolation leads to a result similar to the original one; Least-squares produces spurious oscillations which were not present in the original data.

Frequency descriptors: The 14 frequency descriptors include pairwise variability indices inspired by Grabe and Low [Grab 02]. Hereby, the set $A = \{i : f_i, f_{i+1} \in \mathbb{R}\}$ contains the indices of all valid inputs which also have a valid right neighbour:

$$\mathrm{pvi}(\boldsymbol{f}) = \frac{1}{|A|} \sum_{i \in A} |f_{i+1} - f_i|, \tag{7.23}$$

$$\mathrm{pvi2}(\boldsymbol{f}) = \sqrt{\frac{1}{|A|} \sum_{i \in A} (f_{i+1} - f_i)^2}, \tag{7.24}$$

$$\mathrm{npvi}(\boldsymbol{f}) = \frac{1}{|A|} \sum_{i \in A} \frac{|f_{i+1} - f_i|}{\frac{1}{2}(f_{i+1} + f_i)}, \tag{7.25}$$

$$\mathrm{npvi2}(\boldsymbol{f}) = \sqrt{\frac{1}{|A|} \sum_{i \in A} \left(\frac{f_{i+1} - f_i}{\frac{1}{2}(f_{i+1} + f_i)} \right)^2}. \tag{7.26}$$

The normalized versions npvi and npvi2 are only used if input is known to be positive a priori.

The remaining frequency descriptors are energies in 10 frequency bands. First, for the sake of simplicity, missing values are interpolated by zeros. Depending on the distribution of missing values throughout the input, that will smear the true frequencies; however, for our short-time signals, the impact should be moderate, since we can expect missing values to occur in blocks (e. g. unvoiced periods for F0), and not scattered throughout the input. Thus, the true frequencies will be smeared across the frequency range to some extent, but artefacts such as false high frequencies (that would result from scattered or recurring missing values) should not show up too strongly. The interpolated input sequence is multiplied with the Hann window w_n of size N, cf. (4.1). To allow straightforward application of the FFT, the input is padded with $N' - N$ zeros so that $N' \geq N$ is a power of two; additionally, $N' \geq 32$ guarantees a minimum frequency resolution. Then, the power spectrum $P_k = |F_k|^2$ with $0 \leq k < M = \lceil (N' + 1)/2 \rceil$ is computed according to (4.2) and normalized by the original length and the mean energy of the window:

$$P'_k = \frac{1}{N \cdot \frac{\sum_{n=0}^{N-1} w_n^2}{N}} P_k = \frac{1}{\sum_{n=0}^{N-1} w_n^2} P_k. \tag{7.27}$$

Lastly, the information contained in the power spectrum is compressed by a triangular filter bank, i. e. weighted by triangular filters and integrated, cf. Figure 7.2. The resulting band energies are a little similar to the mel filter spectrum in the computation of MFCC (cf. Section 4.1.2): Like there, the band energies compactly represent the spectrum. Note, however, that here, it is the spectrum of the short-time features that is processed instead of the raw speech signal. The computation of the band energies is illustrated in Figure 7.3. All in all, between 49 and 53 descriptors (one less if segments are known to be of constant length; three less if signal is not positive a priori).

Special cases: When the segment is empty (i. e. zero length), all descriptors are undefined. If all values in $\boldsymbol{f}$ are undefined, all descriptors are undefined as well, except

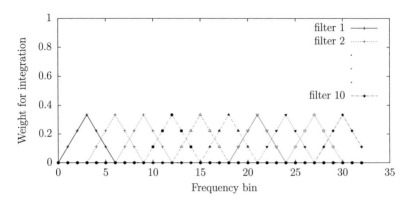

Figure 7.2: Frequency band descriptors: filter bank used for compressing the power spectrum. The filters have 50 % overlap and span the entire (non-redundant) frequency range; each filter is normalized to sum 1. By intention, the first frequency bin (which is just the mean of the input) gets a zero weight while the last frequency bin gets a positive weight. In this example, $N' = 64$, i.e. the last frequency bin, corresponding to the Nyquist frequency (which is half the sampling frequency of the short-time feature at hand) is $M - 1 = 32$.

for 'length' and 'finite'. When the length of the segment is exactly one, 'slope', 'regerr' and all 'pvi' measures are undefined. The 'pvi' measures are also undefined if there is not at least one pair of valid neighbours. The 'pausebefore' measures are undefined if the current segment is the first in a row; the 'pauseafter' measures are undefined if the current segment is the last in a row.

Invariance properties: All normalizations given above have the goal of achieving approximate invariance, either against time scaling, e. g.

$$\boldsymbol{f} = (1, 10)^{\mathsf{T}} \quad \text{vs.} \quad \boldsymbol{f} = (1, 1, 10, 10)^{\mathsf{T}} \tag{7.28}$$

or against duration given stationary input, e. g.

$$\boldsymbol{f} = (1, 10)^{\mathsf{T}} \quad \text{vs.} \quad \boldsymbol{f} = (1, 10, 1, 10). \tag{7.29}$$

Specifically,

- the statistical descriptors are approximately invariant against both scaling and duration,

- the duration and shape descriptors (except for 'length', 'pausebeforeabs', and 'pauseafterabs') are approximately invariant against scaling, and

- the frequency descriptors are approximately invariant against duration (cf. also Figure 7.3).

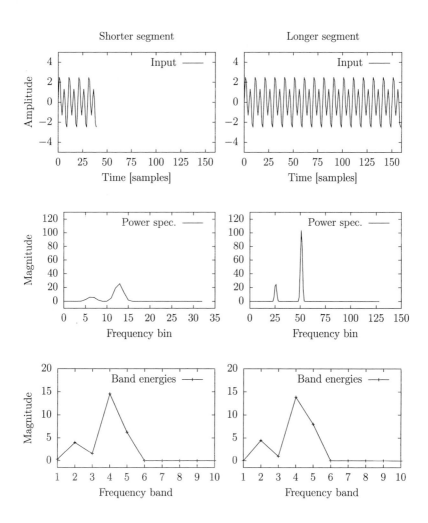

Figure 7.3: Frequency band descriptors for a shorter input segment (left column; 40 values) and a longer input segment (right column; 160 values). In both cases, the input (top row) is a mixture of the two frequencies $0.2 \cdot f_{\mathrm{nyquist}}$ and $0.4 \cdot f_{\mathrm{nyquist}}$. For the shorter segment, these two frequencies appear strongly smeared in the power spectrum, while they are quite distinct for the longer segment (middle row; for windowing, padding and normalization see text). Nevertheless, through the smoothing by the filter bank (cf. Figure 7.2), the resulting band energies (bottom row) are quite similar.

With respect to translation, e. g.

$$\boldsymbol{f} = (1, 10, 1, 1)^{\mathsf{T}} \quad \text{vs.} \quad \boldsymbol{f} = (1, 1, 10, 1)^{\mathsf{T}}, \tag{7.30}$$

the statistical and frequency descriptors are approximately invariant, while most duration and slope descriptors are not.

7.1.2   Features from generic descriptors

We now describe how the generic descriptors are used to compute suitable acoustic-prosodic features for the tasks at hand. First of all, we perform a segmentation of the utterance using forced alignment of the target utterance (cf. Section 4.5.4). That involves the use of the acoustic model (the HMMs) of a speech recognizer, and a pronunciation lexicon; it results in the boundaries of pauses, words, syllables, and phonemes. Note that hereby, we implicitly assume that the learner (as a cooperative user) produces the actual target utterance; in other cases one could perform a semi-free recognition allowing some substitutions, deletions and insertions, or a virtually free recognition solely guided by the language model. Additionally, we obtain a segmentation into voiced and unvoiced (including silence) segments from the RAPT algorithm (cf. Section 4.1.4).

The following 8 short-time features are used:

f0: The logarithm of the fundamental frequency as estimated by the RAPT algorithm, normalized by subtracting the mean over the speaker. 'f0' is undefined outside voiced regions; the mean is computed only on voiced frames.

ene: the logarithm of the intensity, cf. (4.5), normalised by subtracting the mean over the speaker. The mean is computed either over all frames, or only on speech frames according to the segmentation.

enevoiced: the logarithm of the intensity for voiced frames, undefined elsewhere; normalization is done as for f0.

hnr: Although we did not define voice quality as one of the core prosodic features in Section 1.2.2, we include the harmonics-to-noise ratio (HNR, [Yumo 82]), as it may play some role in accents and boundaries (laryngealizations), and comes for free as a by-product of the RAPT algorithm. For each frame, we use the NCC value $\phi_{\hat{k}}$ for the lag $\hat{k}$ that corresponds to the F0, cf. (4.6). A measure for the HNR is then given by

$$10 \cdot \log_{10} \left(\frac{\phi_{\hat{k}} + \epsilon_1}{1 - (\phi_{\hat{k}} - \epsilon_2)} \right). \tag{7.31}$$

Hereby, the constants $\epsilon_1 = 0.1$ and $\epsilon_2 = 10^{-4}$ are safeguards to avoid numeric problems that might result from outliers with $\phi_{\hat{k}}$ outside $[0.1; 0.9999]$; for normal ranges, their effect is negligible. 'hnr' is undefined outside voiced regions; normalization is done as for f0.

Group	Calculated from
Current syllable	STF × SSeg × Desc
Context concatenation	STF × SSeg × Desc × 4 syllables
Context embedding	STF × SSeg × Desc × {'mean', 'slope'}

Table 7.2: Features calculated per syllable. STF: short-time features, SSeg: syllable segments, Desc: descriptors.

mfcc0-mfcc4: the first 5 MFCCs, normalized by subtracting the means over the speaker. The means are computed either on all frames or just on speech frames according to the segmentation; 'mfcc0'-'mfcc4' are undefined for non-speech frames.

For encoding *local information*, features are computed for each syllable; cf. Table 7.2 for an overview. From the current syllable, we compute the generic descriptors (cf. Section 7.1.1) for all short-time features above, using the 4 following segment definitions:

syl: the whole interval of the syllable as given by the segmentation,

sylfix: a fixed-size interval of duration 0.2 sec, centred around the middle of the syllable (the idea is to introduce some robustness against segmentation errors by covering some minimal duration, but not much more than one syllable, assuming most syllables to be longer than 0.1 sec),

nuc: the interval of the nucleus of the syllable as given by the segmentation, and

nucfix: a fixed-size interval of duration 0.05 sec, centred around the middle of the current nucleus.

Since the descriptors have been designed to intrinsically cope with missing data, all descriptors can normally be computed even if the short-time feature contains some undefined values in the segment (e. g. f0 during unvoiced frames). In special cases, however, that can fail: If there is no valid input value at all, most descriptors are undefined; if there is just one valid input, or no valid neighbours, a few of the descriptors are undefined. We discriminate between three ways to handle this problem.

Early imputation: If a short-time feature is completely undefined during the current segment, it is substituted by zero throughout the segment. If just one value is defined, the (otherwise undefined) descriptors 'slope' and 'regerr' are set to zero. If there are no defined neighbours, the (otherwise undefined) 'pvi' descriptors are zeroed.

Late imputation: Imputation is done at a later stage: any higher-level feature that is undefined for the current instance is substituted by a default value before being passed on to classification or regression methods. The default value is calculated as the mean value over all instances of the training set that contain no undefined feature at all.

Global interpolation: As suggested by Kiessling [Kies 97], the short-time features are interpolated linearly over the whole utterance. At the tails, extrapolation with the nearest defined neighbour is used. If a short-time feature is undefined throughout the utterance, it is set to zero everywhere (zero has some justification as a default value, since all short-time features are normalized). The interpolation is performed after normalization, but before the computation of any descriptors. Thus, global interpolation 1) relieves the descriptors of having to handle undefined values and 2) solves the rare cases of undefined descriptors. The disadvantage is that the interpolated values distort the results, which may not be beneficial for classification.

To account for coarticulation, the 'trading relation' of prosodic parameters (prosodic functions can be realized by trading different means, cf. [Kies 97, p. 27, 168]), and interactions between rhythm and syllable prominence [Nieb 09], information about the context is included. We distinguish two approaches for this.

Context concatenation: The neighbourhood is provided to the classifier explicitly by using the features of the two left and two right neighbouring syllables. This approach is most exhaustive; however, there is a problem for the two very first of last syllables in the utterance: here, not all neighbours exist. We repair this either by (1) early imputation by defaults on the level of short-time features, assuming an input sequence of zeros (as long as the average segment in the current utterance), (2) imputation on utterance level, using the average of all defined syllables as a substitute for missing neighbours, or (3) late imputation, substituting missing features by the mean on all training data. An alternative would be to train a separate classifier (or regressor) for each neighbourhood configuration; however, that there are 9 such configurations (cf. Table 7.3), and there will be relatively few training examples for all but the full neighbourhood configuration (row '9'). We therefore do not pursue this approach.

Context embedding: This approach encodes the information contained within the neighbourhood by features that are always well-defined. For each of the individual syllable features, we compute the descriptors 'mean' and 'slope' for the 5-point neighbourhood centred around the current syllable. Since the mean needs just one valid input to be valid, and slope just two (cf. Section 7.1.1), that solves the problem of missing neighbours if the utterance contains at least two syllables (otherwise, the task of word accent detection, for instance, does not apply).

For both methods, we substitute the 'pausebefore' features of the very first syllable, and the 'pauseafter' features of the very last syllable, which are all undefined, by zeros.

Features for encoding *global information* are computed for each utterance, cf. Table 7.4. From the whole speech segment (starting at the beginning of the first word and terminating at the end of the last word), descriptors are computed for each of the short-time features (cf. Page 138), cf. row 'Whole speech segment' in Table 7.4. Another set of features is computed from two fixed-length segments of duration 1 sec: one starting at the beginning of the speech interval, and the other terminating at the

Context number	Existing neighbours					N_{syl}
	-2	-1	0	1	2	
1			x			1
2		x	x			2
3			x	x		2
4	x	x	x			≥ 3
5		x	x	x		3
6			x	x	x	≥ 3
7	x	x	x	x		≥ 4
8		x	x	x	x	≥ 4
9	x	x	x	x	x	≥ 5

Table 7.3: The possible 5-syllable neighbourhoods. N_{syl} is the number of syllables in the utterance; '-2' is the second left neighbour, '-1' the left neighbour, '0' the current syllable, and so on.

Group	Calculated from
Whole speech segment	STF × Desc
Fixed-length tails	STF × Desc × 2 tails
Syllable tails concat.	STF × SSeg × Desc × 5 syllables × 2 tails
Syllable tails embed.	STF × SSeg × Desc × {'mean', 'slope'} × 2 tails
Syllable aggregation	STF × SSeg × {Dur, Shape} × {'mean', 'sd', 'pvi'} + STF × SSeg × {Stat, Freq} × {'mean', 'sd'}
Stressed syllable aggreg.	{ <same as above> } × 5 syllables

Table 7.4: Global features calculated per utterance. STF: short-time features, Desc: descriptors, SSeg: syllable segments, Dur: duration descriptors, Shape: shape descriptors, Stat: statistic descriptors, Freq: frequency descriptors.

end of the speech interval, cf. row 'Fixed-length tails' of Table 7.4. Additionally, the first and last 5 syllables of the utterance are encoded by concatenating the respective syllable features, cf. row 'Syllable tails concat.' of Table 7.4. If the utterance contains less than 5 syllables, some of these features will be undefined; they are handled in the same way as done for the 'Context concatenation' for the syllable features above. Also the context embedding technique by 'mean' and 'slope' is used again, cf. row 'Syllable tails embed.'

Then, we aggregate descriptors from all syllables (computed for all short-time features, and for all syllable segments) by applying selected descriptors *again* (cf. row 'Syllable aggregation' of Table 7.4): the duration and shape descriptors of all syllables are aggregated by 'mean', 'sd', and 'pvi'; the statistic and frequency descriptors of all syllables are aggregated just by 'mean' and 'sd'. The selection was done to keep the final number of features manageable, and to keep just most useful combinations: When aggregating over all syllables, we look for quantities invariant to duration; therefore, we selected the two descriptors 'mean' and 'sd' from the statistic group of descriptors (which are invariant to duration). The 'pvi' descriptor, which encodes local variability, was selected just to aggregate over duration and shape descriptors (which are not duration invariant), but not to the duration-invariant statistic and frequency descriptors. The assumption was that local differences (pvi) of duration invariant quantities (statistic and frequency descriptors) are not very informative. Finally, we aggregate in the same way just over the *stressed* syllables [Hön 10a], including their ±2 neighbourhood, cf. row 'Stressed syllable aggreg'. A syllable is assumed to be stressed if it bears a primary or secondary word accent according to canonical (but not necessarily actual) pronunciation; for mono-syllabic words, the presence of a primary or secondary phrase accent according to the distribution of prototypical phrase accents (cf. Sections 5.1.1 and 5.2.1) is taken.

7.1.3 Text dependent features

The appropriateness of prosody will often depend on the structure of the spoken word or sentence. For example, at some word boundaries a phrase boundary with a larger pause is perfectly acceptable, while in other cases (e. g. after 'call' in 'Please call Stella'), a pause will confuse the listener. To allow our assessment modules to exploit that knowledge, we compute some text-dependent features.

For encoding *local text structure*, we compute features for the current syllable, cf. Table 7.5. For each syllable in the ±2 neighbourhood, a binary feature indicates the presence (1) or absence (0) of any word accent, according to canonical[3] (but not necessarily actual) pronunciation. Another group of features is used for indicating just primary word accent. Additionally, for each of these syllables, a feature indicates whether the associated word bears any phrase accent in the prototypical realization (cf. Sections 5.1.1 and 5.2.1). Another group of features indicates just primary phrase accents. Note that acceptable configuration of phrase accents and boundaries is usually far from unique; still, the prototypical version contains some useful information (for instance, usually no pause should be inserted when neither minor nor major

---

[3] We take the simplifying assumption that only a single word accent configuration is canonically acceptable for each word.

Group	Calculated from
Word accent	5 syllables
Primary word accent	5 syllables
Phrase accent	5 syllables
Primary phrase accent	5 syllables
Word boundary	6 syllable boundaries
Minor phrase boundary	6 syllable boundaries
Major phrase boundary	6 syllable boundaries
Sentence boundary	6 syllable boundaries
Utterance boundary	6 syllable boundaries
Exclamation	6 syllable boundaries
Question	6 syllable boundaries
Ellipsis	6 syllable boundaries

Table 7.5: Text features computed for the current syllable and its ± 2 neighbourhood.

phrase boundary are annotated). Next, for the 6 syllable boundaries surrounding the ± 2 neighbourhood, features indicating the presence or absence of word boundaries, minor/major phrase boundaries (according to the prototypical realization), end of sentence (can occur within utterance, cf. e.g. Page 209), and utterance boundaries are computed. Similarly to the word and phrase accents, these are organized hierarchically, i.e. utterance boundary implies end of sentence, end of sentence implies major phrase boundary, major boundary implies minor boundary, and minor boundary implies word boundary. The idea behind this hierarchy is to encode the similarity of these phenomena. Finally, for each of the syllable boundaries, we add binary features indicating whether there is a word boundary with an associated exclamation mark[4], a question mark, or an ellipsis within a sentence (indicating a hesitation, cf. e.g. Page 207).

Information about the *global text structure* is encoded by a feature vector computed per utterance, cf. Table 7.6 for an overview. First, the number of words and syllables, and (redundantly) the proportion of syllables and words are computed. Then, the beginning and end of the utterance are encoded by adding the syllable text features of the third and antepenultimate syllable. If the utterance contains less than 5 syllables, some of these features will be undefined; again, these cases will be discussed below. Next, we add, relative to the number of syllables: number of any word accents, number of primary word accents, number of any phrase accents, number of primary phrase accents, number of word boundaries, number of minor phrase boundaries, number of major phrase boundaries, number of sentence ends, and number of utterance boundaries (some of these are redundant, e.g. the last one is indirectly proportional to the number of syllables). Again, the same hierarchy as above is applied, i.e. number of word boundaries $\geq$ number of minor boundaries $\geq$ number major boundaries, and so on. Finally, we add, relative to the number of syllables, the number of exclamation, question, and ellipsis marks.

---

[4] There are virtually no commands in the corpora used, so a distinction between exclamation and command is not necessary.

Description or Group
Number of words
Number of syllables
Syllables per word
Syllable structure tails
Word accents per syllables
Primary word accents per syllables
Phrase accents per syllables
Primary phrase accents per syllables
Word boundaries per syllables
Minor phrase boundaries per syllables
Major phrase boundaries per syllables
Sentence ends per syllables
Utterance boundaries per syllables
Exclamations per syllables
Questions per syllables
Ellipses per syllables

Table 7.6: Global text features computed per utterance.

7.1.4   Specialized rhythm features

A number of acoustic parameters have been suggested for characterizing native language rhythm (cf. Section 2.1.3). These are promising candidates for characterizing non-native rhythm, too (cf. Section 3.2). Although our generic features should contain the same information (at least implicitly), we still compute some parameters explicitly, for the sake of enhanced interpretability. Table 7.7 gives an overview.

Tempo features: A simple but fundamental property of speech is how fast something is said. Tempo is not necessarily related to rhythm directly, but for L2 speakers it will be highly correlated to proficiency and thus, to any global pronunciation score. We compute the rate of speech (number of syllables per length of speech interval), the articulation rate (number of syllables per speech time, i.e. per length of speech interval minus pauses), and (redundantly) the proportion of pauses (ratio of pause duration and length of speech interval).

Pair-wise variability indices (PVI): Local variability of durations has been suggested as a cue by Grabe and Low [Grab 02]. As in the original paper, we compute the raw and normalized indices, see (7.23) and (7.25), for the durations of consecutive vocalic and consonantal segments (as determined from the segmentation).

Global proportions of intervals (GPI): Further, we compute Ramus' %V, i.e. the proportion of vocalic speech among all speech, ΔV, and ΔC, i.e. the standard deviation of the duration of vocalic and consonantal segments [Ramu 02]. We also compute Dellwo's varcoΔC, i.e. ΔC normalized by dividing through the average dur-

Group	Feature
Tempo	speech rate
	articulation rate
	pause proportion
PVI	rPVIv
	nPVIv
	rPVIc
	nPVIc
GPI	percentV
	deltaV
	deltaC
	varcoV
	varcoC

Table 7.7: Specialized language rhythm features. The prefixes 'r' and 'n' indicate normalized and raw versions, the postfixes 'v'/V' and 'c'/'C' denote vocalic and consonantal segments, respectively.

ation of consonantal segments [Dell 03], and add the equivalent for vocalic segments [Whit 07a].

7.2 Classification and regression

We now describe how we apply classification and regression methods in order to convert the features introduced above into discrete classes or continuous values we can use for pronunciation assessment. The focus is on methods; details of implementation will be given in Chapter 8.

7.2.1 Word accent position

For word accent, we can identify two tasks: the first one is error detection, i. e. just deciding per word whether there is any error; the second one is diagnosis, which involves specifying which word accent configuration was realized instead of the canonical one. We opt here for diagnosis, because it is potentially more useful for the learner; besides, errors can be derived from diagnosis results. For error detection, we can discriminate between a *strict version* where the distinction between secondary and primary accents matters, and a *tolerant version* which accepts approximately correct configurations. Our definition of approximately correct word accent allows confusions between unaccented and secondary accent, and confusions between secondary and primary accent; it is equivalent to the 'A-P-N' criterion in [Li 12]. A third alternative that lies in between is only checking the position of the primary word accent.

At least for English, different word accent positions occur canonically, i. e. in native speech data. Under the simplifying assumption that native speakers will produce only correct word accent configurations, it is therefore conceivable to train a word accent recognition system exclusively with native, un-annotated data. Solely the transliteration, i. e. what has been said, plus a pronunciation dictionary with word accent information is needed. This is a very attractive possibility, as collecting non-native material that is annotated for word accent errors is costly. *Evaluating* how well the system recognizes errors has to be done using such annotated non-native data nevertheless; however, much less data is needed for evaluation than for training. Yet, care has to be taken during construction, because there is a mismatch between training and target data. Canonical word accent is highly dependent on the canonical vowel of the syllable, e. g. in English, a schwa is a safe sign for an unaccented syllable. If information about the canonical vowel is supplied to the classifier, it can take a short cut and use that information to predict word accent in native data with high accuracy; however, it will fail to take into account the actual pronunciation and to detect word accent errors in non-native data. In this sense, our MFCC features (cf. 7.1.2) are very suitable because they inform the classifier about the *actually* pronounced vowel (e. g. to perform implicit intrinsic loudness normalization) but will not leak information about the canonical vowels (which would enable the mentioned short cut).

Determining the word accent configuration of a word is most directly cast as a classification problem per word, with a separate classifier for each word count [Hön 09]. If we were just interested in the position of the primary accent, a word with two syllables would constitute a 2-class problem, a word with three syllables a 3-class problem, and so on. This approach has a serious drawback, however: for words with several syllables, not enough training examples will be available. For the vocabulary of the C-AuDiT corpus (cf. Sections 5.1 and A.1), for instance, there is no 4-syllabic word that has any accent on the last syllable according to canonical pronunciation. That means when training with native data, we have a definite gap in our observations, and even when training with non-native data, many classes (word accent configurations) will not have enough observations. When additionally discriminating between primary and secondary accents, the problem gets even more severe.

We therefore take a simpler approach that first works out the probable accent of each syllable and then does a post-processing to arrive at a decision on word level. In preliminary experiments [Hön 09], we found that the more complex modelling per syllable count gave only a minimal improvement compared to this simpler approach (even for words with few syllables, i. e. sparseness of training data was not a problem). Thus, the simplification makes sense because it allows to reasonably approach in the first place (1) words with several syllables and (2) a distinction between primary and secondary accent.

For determining the accent of a syllable, we apply our generic acoustic-prosodic features. Specifically, we use the local feature vector associated to the syllable, cf. Section 7.1.2. To supply even more context than already contained in that set, we can also add the global feature vector of the utterance. Additionally, we use the associated local and global text features, cf. Section 7.1.3. For most experiments (especially when training on native data), we omit the local text features informing about canonical word accent.

We use an SVM (cf. Section 4.3) to predict the accent of the syllable from the features, with the three possible classes 'no accent', 'secondary accent', and 'primary accent'. When training with native data, we use the canonical word accents according to the pronunciation lexicon; for non-native data we use the actually produced accents according to the annotation (cf. Section 6.1.1). Only syllables from multi-syllabic words are used for training. A one-versus-rest scheme is used to implement a three-class classifier with three binary classifiers (cf. Section 4.3.2). In all cases, we simulate a balanced training set (with equal a priori probabilities for each class) using *instance weights*[5], in order to remove possible bias toward the canonical accent configuration when training with native data. In order to achieve this, each $\boldsymbol{x}_i$ in (4.49) is substituted by $w_{y_i} \cdot \boldsymbol{x}_i$ with suitable class-dependent scalar weights w_{y_i}.

A word level result is obtained by combining the individual syllable results, with the simplifying assumption of statistical independence. Thus, the a posteriori density for a certain word accent configuration $\boldsymbol{a} = (a_1, a_2, \ldots, a_S)^\mathsf{T}$ can be factorized (a_i is the accent class of syllable i, S is the number of syllables, $\boldsymbol{X} = (\boldsymbol{x}_1, \boldsymbol{x}_2, \ldots, \boldsymbol{x}_S)$ are the feature vectors):

$$
\begin{aligned}
P(\boldsymbol{a}|\boldsymbol{X}) &= \frac{P(\boldsymbol{a}) \cdot p(\boldsymbol{X}|\boldsymbol{a})}{p(\boldsymbol{X})} & (7.32) \\
&= \frac{P(\boldsymbol{a}) \cdot p(\boldsymbol{x}_1, \boldsymbol{x}_2, \ldots, \boldsymbol{x}_S | a_1, a_2, \ldots, a_S)}{p(\boldsymbol{X})} & (7.33) \\
&= \frac{P(\boldsymbol{a}) \cdot \prod_{i=1}^{S} p(\boldsymbol{x}_i | a_i)}{p(\boldsymbol{X})}. & (7.34)
\end{aligned}
$$

When forced to decide for a diagnosis result, one could assume uniform a priori probabilities $P(\boldsymbol{a})$ and just decide for the accent configuration with maximum conditional density $p(\boldsymbol{X}|\boldsymbol{a})$. However, we cannot assume our probability estimates to be perfectly realistic, and care should be taken when reporting a supposed pronunciation error to the learner. Therefore, we use the *probability of correct pronunciation* [Hön 09], i. e. the probability of the canonical word accent configuration $\boldsymbol{a}^\star$

$$
\begin{aligned}
P(\boldsymbol{a}^\star|\boldsymbol{X}) &= \frac{P(\boldsymbol{a}^\star) \cdot p(\boldsymbol{X}|\boldsymbol{a}^\star)}{p(\boldsymbol{X})} & (7.35) \\
&= \frac{P(\boldsymbol{a}^\star) \cdot p(\boldsymbol{X}|\boldsymbol{a}^\star)}{\sum_a P(\boldsymbol{a}) \cdot p(\boldsymbol{X}|\boldsymbol{a})} & (7.36)
\end{aligned}
$$

and report a word accent error (and the diagnosis, i. e. most likely accent configuration) if that probability is below a certain threshold. This formulation is used for the strict version; for the tolerant version, we calculate the *probability of approximately correct pronunciation*, i. e. the total probability of all tolerated word accent configurations $\tilde{\boldsymbol{a}}$:

$$
\sum_{\tilde{\boldsymbol{a}}} P(\tilde{\boldsymbol{a}}|\boldsymbol{X}). \tag{7.37}
$$

The optimal threshold depends on the costs of missed and falsely reported errors; however, these are difficult to quantify in the context of language learning. In practice, one will select a threshold that shows—according to pedagogical and/or commercial considerations—an acceptably low false alarm rate (e. g. 5 %) on the test set.

---

[5]`https://www.csie.ntu.edu.tw/~cjlin/libsvmtools`, last visited September 8th, 2017

We assume uniform[6] a priori probabilities for all legal word accent configurations and use a zero probability for the illegal ones. What is a legal configuration depends partly on conventions; we choose to allow any distribution of accents as long as there is exactly one primary accent in the word. That means that the sums in (7.36) and (7.37) can be reduced to $S \cdot 2^{S-1}$ summands, which is well manageable for realistic syllable counts $S < 10$, as each of the involved $3 \cdot S$ conditional probabilities $p(x_i|a_i)$, cf. (7.34), has to be evaluated only once and can then be retrieved from a lookup table. The SVM does not provide true probabilities; we use the pseudo-probabilities estimated from the signed distances to the hyperplane as suggested by Platt (cf. Section 4.3.3).

7.2.2 Rhythm assessment

For the automatic assessment of rhythm we do not attempt to set up a method that can be constructed using native, un-annotated data only. Instead, we predict pronunciation scores using a regression system that is trained directly on the non-native recordings, with the human labels as target scores, cf. Sections 6.1.2 and 6.2.

In the first approach, we compute a single feature vector from the whole utterance. We use the global version of our generic acoustic-prosodic features (cf. Section 7.1.2), the global text features (cf. Section 7.1.3) and the specialized rhythm features (cf. Section 7.1.4). SVR (cf. Section 4.4) is used to learn the mapping from feature vectors to rhythm scores.

One possible shortcoming of this approach is that information about locality and order is lost. For example, if there is a long pause at a word boundary which is marked as 'major phrase boundary' in the prototypical realization (cf. Sections 5.1.1 and 5.2.1), the appropriateness of that pause is not necessarily reflected in global features such as mean or standard deviation of pause duration. The global text features contain the frequency of word boundaries (cf. Section 7.1.3), but the information about the coincidence of acoustics and text is lost. This is partly repaired by aggregating over stressed syllables in the global features; however, that allows to retrieve only a part of such coincidence information, and it is difficult to capture more aspects in global feature vectors, also because that would further increase the dimension of the features.

Our second approach therefore uses a *divide and conquer* strategy: First, the utterance is divided into snippets, which are scored individually; then, the results are combined to arrive at a single score [Hön 12a]. As snippets, we use all syllables plus their ± 2 syllable neighbourhoods. For describing each snippet, we use the same features that we already used for classifying accents per syllable (cf. Section 7.2.1), extracted for the central syllable of the snippet: the associated local, and the global acoustic-prosodic features, plus the associated local, and the global text features. The score is predicted using SVR; as we do not have a more local annotation for rhythm, we use the score of the whole utterance as a target for each snippet. The

---

[6]Unless one has a strong expectation of the word accent errors the group of learners is likely to make, it seems wiser not to bias the recognition of the word accent configuration too strongly. Word accent errors depend not only on the L1 of the speaker, but also on the speaker's lexical knowledge and awareness of the phenomenon; also, the a priori probabilities for a given configuration will depend on the canonical pronunciation. Therefore, they are difficult to estimate reliably.

individual results are combined by averaging; cf. [Grop 12] for a more intelligent, weighted combination using confidences.

This chapter detailed the approaches proposed for automatic pronunciation assessment. The next chapter will evaluate whether they are suitable for that goal, and how reliable they are; also, where specific design choices were left open we will identify the best ones empirically.

8

Experimental results

In this chapter the methods proposed for pronunciation assessment (cf. Chapter 7) are experimentally evaluated, using the collected recordings (cf. Chapter 5) and annotations (cf. Chapter 6).

8.1   Segmentation

For all experiments, we require a segmentation of the utterance into syllables and syllable nuclei in order to compute the acoustic-prosodic features. As indicated above, we use the forced alignment of the target text, i. e. the most likely phoneme segmentation of the target text given the acoustic observations, the acoustic model (phoneme HMMs) of a speech recognizer, and a pronunciation lexicon. We use the merged pronunciation lexica from the C-AuDiT and AUWL projects; for simplicity, we use just a single pronunciation for each word, discarding existing alternative pronunciations. Syllable boundaries are part of the lexicon; nuclei are identified as the vocalic part of syllables; where no vowel exists, a suitable substitute is used (/m/ in the interjection 'hmm').

This approach assumes that the exact target text has indeed been produced; in fact, this is not the case for all recordings, according to the annotation (cf. Sections 6.1 and   5.2.3). We therefore exclude those cases from the evaluations. For C-AuDiT, we exclude a recording if at least one labeller indicated at least one word editing. For AUWL, we use just the 'clean' material, excluding the 20 % classified as 'usable'. In an application, this step could be done automatically using a speech recognizer and a language model suitably constructed for the target text.

We use the *Kaldi* system for training acoustic models and computing forced alignments. The models are estimated using the combined native data of C-AuDiT and AUWL. For estimation, transliterations of the recordings are necessary (cf. Section 4.5.4). Again, we use the target texts under the assumptions that the speakers did not make any reading errors. In fact, even for the native speakers that assumption does not always hold; however, this time we have no annotation of word errors at our disposal (it was not deemed worthwhile, given the low frequency of errors and the cost of annotation). Although the errors are few and would deteriorate the quality of the models just a little, we exploit information that is generated anyway during the training process to identify erroneous recordings in a semi-automatic way.

First, we train the models using all available recordings (as mentioned, the errors are rare, and the resulting models well usable). The iterative learning of the segmentation of the training data (cf. Section 4.5.4) involves a forced alignment of the transliteration. For efficiency reasons, this step is done using beam search instead of the full Viterbi search, cf. Section 4.5.2. If there is a large mismatch between the acoustic observations and the assumed sequence of acoustic models, beam search may fail to produce a state sequence that includes the final state (the explicit end state after the last phoneme). The likelihood of such an alignment failure depends on the *beam size* which determines how many δ_{t+1} are kept in each iteration, cf. (4.94). The failure of beam search to produce a valid forced alignment is an indication of a wrong transliteration. In Kaldi, forced alignment of each utterance is first attempted with a relatively small beam size. If that fails, a larger beam size is used (which normally does not fail even if the transcription is wrong). We identify those recordings which lead to an alignment failure with the small beam size[1], and manually check them for reading errors. We did this procedure for all data (not just the native utterances) and thus excluded 21 recordings from acoustic model training and later processing for pronunciation assessment. In some cases reading errors are not the problem but recording failures such as truncations or glitches (intervals of samples dropped by the sound driver), which explains why we also found cases in the non-native material even though labellers did not mark the case as unusable (presumably because they did not regard the problem as being severe enough).

We use different HMMs per phone depending on the position in the word (beginning, middle, end, or singleton); apart from that, we do not use context (so-called mono-phone models, in contrast to context-dependent models such as tri-phone models that depend on the neighbour phonemes). Diphthongs such as /aɪ/ are modelled by dedicated HMMs, i. e. not as the concatenation of the two HMMs for /a/ and /ɪ/. All phonemes are modelled by linear HMMs with 3 states (and an explicit end state that does not generate observations). As a consequence, the segmentation of any phone (and thus any nucleus or syllable) spans at least three frames. The topology of the silence HMM is more flexible, and also allows some backward recursions:

$$(a_{ij}) = \begin{pmatrix} \star & \star & \star & \star & \\ & \star & \star & \star & \star \\ & \star & \star & \star & \star \\ & \star & \star & \star & \star \\ & & & & \star \end{pmatrix} \tag{8.1}$$

(the explicit end state can only be reached from the last emitting state). That topology possibly improves the modelling of different silence durations, and different stationary and transient noises. Minimum duration of silence is three frames again. We limit the total number of Gaussian mixtures to 1000, which results in an average of two mixtures per state (we have around 170 word position dependent phonemes).

The acoustic observations are standard: 13 MFCCs (23 filters up to 8 kHz), plus deltas (slope of regression line through 5 consecutive MFCCs) and delta-deltas (slope

---

[1]We look at the last alignment of the iterative training procedure and use the beam size 10 (`gmm-align-compiled -beam=10`) of the `egs/wsj/s5` recipe.

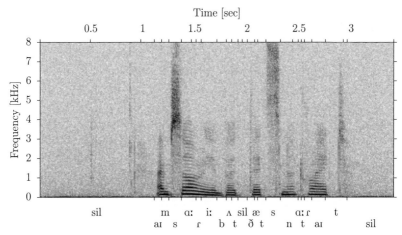

Figure 8.1: Segmentation obtained by forced alignment for 'I'm sorry, but that's not right' spoken by a female, non-native speaker. Silence is denoted by 'sil'. Each second segment identifier (i.e. 'sil' or an IPA phoneme) is typeset with a vertical offset to avoid overlap. At least in this example, the keyboard sound around 0.5 sec and the lip smacking/breathing around 1.0 sec are assigned to silence as desired.

of regression line through 5 consecutive deltas). We use a large beam width[2] for computing the alignment. With that, the beam search did not fail for any of the recordings used. According to manual inspection on a random basis, the resulting segmentations are very accurate. Also, the silence HMM seems to successfully learn to cover non-speech events such as keyboard clicks or lip smacks, even though those are not explicitly transliterated and modelled. An example segmentation is depicted in Figure 8.1.

We did not do a formal analysis of the quality of the alignments. First, in an application, the system must make do with the automatic segmentation anyway. Second, that would require the manual creation of a reference segmentation, which would be costly, so we did not deem it worthwhile. Besides, forced alignment is well-established for the purpose of segmentation for prosodic analysis [Kies 97].

8.2 Word accent position

We first focus on and optimize the classification of accent on syllable level based on the local acoustic (cf. Table 7.2) and textual (cf. Table 7.5) features. This makes sense as our approach (cf. Section 7.2.1) combines syllable-level results to arrive at a decision on word level; and we assume that a higher recognition rate on syllable level will generally lead to a better performance in error detection and diagnosis on word level as well.

---

[2]`gmm-align-compiled -beam=400`

We measure classification performance as the average of the recognition rates (recalls) of all classes; this has been called *average of the class-wise recognition rates* (CL) [Batl 96] or *unweighted average recall* (UAR) [Schu 09]. It is invariant against imbalanced classes in so far as the *chance baseline* (the best performance of a trivial classifier guessing randomly, or for the most frequent class) can be stated independently of the data: for K classes, it is $1/K$. Also, it is the natural choice in our case as we aim for a classifier not biased towards the more frequent classes.

Note that in all experiments on accents (both syllable and word level), we ignore not only utterances with any word error, but also syllables whose associated ± 2 neighbour words exhibit any annotated syllable insertions or deletions, as these violations of the assumptions behind forced alignment may produce erroneous segmentations.

For evaluation, we estimate *speaker-independent* performance, i. e. we test on data from speakers that were not used for estimating classifier parameters or meta-parameters. In order to do so in the most data-efficient way, we perform cross-validation with the constraint that in each fold, training and test data have to be disjunct with respect to speakers. For the final performance, we do not average the classification rates of the folds, but rather compute a single classification rate on the combined results (predictions of classifiers) of all test folds. For UAR, this does make a (usually tiny) difference to averaging, and for evaluating regression later, this procedure can be important to avoid optimistic results[3]. Meta-parameters (such as the complexity C of SVMs, cf. (4.3.3)) have to be tuned on data not used for estimating the actual parameters of the classifier (such as β, β_0 of SVMs). In order to do so, we optimize the meta-parameters for each fold with the help of a nested cross-validation on the associated training set. For describing the involved sets of data in each fold, we use TEST for the data used for testing in the outer evaluation loop, VALI for the data used for meta-parameter optimization in the inner loop, TRAIN for the data used for training in the inner loop, and VALITRAIN for the data used for training in the outer loop. If N folds are used in both loops, there are N^2 folds; the fraction of data that can be used for VALITRAIN is, assuming each speaker contributed an equally large mount of data, $\frac{N-1}{N}$ and for TRAIN $(\frac{N-1}{N})^2$, cf. Table 8.1 for an illustration. If the loops are constructed to leave one speaker out at a time, and there are S speakers, the number of folds is $S \cdot (S-1)$; the fraction $\frac{S-1}{S}$ is available for VALITRAIN, and the fraction $\frac{S-2}{S}$ for TRAIN, cf. Table 8.2 for illustration. Over the course of the folds, all data is covered exactly once for TEST and VALITRAIN, $N-1$ or $S-1$ times for VALI, and $(N-1)^2$ or $(S-1)(S-2)$ times for TRAIN.

We use the python package *scikit-learn* [Pedr 11] for training and evaluation of the machine learning algorithms. For linear SVM and SVR, we use the variants that make use of the *liblinear* library [Fan 08]. For all machine learning algorithms, we first scale all features individually to unit standard deviation, and then globally such that the average Euclidean length (of a whole feature vector) is unity. The scaling factors are estimated on the respective training set. The individual scaling is important to

---

[3]Consider the extreme case of cross-evaluating a regressor when the test folds contain just two instances: Then, Pearson (and Spearman) correlation is either 1, -1 or undefined. Thus, there is a chance that the result is biased towards 1.

Fold	TEST	VALITRAIN	VALI	TRAIN
1			DE	FGHI
2	ABC	DEFGHI	FG	DEHI
3			HI	DEFG
4			AB	CGHI
5	DEF	ABCGHI	CG	ABHI
6			HI	ABCG
7			AB	CDEF
8	GHI	ABCDEF	CD	ABEF
9			EF	ABCD

Table 8.1: Nested cross-validation with 3x3 folds assuming the data consists of 9 speakers A–I.

Fold	TEST	VALITRAIN	VALI	TRAIN
1			B	CD
2	A	BCD	C	BD
3			D	CB
4			A	CD
5	B	ACD	C	AD
6			D	AC
7			A	BD
8	C	ABD	B	AD
9			D	AB
10			A	BC
11	D	ABC	B	AC
12			C	AB

Table 8.2: Nested leave-one-speaker-out cross-validation with 4 speakers A–D.

ensure equal importance of all features in the presence of regularization; the global scaling simplifies the search for optimal meta-parameters.

8.2.1   Normalization

There are a number of ways to perform normalization of the short-time features. In all cases, we compute some mean value and subtract that from the signal. We experiment with the following choices.

Scope for mean computation: the mean is computed either over the whole signal, or just during speech. The choice only applies to 'ene' and 'mfcc0–4', because the other short-time features are undefined (and thus ignored for the purpose of mean calculation) outside voiced segments anyway.

Scale for mean computation: the mean value can either be computed in the final (logarithmic) domain of the short-time features, or in the original (linear) domain. Seen from the perspective of the final logarithmic domain, averaging in the linear domain will result in an approximation of the peaks (which should be related mostly to actual speech) rather than the valleys (which should be highly influenced by noise). To apply that idea to MFCCs, we back-transform the zero-padded MFCCs with inverse DCT to 23 (smoothed) logarithmic filter bank values, exponentiate, average, take the logarithm, and apply the forward DCT again.

For evaluating the suitability of the choices, we look at a simplified problem on syllable level: the binary classification problem of predicting whether there is any (primary or secondary) stress. For simplicity, we apply linear discriminant analysis (LDA), a variant of the Gaussian classifier (cf. Section 4.2), that assumes equal covariance matrices for each class, which results in linear decision boundaries. For robustness, shrinkage is applied to the covariance matrices, which acts as a regularization. We use automatic shrinkage selection[4] based on Ledoit-Wolf lemma [Ledo 04], and thus can skip the validation loop to optimize meta-parameters. We report the UAR for a subset of the native C-AuDiT data (1000 utterances, 4287 pertinent syllables that are parts of multi-syllabic words). To concentrate on the suitability of normalization (consider, for example, that some features such as 'sd' or 'slope' are invariant against mean subtraction), we just use a single feature: the average value of the current short-time feature during the nucleus. Table 8.3 gives the results.

When using no information from segmentation (columns 'all frames'), computing the mean in the original linear domain is indeed useful: it is better than doing that in the final logarithmic domain in 6 out of 8 cases (typeset in bold face). For energy, the difference is most striking (UAR 65.4 % vs. 57.4 %). If the segmentation is used to concentrate on speech (columns 'speech frames'), that trick is not necessary any more, and it is indeed a bit better to normalize in the final logarithmic domain (better in 6 out of 8 cases; typeset in bold face). When all short-time features are combined (row 'all'), the best UAR with 69.4 % is achieved (underlined; to be compared with 68.8 % when not using segmentation, and normalizing in linear domain). Since we

---

[4]`http://scikit-learn.org/stable/modules/lda_qda.html`, last visited September 8th, 2017

Short-time features	none	all frames		speech frames	
		linear	log	linear	log
ene	57.4	**65.4**	57.4	**65.3**	64.8
enevoiced	58.2	**66.4**	66.3	**66.4**	66.3
f0	54.4	61.1	**61.2**	61.1	**61.2**
mfcc0–5	64.2	**68.7**	68.3	68.3	**69.3**
mfcc1–4	63.1	**66.0**	65.0	65.9	**68.0**
mfcc0	58.5	**62.8**	62.6	63.5	**67.4**
hnr	57.0	55.4	**57.5**	55.4	**57.5**
all	65.0	**68.8**	67.7	68.6	<u>**69.4**</u>

Table 8.3: Effects of different normalizations for the classification of accented syllables: no normalization (column 'none'); computation of the mean over all frames, or just speech frames; calculation of the mean in linear or logarithmic domain. As higher-level features, just the mean values of the nucleus segment are used (no context, no global features). The figure given is the unweighted average recall [%] of the two-class problem (no accent vs. primary or secondary accent) on syllable level, i.e. chance baseline is 50 %. Data is a subset of the native C-AuDiT recordings, assuming canonical pronunciations. Note that for 'enevoiced', 'f0', and 'hnr', there is no difference between the scope of mean computation (all frames/speech frames), because they are computed only on voiced frames, which are in the majority of cases a subset of the speech frames.

have the segmentation at our disposal anyway, the conclusion is to use it, and perform normalization in the logarithmic domain. Nevertheless, the suitability of the linear method in absence of a segmentation is noteworthy, and may be useful in other contexts (e.g. instead of training a speech recognizer using standard cepstral mean subtraction, which is performed in the logarithmic domain).

8.2.2 Undefined short-time features

The first issue that can lead to undefined short-time features is easy to fix: Sometimes, the speech signal is exactly zero all over the short-time analysis frame[5], leading to zero intensity and thus, to a logarithmic intensity of $-\infty$, cf. (4.5). We fix this by adding a lower bound before taking the logarithm; the bound is chosen to correspond to the energy of the signal $(1, -1, 1, -1, \ldots)$.

A more fundamental problem is that the short-time features 'f0', 'enevoiced' and 'hnr' are undefined when speech is unvoiced—and unvoiced parts are quite common even in nuclei, cf. Figure 8.2 for an example. The descriptors (cf. Section 7.1.1) have been designed to cope with missing values as best as possible, but the missing values will nevertheless have some impact on the resulting higher-level features. Another problem is that in rare cases, a whole segment is classified as unvoiced—either rightfully or due to errors introduced by the RAPT algorithm (cf. Section 4.1.4). Then,

---

[5]All-zero intervals can e.g. be caused by buffer or timing failures of the sound driver, or by misguided attempts of the sound driver to perform noise suppression.

all descriptors are undefined.[6] If there is just one voiced frame in a segment, the descriptors 'slope' and 'regerr' are undefined; if no pair of voiced neighbours exists, the 'pvi' descriptors are undefined.

We identified three methods to cope with these problems in Section 7.1.2: early imputation, late imputation, or global interpolation. We first compare early imputation (i. e. using default values on the level of short-time features) with late imputation (i. e. using default values on the level of higher-level features). We now use all features from the current syllable; otherwise, the set-up is the same as above. The results are given in Table 8.4. Overall, the differences are small, which is because undefined values are rare (as we have not yet included features calculated from context syllables). In 15 cases, early imputation is better, in 19 cases, late imputation is better, and in 6 cases, there is a tie (the better result is typeset in bold face, respectively). Thus, late imputation seems to be a little bit better; that is also the case for the most relevant result: for all short-time features and all descriptors for both nuclei and syllables, a UAR of 86.4 % is obtained (last row, underlined; to be compared to with 86.3 %). Therefore, we decide to use late imputation rather than early imputation for the present purpose.

For the 'dct' descriptors, we used linear interpolation inside the segment to cope with missing values, cf. Page 133. A different strategy is to choose the DCT coefficients such that the reconstruction has the least squared error on the defined points. Table 8.5 compares the two approaches; the recognition rates approach the chance baseline for the least-square technique; linear interpolation is better in all cases (typeset in bold face). Thus, the approach has to be discarded. Probably, the spurious oscillations (cf. Figure 7.1) introduced by the least-squares criterion are the reason for the disastrous effect.

For the 'band' descriptors, undefined values are substituted by zeros. An alternative approach is to apply defect interpolation in the frequency domain; we apply the approach[7] of Aach and Metzler [Aach 01]. Table 8.6 investigates the usefulness of that approach. Defect interpolation seems to be a little better than using zeros: it is better in 9 out of 15 cases. However, the difference for the most relevant case (using all short-time features, and both nuclei and syllables) is small (last row: UAR 86.4 % (underlined) vs. 86.3). Given the additional computational effort needed for the methods, we decide to discard it. Nevertheless, the result is noteworthy, and applying defect interpolation in the context of feature extraction might be useful in other contexts.

Since we discarded any special handling for the purpose of computing the 'dct' or 'band' descriptors, we now compare late imputation with global interpolation (which would make the special handling obsolete as it removes any undefined values on short-

---

[6]As a side note, it may be mentioned that we use the special floating point value *NaN* (not a number) for undefined signals and features. This is very handy as any calculation involving a NaN value will result in a NaN value again; thus, the property 'undefined' is automatically passed on to subsequent modules, without the necessity for additional variables or conditional statements in the implementation.

[7] For line selection, we use simplified criterion $|G^{(i-1)}(s^{(i)})|$ mentioned in [Aach 01], and as many iterations as data points, which results in a quadratic complexity in the length of the segment (not a problem for our segment lengths). In rare cases, the iterative scheme does not converge; we prevent this by aborting early if the same line is selected twice in succession, or if the error does not decrease.

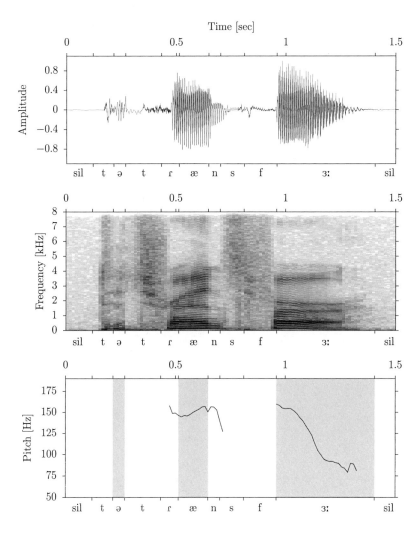

Figure 8.2: Segmentation of a male native speaker's realization of 'to transfer', shown in the signal (top), spectrogram (middle) and F0 (bottom). The nucleus segments are visualized in the bottom by grey rectangles; during the first one (/ə/ in 'to'), no voicing is detected by the RAPT algorithm, which could be regarded as an error, since perceptually, some voicing is noticeable.

STF	SSeg	Descriptors	early	late
f0	nuc	dct	**62.5**	60.7
		band	**61.2**	60.7
	syl	dct	63.8	**63.9**
		band	**58.8**	58.3
	nuc+syl	statistics⁻	70.6	70.6
		shape⁻	67.4	67.4
		frequency⁻	**63.1**	62.5
		all	**83.1**	82.8
enevoiced	nuc	dct	67.7	**67.9**
		band	**62.4**	62.0
	syl	dct	72.8	**72.9**
		band	**65.4**	65.1
	nuc+syl	statistics⁻	72.6	**72.7**
		shape⁻	75.6	**75.7**
		frequency⁻	**70.5**	68.8
		all	85.2	85.2
hnr	nuc	dct	60.0	**60.2**
		band	**61.3**	60.9
	syl	dct	62.7	**62.8**
		band	**61.9**	61.7
	nuc+syl	statistics⁻	69.5	**69.8**
		shape⁻	67.7	**67.9**
		frequency⁻	65.0	**65.1**
		all	**81.4**	81.3
f0+enevoiced+hnr	nuc	dct	68.8	68.8
		band	**63.5**	63.1
	syl	dct	75.0	**75.1**
		band	66.4	66.4
	nuc+syl	statistics⁻	76.1	**76.4**
		shape⁻	78.2	**78.4**
		frequency⁻	70.2	**70.4**
		all	85.5	**85.6**
all	nuc	dct	**71.7**	71.6
		band	**67.3**	67.1
	syl	dct	80.6	**81.0**
		band	78.4	78.4
	nuc+syl	statistics⁻	80.5	**80.6**
		shape⁻	84.7	**85.0**
		frequency⁻	**80.1**	80.0
		all	86.3	**_86.4_**

Table 8.4: Comparing early and late imputation (% UAR of two-class syllable accent; subset of native C-AuDiT-data, chance baseline 50 %). Results are given for subsets of descriptors with a clear semantic ('statistics⁻': all statistic descriptors, cf. Table 7.1, except 'finite'; 'shape⁻': 'slope', 'regerr' and the dct descriptors; 'frequency⁻': 'pvi', 'pvi2', and the band descriptors). Note that 'all' refers to all descriptors, not just the union of those subsets. STF='all' refers to all eight short-time features (i. e. including 'ene' and 'mfcc0–4'). Typographic emphasis: see text.

Short-time features	SSeg	linear int.	lsq
f0	nuc	**62.5**	52.1
	syl	**63.8**	51.2
enevoiced	nuc	**67.7**	52.0
	syl	**72.8**	51.6
hnr	nuc	**60.0**	50.0
	syl	**62.7**	50.8

Table 8.5: Using linear interpolation (within the input segment) vs. the least-squares method (column 'lsq'; see text) for computing DCT descriptors in the presence of undefined values (% UAR of two-class syllable accent; subset of native C-AuDiT-data, chance baseline 50 %).

Short-time features	SSeg	Descriptors	zeros	defect interp.
f0	nuc	band	**61.2**	60.9
	syl	band	58.8	**60.9**
	nuc+syl	all	83.1	**83.3**
enevoiced	nuc	band	**62.4**	61.9
	syl	band	65.4	**66.2**
	nuc+syl	all	**85.2**	85.1
hnr	nuc	band	**61.3**	61.0
	syl	all	61.9	**64.6**
	nuc+syl	all	**81.4**	81.3
f0+enevoiced+hnr	nuc	band	63.5	**64.0**
	syl	band	66.4	**68.2**
	nuc+syl	all	**85.7**	85.5
all	nuc	band	63.5	**64.0**
	syl	band	66.4	**68.2**
	nuc+syl	all	86.3	**<u>86.4</u>**

Table 8.6: Using imputation by zeros vs. defect interpolation in the frequency domain for the purpose of frequency band descriptors (% UAR of two-class syllable accent; subset of native C-AuDiT-data, chance baseline 50 %).

time level). The results of these experiments are given in Table 8.7. Late imputation seems to be a little better on the nucleus segments, especially for f0 (dct descriptors: UAR 62.5 % (underlined) vs. 61.6 %; band descriptors: UAR 61.2 % (underlined) vs. 58.9 %). Linear interpolation, on the other hand, seems to be better on syllables (f0: UAR 64.6,% (underlined) vs. 63.8,% for dct descriptors, and 66.5 % (underlined) vs. 58.8 for band descriptors). When using all descriptors and looking at single short-time features, late imputation wins for 'f0' (UAR 83.1 % (underlined) vs. 81.5 %), and interpolation wins for 'enevoiced' and 'hnr' (UAR 85.9 % (underlined) vs. 85.2 % and 81.5 % (underlined) vs. 81.4 %). Overall, interpolation seems to be slightly ahead (in 27 of 40 cases; typeset in bold face); when using all short-time features and descriptors[8] (last row) it results in a UAR of 86.6 % (underlined) vs. a UAR of 86.3 %. Since the picture is a little ambiguous, an obvious possibility is not to decide between the two possibilities but combine the features from both procedures, cf. column 'both'. Despite improvements for most configurations (in 30 out of 40 cases, the combination is better than either imputation or interpolation alone; typeset in bold face in last column) that strategy does not win when using all short-time features and descriptors (UAR 86.4 % vs. 86.6 % for linear interpolation alone). We therefore decide for using interpolation only.

8.2.3   Context

For including features capturing the information from neighbouring syllables, we test the two strategies described in Section 7.2.1: Context concatenation, which has to deal with missing values, and embedding, which avoids missing values in the first place. As the dimension of the feature vectors increases substantially through the inclusion of context features, we switch to using SVM instead of LDA. For SVM we need to optimize the meta-parameter C in the inner cross-validation loop; to get stable results for the relatively small subset, we use 4 outer and 4 inner folds. Apart from that, we stick to the set-up used so far (i. e. two-class problem, subset of native data). We use a linear kernel and $C \in \{0.01, 0.1, 1, 10\}$. Note for comparison to previous results that by using 4 folds instead of 2, the UAR of 86.6 % resulting from the optimizations above (cf. Table 8.7) increases to 87.6; using SVM instead of LDA further improves UAR to 88.8 %.

Table 8.8 gives the results of these experiments. The (always well defined) context embedding features (row 'embedding') improve results quite a bit compared to using no context at all. For example when using all short-time features and descriptors, results improve from a UAR of 88.8 % (the comparable figure for no context) to a UAR of 90.9 % (lower right cell), which is a 19 % relative reduction of the error rate. Better results, however, are obtained from the context concatenation features (rows 'concatenation'), even though we then have to deal with missing neighbours. In Table 8.8 we compare early imputation on the level of short-time features (column

---

[8]Note that the duration descriptors are computed for all short-time features, and thus occur repeatedly in the resulting feature set. We do *not* remove those duplicates, since that deteriorated performance. This result seems absurd at first; however, on second thought it makes sense: when removing the duplicates from a large feature vector, the relative count of the important duration features such as length, onset and offset decreases. Combined with the regularization of SVM, which gives equal influence to all features, that can lead to a deterioration of performance.

STF	SSeg	Descriptors	late	lin. int.	both
f0	nuc	dct	**62.5**	61.6	62.3
		band	**61.2**	58.9	**62.2**
	syl	dct	63.8	**64.6**	64.9
		band	58.8	**66.5**	66.2
	nuc+syl	statistics⁻	70.6	**71.9**	**73.5**
		shape⁻	67.4	**70.3**	70.1
		frequency⁻	63.1	**65.6**	**67.1**
		all	**83.1**	81.5	**84.1**
enevoiced	nuc	dct	67.7	**67.9**	**68.0**
		band	**62.4**	62.2	**63.4**
	syl	dct	72.8	**74.6**	**74.9**
		band	65.4	**69.2**	**70.0**
	nuc+syl	statistics⁻	72.6	**74.5**	**75.3**
		shape⁻	75.6	**76.9**	**77.3**
		frequency⁻	70.5	**71.8**	**74.1**
		all	85.2	**85.9**	**86.6**
hnr	nuc	dct	60.0	**60.1**	60.1
		band	**61.3**	61.1	**61.7**
	syl	dct	**62.7**	62.1	62.7
		band	61.9	**65.6**	**66.5**
	nuc+syl	statistics⁻	69.5	**72.3**	**74.0**
		shape⁻	**67.7**	66.9	67.3
		frequency⁻	65.0	**66.8**	**69.3**
		all	81.4	**81.5**	**82.3**
f0+enevoiced+hnr	nuc	dct	**68.8**	68.5	**68.9**
		band	63.5	**64.2**	**65.0**
	syl	dct	75.0	**77.3**	**77.7**
		band	66.4	**72.3**	**72.9**
	nuc+syl	statistics⁻	76.1	**79.1**	**80.9**
		shape⁻	78.2	**80.2**	79.9
		frequency⁻	70.2	**75.5**	**76.2**
		all	85.5	**86.0**	**86.1**
all	nuc	dct	**71.7**	71.5	71.5
		band	**67.3**	67.1	67.1
	syl	dct	80.6	**81.0**	**81.3**
		band	**78.4**	77.8	**78.5**
	nuc+syl	statistics⁻	80.5	**81.6**	**81.7**
		shape⁻	84.7	84.7	**84.8**
		frequency⁻	**80.1**	79.8	**80.2**
		all	86.3	**86.6**	86.4

Table 8.7: Late imputation of higher-level features vs. global linear interpolation (column 'lin. int.') of the short-time features (% UAR of two-class syllable accent; subset of native C-AuDiT-data, chance baseline 50 %). Column 'both' uses the union of features computed with both approaches. For more explanations, cf. Table 8.4.

'early') with late imputation on the level of higher-level features using global defaults (column 'late'). Early imputation seems to do a little better: 'early' wins in 17 out of 33 cases, and 'late' wins in 15 cases, and there is one tie (the winner is typeset in bold face). Especially when using all short-time features and descriptors (last row), 'early' is ahead with a UAR of 93.0 % (underlined) vs. 92.7 %. That figure is a 37.5 % relative reduction of error compared to using no context at all.

Imputation of higher-level features on utterance level (the second method mentioned on Page 140) was not competitive (92.4 % UAR for all short-time features and all descriptors; not contained in Table 8.8). Neither did a combination of context concatenation and context embedding features improve results over that of context concatenation alone (92.8 % UAR vs. 93.0 %; not contained in Table 8.8).

There is one relatively clear exception to the predominance of early imputation: the method performs worse than late imputation for duration features (85.7 % UAR vs. 88.5 % (underlined), second row). This can be explained by inappropriate default values generated for 'onsetpos', 'offsetpos' and the 'pause' features. In an improved version of the default features, we therefore substitute those features by their mean across all syllables in the current utterance. Thus, the performance of the duration features rises from a UAR of 85.7 % to 88.3 % (not contained in Table). In combination with all features, the difference is not noticeable (93.0 % UAR; not contained in Table); we nevertheless keep the improved version for the following experiments.

Next, we tried to enhance the feature set with the 'nucfix' and 'sylfix' segments, and global features. To speed up computation time, we just used a 2x2 cross-validation here; that reduced the baseline from a UAR of 93.0 % to 92.3 %. Adding features from 'nucfix' segments did not help (91.8 %); only the 'sylfix' segments improved results a bit (92.4 %). Since adding the 'sylfix' features increases the number of features by 50 %, and the improvement is negligible, we discard that idea. Adding global utterance features did not yield an improvement (91.4 % when using all global features; 92.1 % when adding the global features without syllable tails concatenation or embedding).

8.2.4   Word level

We now combine the results on syllable level to derive information about the accent configuration on the word level as described in Section 7.2.1. For simplicity, we start with the smaller feature set without context as optimized above (i. e. using linear interpolation of short-time features on utterance level, and no text features yet). We model all three accent classes and use LDA as in Section 8.2.1 since it readily provides the required class probabilities $p(\boldsymbol{x}_i|a_i)$, cf. (7.34). We use just the annotations of labeller 1 (multiple labellers will be treated below) and apply the strict evaluation policy (i. e. any change in primary or secondary accent is considered an error). In the first series of experiments, we train the syllable classifier with a subset of the native data (the same 1000 utterances used above, 11 speakers), and test the detection of word accent configuration errors on a subset of the non-native data (2000 randomly drawn non-native utterances from 22 speakers). In the second series of experiments, we perform a two-fold speaker-independent cross-validation on the subset of non-native data (which results in 11 speaker for training in each fold; therefore, the

Short-time features	Descriptors	concatenation		embedding
		early	late	
(any)	duration⁻	85.7	**88.5**	83.6
f0	statistics⁻	86.6	**87.2**	85.0
	shape⁻	**75.3**	75.1	73.5
	frequency⁻	**73.8**	71.2	70.7
	all	86.6	**87.2**	85.0
ene	statistics⁻	80.5	**82.4**	79.8
	shape⁻	81.6	**83.1**	81.6
	frequency⁻	79.3	79.3	76.6
	all	89.6	**90.0**	88.6
enevoiced	statistics⁻	**82.6**	82.2	79.7
	shape⁻	**84.6**	84.5	82.2
	frequency⁻	**76.7**	75.9	74.4
	all	**90.2**	89.9	88.6
hnr	statistics⁻	**79.0**	76.1	74.4
	shape⁻	69.8	**70.2**	68.4
	frequency⁻	**73.4**	72.4	69.9
	all	87.3	**87.8**	84.5
mfcc	statistics⁻	**87.6**	87.4	85.4
	shape⁻	88.1	**89.2**	87.7
	frequency⁻	**85.3**	84.2	83.1
	all	**93.1**	92.5	90.2
mfcc0	statistics⁻	81.6	**82.0**	81.1
	shape⁻	85.2	**86.0**	83.8
	frequency⁻	**81.7**	81.3	80.0
	all	90.7	**90.8**	88.7
mfcc1–4	statistics⁻	**86.9**	85.1	83.5
	shape⁻	86.0	**87.0**	84.4
	frequency⁻	**84.1**	83.0	81.7
	all	**91.9**	90.8	88.7
all	statistics⁻	88.0	**88.3**	86.4
	shape⁻	89.1	**89.7**	87.9
	frequency⁻	**85.7**	85.0	82.8
	all	**93.0**	92.7	90.9

Table 8.8: Representing context by concatenation vs. embedding (% UAR of two-class syllable accent; subset of native C-AuDiT-data, chance baseline 50 %). For concatenation, missing neighbours are handled by imputation of short-time features (row 'early') or higher-level features (row 'late'). 'duration⁻': duration descriptors with a clear semantic, i. e. 'length', 'onsetpos', 'offsetpos' and 'pause' descriptors. For more explanations, cf. Table 8.4.

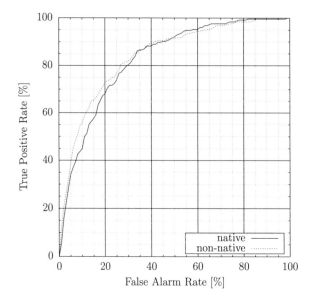

Figure 8.3: Receiver-Operator-Characteristic for detecting erroneous word accent configurations on word level (LDA, strict error policy, features without context, performance evaluated on the same labeller that is used for training). Training is done with 11 native or 11 non-native speakers.

results of native and non-native training should be comparable). Figure 8.3 shows the receiver-operator-characteristic (ROC) [Fawc 04] of that first set-up of our system. Training with un-annotated native data is worse than training with annotated, non-native data, but the results are not too far away: when the false alarm or *false positive rate* (FPR) rate is adjusted to 5 %, the *true positive rate* (TPR) is 34.3 % for native and 39.0 % for non-native training data. Note that we generate a single ROC curve from the cross-validation by combining the individual ROC curves of each test fold. In order to do so, each ROC curve is re-sampled on 101 points on the x-axis (false alarm rate); then, the y-values of the curves (true positive rates) are simply averaged (weighted by the number of tested instances). This method is suggested in the documentation[9] of scikit-learn [Pedr 11]. It is more robust than performing a single ROC analysis on probabilities collected across all folds, since the probabilities (at least the ones later derived from SVMs) may be scaled differently. On the other hand, the test folds need to be large enough for performing a ROC analysis; in particular, they should contain enough positives (i.e. pronunciation errors). In our case, the folds are large enough and we found the method perfectly suited.

---

[9]http://scikit-learn.org/stable/auto_examples/model_selection/plot_roc_crossval.html, last visited September 8th, 2017

Text features	native		non-native	
	UAR	TPR	UAR	TPR
none	61.0	34.3	61.6	39.0
word accents	62.7	28.1	<u>80.0</u>	*17.7*
phrase accents	63.0	33.1	63.6	39.8
boundaries	62.9	29.5	64.1	38.2
word boundaries	64.2	<u>40.6</u>	65.0	<u>47.2</u>
other	60.8	34.3	61.9	40.6
all	80.0	*4.7*	80.0	21.3
all except word accent	67.2	37.4	66.6	<u>48.0</u>

Table 8.9: Using different text features along with the acoustic features (no context, linear interpolation): Syllable-level accent classification rate (% UAR of three-class problem) and the true positive rate (% TPR) of detecting erroneous word accent configurations at a false positive rate of 5 %. Training is done on 11 native or 11 non-native speakers. 'boundaries' comprises utterance, sentence and phrase boundaries. 'other' the features indicating exclamation, question and ellipsis marks. The text features relate either to the current syllable or to the left and right syllable boundary. Chance baselines are 33.3 % for UAR and 5 % for TPR. Typographic emphasis: see text.

We can now dare to test the usefulness of text features for improving the performance of our system—at least when using native data to train the syllable models, this would not have been constructive as the classifier may use text features as a shortcut to predict canonical rather than actual pronunciation, and thus failing to detect errors. The system is set up as above, except that we now add text features (cf. Table 7.1.3); for a start, we just take those relating to the current syllable (and its left and right syllable boundary). Table 8.9 gives the results of these experiments; performance is given as the TPR at FPR=5 %.

First, it has to be noted that the recognition rate for the three-class problem is much lower than for the two-class problem: UAR is 61.6 % while it was 86.6 % (cf. Table 8.7) for the two-class problem (native data). This is a considerable drop as the error rate is now only 42 % (relative) lower than the chance baseline[10] while for the two-class problem it was 73 % (relative) lower[11]. The reason is that secondary accent is often confused with the other accent classes; most often, it is recognized as primary accent, as becomes clear when looking at the confusion matrix, cf. Table 8.10.

When training with non-native data (columns 'non-native' in Table 8.9), the features informing about the (canonical) word accent strongly improve the classification rate on syllable level (from a UAR of 61.6 %, row 'none', to 80.0 %, underlined, row 'word accents'), but as expected, that is just a short-cut which deteriorates the detection of actual pronunciation errors: TPR drops to 17.7 % (typeset in italics). Otherwise, nearly all text features help the detection of word accent errors. Most helpful is the pair of word boundaries surrounding the current syllable: these improve the TPR from 39.0 % to 47.2 % (row 'word boundaries; underlined). The combination

---

[10] $100\% - (100\% - 61.6\%)/(100\% - 33.3\%) = 42\%$

[11] $100(100\% - 86.6\%)/(100\% - 50\%) = 73\%$

Reference	Cases	Prediction [%]		
		no accent	primary	secondary
no accent	4027	76.4	13.7	9.9
primary	3042	12.7	73.7	13.6
secondary	251	27.1	38.2	34.7

Table 8.10: Confusion matrix for syllable accent as a three-class problem (61.6 % UAR; non-native data; no text features, cf. row 'none' in Table 8.9).

of all text features except word accent improves TPR further to 48.0 % (underlined, last row).

When training with native data (columns 'native'), there is a two-fold mismatch: First, no accents diverging from the canonical are annotated on syllable level; second, there is a substantial acoustical mismatch between native and non-native speakers. The latter shows in the results without text features (row 'none'): compared to non-native training data, the TPR drops (as already mentioned above) from 39.0 % to 34.3 %. The mismatch concerning syllable accents shows in the fact that now, most text features deteriorate error detection[12]. When taking all, TPR even drops down to 4.7 % (row 'all', typeset in italics). Only word boundaries remain useful (they increase TPR from 34.3 % to 40.6 %; row 'word boundaries', underlined); the combination of all text features except word accents slightly deteriorates (to a TPR of 37.4 %; last row).

Summing up, when training with non-native data, there is enough divergence from canonical pronunciations to make the classifier profit from most text features, while with native data, it seems best to restrict the choice to word boundaries.

We now determine one more parameter of our system. While for the 'strict' and 'tolerant' version of assessing the word accent configuration (cf. Section 7.2.1), the only reasonable choice seems to model three classes on syllable level (even though we have seen that secondary accents are easily confused), we have the choice between two and three classes for the 'primary' version (assessing only the position of the primary word accent).

For the two-class case, we have to decide what to do with the secondary accents in our training data: we can either cast them to 'no accent' or 'primary accent', or discard them for training purposes. For evaluation, we always cast down to 'no accent'. Table 8.11 compares the available choices. First of all, for the non-native data, the detection rate is lower for the 'primary' task than for the 'strict' task: TPR at FPR 5 % decreases from 40.6 % (cf. Table 8.9) to 38.5 % (row '3' in Table 8.11). For training with non-natives, the detection rate rises, from 48.0 % (cf. Table 8.9) to 51.6 % (row '3' in Table 8.11; underlined).

With regard to modelling strategy, one can see that when training with the mismatched native data, it makes sense to simplify the syllable modelling: the two-class approach is better than the three-class approach, for all three choices of how to cast

---

[12]For word boundaries alone, the change is not as dramatic as for the non-native data; a likely explanation is an interplay of the hierarchical coding of primary and secondary word accents (cf. Section 7.1.3) and the linearity of the classifier. If a non-linear classifier such as a SVM with an RBF kernel is used, UAR indeed rises to 78.7 %.

# modelled classes	secondary acc.	native		non-native	
		UAR	TPR	UAR	TPR
3	(modelled)	64.2	38.5	66.6	<u>51.6</u>
2	up	86.0	43.9	86.3	48.8
	down	85.0	<u>45.1</u>	85.1	50.8
	discard	86.7	44.7	87.1	50.4

Table 8.11: Using different modelling for detecting errors in primary word accent position: Syllable-level accent classification rate (% UAR) and the true positive rate (% TPR) of detecting errors in primary word accent position at a false positive rate of 5 %. Training is done on 11 native or 11 non-native speakers. Features are the respectively optimal ones (separately for native/non-native training data) according to Table 8.9. Chance baselines: 33.3 % for UAR in the three-class case and 50 % in the 2-class case; 5 % for TPR.

secondary accents in the training data. Down-casting to 'no accent' seems to be the best: Although the recognition rate at syllable level is lower (85.0 % UAR) than for up-casting or discarding (86.0 % and 86.7 %, respectively), it yields the best error detection rate with a TPR of 45.1 % (underlined). The lower UAR makes sense as secondary accent is less easily classified as 'no accent' than 'primary accent', cf. Table 8.10. The higher TPR can be explained, on the other hand, by the fact that teaching the classifier to map secondary accents to 'no accent' is better in line with the task of detecting just primary accent.

When training with matched non-native data, the best strategy is to actually model all three classes on syllable level: all the two-class approaches are worse; the best choice (down-casting secondary accents) decreases TPR from 51.6 % (underlined) to 50.8 %. Apparently, modelling the three classes as they are is best if matched training data is available. The fact that secondary accent is easily confused does not matter; it reflects the intrinsic difficulties of the problem.

So far, we have only used a single labeller for training the classifier with non-native training data. Any human labeller will make errors, and combining multiple labellers should remove some of these errors. Therefore, we seek for a method to merge multiple annotations. We identify the following three strategies; note that for simplicity, all operate on syllable level (not on word level).

Majority voting: the accent annotated by most labellers is taken. In case of a tie, randomization is used. The disadvantage of this strategy is that generally, labellers have a low probability to annotate an accent diverging from the canonical pronunciation (around 8 % on the C-AuDiT data). Therefore, the probability that annotated deviations coincide is low, so that after a majority voting, few annotated deviations might remain.

Pessimistic: a single labeller deviating from the canonical accent suffices to assume a change in accent. Majority decision is applied to those labellers deviating from the canonical accent. Ties are again broken by randomization.

Proportional: a change in pronunciation is assumed if more labellers than expected annotated a deviating accent. Unfortunately, we cannot test suitability of that

# labeller folds	2	3	9	9 (∗)
# training labellers	4–5	6	8	1
majority merging	43.6	45.2	45.4	-
pessimistic merging	47.5	47.7	47.9	-
no merging	-	-	-	43.7

Table 8.12: Different strategies to merge up to 8 of 9 labellers for training (for testing, one labeller is used in turn), evaluated with cross-evaluation over the labellers. Data is the reduced subset of non-native data; the system is the context-less system with text features optimized for non-native training data; as above, classifier is LDA, task is strict word accent error detection. The given figure is % TPR at an FPR of 5 %. (∗) here, a single labeller is used for training in turn.

idea on our data: As mentioned above, the a priori probability for a change of syllable accent is only around 8 % on our data; therefore, already one of the (up to ten) labellers suffices to pass the threshold. Therefore the method is equivalent to the pessimistic strategy on our data.

We test the majority and the pessimistic strategy on a subset of the data that has been annotated by many labellers: the reduced set of 24 sentences per speaker, cf. Section 5.1.2. After removing the utterances with word errors, 1274 of the 24 × 58 = 1392 utterances remain. Nine out of the ten labellers have annotated most of that subset; we therefore restrict ourselves to those. Evaluation is just performed on the subset of 3899 words that are annotated by all 9 labellers.

In order to achieve an unbiased comparison, we do not evaluate detection performance on the labellers used for training; rather, we embed or system evaluation inside another cross-evaluation over the labellers. In each fold of the labeller cross-evaluation, the system is trained with the merged training labellers, and tested separately with each of the test labellers (assuming one test labeller as the ground truth at a time). The results (UAR and ROC curves) are again suitably averaged. The resulting measurements of human-machine agreement are directly comparable to pairwise human-human agreement.

Table 8.12 gives the results of these experiments. When using only one labeller at a time (row 'no merging'), a TPR of 43.7 % (at an FPR of 5 %) results. This is substantially lower than the result achieved in Table 8.9 where 48.0 % was achieved with the same configuration. Reasons might be (1) that evaluation is now done on a different subset and (2) that the above comparison on the training labels is biased.

When applying the majority strategy to merge 4 or 5 labellers (2-fold labeller cross-validation), the performance of 43.6 % is even slightly worse than using only a single labeller for training at a time (43.7 %). Apparently, majority merging of detection events is disadvantageous if those events are rare. When merging more labellers at a time, however, an improvement can be achieved, up to a UAR of 45.5 % with the combination of 8 labellers. Much better, however, is the pessimistic strategy: here, already 4–5 labellers improve the TPR from 43.7 % to 47.5 %; performance continues to improve slightly until the maximal number we can test (8 labellers: 47.9 %). We expect that when too many labellers were merged with the pessimistic strategy, the performance would start to degrade at some point, as too many falsely

labeller	strict		primary		tolerant	
	FPR	TPR	FPR	TPR	FPR	TPR
1	3.7	69.3	3.8	76.2	3.3	76.5
3	6.1	82.1	5.7	88.3	4.8	86.1
4	1.4	23.1	1.4	22.8	1.4	25.6
5	4.5	67.2	3.9	68.3	2.7	63.8
6	2.3	45.8	2.1	47.6	1.8	49.1
7	4.3	26.2	1.4	20.1	1.3	22.1
8	6.8	78.8	5.1	81.2	4.2	82.5
9	5.5	78.2	4.5	81.3	4.0	82.5
10	5.2	72.6	5.2	77.3	5.0	79.1
all	4.4	59.5	3.7	61.4	<u>3.2</u>	<u>61.9</u>

Table 8.13: Pairwise human agreement for word accent error detection (% FPR, % TPR). In each pairing, one labeller is assumed as the ground truth and the other is tested. For each single labeller, pairwise comparison with all other labellers are performed; for 'all', all 8 × 9 pairings are considered. Note that there is no line for labeller 2 because that labeller was excluded due to too few annotated recordings.

detected pronunciation errors would be collected. In that case, the proportional strategy could be applied. In any case, a fixed threshold strategy (e. g. assuming deviations only if more than 10 % of the labellers annotated a deviation) should be suitable.

What is the most appropriate word accent error detection task: the strict, primary, or tolerant version? Phonetically and pragmatically, the tolerant version seems to be the most useful. Also, human agreement is highest for the tolerant version, as is shown in Table 8.13 which lists the pair-wise agreement of human labellers for each of the tasks: over all labeller pairs, the tolerant version has the best FPR (3.2 %, underlined, vs. 4.4 % and 3.7 %, respectively for strict and primary) as well as the best TPR (61.9 %, underlined, vs. 59.5 % and 61.4 %, respectively for strict and primary). We therefore concentrate on the tolerant version for the further experiments.

We now use all non-native data of C-AuDiT to evaluate the performance of the optimized system (linear interpolation of short-time features, context concatenation features with improved default features, text features except word accent, pessimistic labeller merging). We use SVM with a linear kernel and evaluate in a 4x4-fold cross-validation, embedded in a cross-validation over the 9 labellers (we use just 2 folds to limit computation time, although we give away some performance, cf. Table 8.12). For (7.34), we need probabilities that the SVM does not provide; as a substitute, we estimate pseudo-probabilities from the SVM outputs (signed distances to the class decision boundaries). We use Platt's method of fitting a sigmoid function to the signed distances [Plat 00]. In order to obtain good probability estimates, the parameters of the sigmoid should be estimated on data not used for training the SVM. One method would be to estimate them on VALI in each validation fold, and then apply the averaged parameters for the output of the SVM trained on VALITRAIN. However, the parameters might not fit well to the new SVM; therefore, a different strategy[13] is applied: All SVMs trained with TRAIN with their associated sigmoid parameters estimated on VALI, are applied on TEST, and the resulting probabilities are averaged arithmetically [Nicu 05, Zadr 02].

The properties of the resulting system are shown in a *detection error trade-off* (DET) curve [Mart 97], a variant of the ROC curve that allows better observation of system contrasts, cf. Figure 8.4. Through the cross-validation over the labellers, the results are now directly comparable to (pairwise) human performance measurements. Recognition rate on syllable level (three-class problem) is now 71.5 % UAR; for error detection at an FPR of 5 % (according to the tolerant criterion), a TPR of 63.8 % is achieved. This is a satisfactory result much better than the one reported in [Hön 09] (although results are not really comparable because we have more data now) and probably at least competitive to the result reported in [Ferr 15] (100 % − 48.4 % = 51.6, % TPR at 5 % FPR). The performance is also not too far away from the average human performance of 61.9 % TPR at 3.2 % FPR (cf. Table 8.13); at the human FPR of 3.2 %, the system has a TPR of 53.4 % (i. e. it detects 13 % (relative) less errors at the same false alarm rate); conversely, for the human TPR of 61.9 %, the system exhibits an FPR of 4.6 % (i. e. it has 43 % more errors at the same true positive rate). The system exceeds the performance of 2 out of the 9 labellers (cf. Figure 8.4, the two crosses above/right of the DET curve of the system).

8.3   Rhythm

As mentioned in Section 7.2.2, our approach to assessing a speaker's prosody is based on directly predicting the human reference scores from an utterance-global acoustic (cf. Table 7.4) and textual (cf. Table 7.6) feature vector. We use linear SVR to map the feature vectors to scores. Again, we evaluate our system in a nested speaker-independent cross-validation, cf. Section 8.2: For each TEST fold, the meta-parameter $C \in \{0.01, 0.1, 1, 10\}$ is optimized by means of a cross-validation on VALITRAIN. Performance is measured as *Spearman's rank correlation coefficient* ρ, computed from the combined results (predictions of regressors) of all test folds (rather than taking the average correlation of the test folds). The same measure is used for tuning C. We use 4 outer and 4 inner folds. We use Spearman's instead of Pearson's correlation coefficient r because of its robustness against outliers.

We assume that the optimization of the local acoustic features for word accent recognition in Sections 8.2.1 to 8.2.3 generalize to the global features and to the task of prosody assessment. Therefore, we use as above: (1) normalization of short-time features on speech frames in logarithmic space, (2) linear interpolation of short-time features on utterance level, (3) only the 'syl' and 'nuc' segments (not 'sylfix' or 'nucfix') (4) the improved version of default values for context features (needed for the stressed syllable aggregation, and tails), and (5) of the two possibilities context embedding and concatenation just the latter one. In contrast to word accent classification above, we do not exclude any text features, since the risk of the system taking a short-cut is not given for the present task. (In word accent classification,

---

[13]The   scikit-learn   class   `CalibratedClassifierCV`   with   `prefit=True`   is   used, http://scikit-learn.org/stable/modules/generated/sklearn.calibration. CalibratedClassifierCV.html, last visited September 8th, 2017.

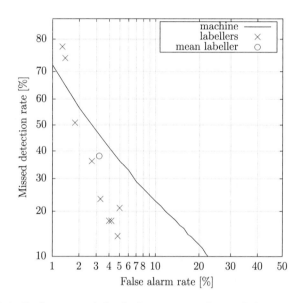

Figure 8.4: Performance of the final system together with human performance, shown in a detection error trade-off curve. The y-axis (missed detection rate) equals $100\% - \text{TPR}$.

the goal of detecting errors was approached indirectly via the syllables' accentedness, which could be comprised by the classifier guessing for canonical accents; here, we are directly modelling the target scores, which is why the problem does not occur.)

8.3.1   C-AuDiT

Table 8.14 gives the results obtained for the *panel* subset of the C-AuDiT and ISLE corpora, which amounts to 448 utterances (without reading errors) from 94 non-native speakers. We use the average of the scores (cf. Section 6.1.2) given for the melody and rhythm questions, as these two ratings are almost equivalent [Hön 10a, Hön 12a].

As expected, the text features alone (row 'text') do not contain much information; possibly, the weak positive correlation of $\rho = 0.089$ for the text features aggregated from all syllables (column 'syl') captures some a priori difficulty of the items to be spoken. Duration information is by far the most important clue: If all segmentations are used for aggregating information (column 'all'), $\rho = 0.737$ is obtained. The aggregation of stressed syllables seems to contribute most with $\rho = 0.721$ (coluumn 'ssyl').

F0 contains relatively weak cues: when using descriptors that should be nearly independent of durations, i. e. the subsets 'statistics$^-$', 'shape$^-$', 'frequency$^-$', and all segmentations, correlations of 0.350, 0.279, and 0.258 are obtained, respectively. If all descriptors are considered (i. e. including all descriptors of row 'duration$^-$'), the result of $\rho = 0.668$ is even worse than using duration features alone. An explanation for this is that the number of duration features (332) is a relatively small fraction of all features (2519), which might limit their influence in the presence of a regularized regression estimator.

Energy is the next more important clue: for the subsets 'statistics$^-$', 'shape$^-$', 'frequency$^-$', and all segmentations, correlations of 0.427, 0.495, and 0.410 are obtained, respectively. Again, however, when considering all descriptors, the result of $\rho = 0.680$ does not improve the duration result.

Spectral information (row 'mfcc1–4') is yet more important than energy: when looking at the individual subsets 'statistics$^-$', 'shape$^-$', and 'frequency$^-$': correlations of 0.522, 0.576, and 0.494, respectively, result, clearly surpassing the respective results using energy or F0. However, in combination with all descriptors, the result is worse ($\rho = 0.603$ vs. 0.668 for F0 and 0.680 for energy), probably because duration is underrepresented again. Contradictorily, the result of $\rho = 0.750$ when using only stressed syllables (column 'ssyl') is better, even though the duration features are still underrepresented in terms of cardinality.

When all short-time features are combined (the four lowermost rows), results improve for all descriptor subsets: $\rho = 0.574, 0.641$, and 0.571, respectively, are obtained for 'statistics$^-$', 'shape$^-$', and 'frequency$^-$', which is higher than any of the results obtained with F0, energy, or MFCCs alone.

Looking at descriptor subsets excluding duration, shape (rows 'shape$^-$') seems to contribute most overall. An exception is f0, where statistics (row 'statistics$^-$') is most important with 0.350 % when using all segmentations (vs. 0.279 and 0.258 for 'shape$^-$' and 'frequency$^-$', respectively).

Short-time features	Descriptors	Segmentation				
		whole	syl	ssyl	tails	all
text		-	**0.089**	0.001	-0.035	-0.031
(any)	duration⁻	0.233	0.613	**0.721**	0.633	0.737
f0	statistics⁻	0.046	0.302	**0.313**	0.251	0.350
	shape⁻	**0.279**	0.170	0.160	0.204	0.279
	frequency⁻	-0.047	**0.259**	0.182	0.131	0.258
	all	0.162	0.571	**0.674**	0.562	0.668
ene	statistics⁻	0.094	0.295	0.332	**0.372**	0.427
	shape⁻	0.141	0.280	**0.401**	0.318	0.495
	frequency⁻	**0.402**	0.276	0.370	0.333	0.410
	all	0.496	0.622	**0.679**	0.579	0.680
mfcc1–4	statistics⁻	0.317	0.441	0.485	**0.491**	0.522
	shape⁻	0.478	0.360	**0.512**	0.452	0.576
	frequency⁻	**0.467**	0.445	0.445	0.344	0.494
	all	0.603	0.627	**0.750**	0.652	0.603
all	statistics⁻	0.523	0.508	0.527	**0.543**	0.574
	shape⁻	**0.592**	0.451	0.582	0.539	0.641
	frequency⁻	**0.581**	0.492	0.562	0.338	0.571
	all	0.674	0.679	**0.764**	0.676	<u>0.773</u>

Table 8.14: Assessment of non-native prosody on C-AuDiT for different short-time features, descriptors, and segmentations ('whole': whole speech segment, 'syl': aggregation of all syllables, 'ssyl': aggregation of all stressed syllables (with their context), 'tails': utterance start and end, 'all': all segments (=union of the aforementioned). The descriptors subsets 'duration⁻', 'statistics⁻', 'shape⁻' and 'frequency⁻' are same as in Tables 8.8 and 8.4. Note that 'all' descriptors contain all descriptors of Table 7.1 (e.g. including duration) plus text features, not just the union of the listed subsets. Similarly, 'all' short-time features comprise all 8 short-time features (cf. Section 7.1.2), not just the union of 'f0', 'ene' and 'mfcc1–4'. For the MFCC features, we want to concentrate on spectral information, therefore 'mfcc0', which is a measure of energy, has been omitted. The figure given is Spearman's rank correlation; chance baseline is 0. Note that as we are using cross-validation, negative correlations are absolutely possible as a consequence of a very weak estimator (producing nearly constant predictions) that overfits to the mean of the training set (http://www.russpoldrack.org/2012/12/the-perils-of-leave-one-out.html, last visited September 8th, 2017, and http://not2hastie.tumblr.com/, last visited September 8th, 2017). Typographic emphasis: see text.

Considering segmentation, the method of aggregating stressed syllables and their context (column 'ssyl') seems to contribute most: it is better than 'whole', 'syl' or 'tails' in 8 out of 17 cases (typeset in bold face), and most of the time almost as good as when using all segmentations (and even better in case of MFCCs). The methods (1) aggregating all syllables (without context, cf. row 'syl') and (2) using the tails of the utterance (row 'tails') perform similar. Using the whole speech segment without any further segmentation (row 'whole') leads to mixed results: is it the worst method in 10 out of 16 cases; on the other hand, it is also the best method in 5 of these 16 cases. So overall, it seems to be the worst method taken in isolation, but to contribute some complementary information nevertheless. An explanation might be that it is the method most robust to segmentation errors (it is only impacted by the voiced/unvoiced segmentation plus the very start and end as segmented by forced alignment).

When using all segmentations with all short-time features and all descriptors (cell at the bottom right, underlined), the best result is obtained, with $\rho = 0.773$ (and $r = 0.704$). This result is visualized in Figure 8.5. This result is slightly better than the one reported in [Hön 12a][14].

In order to compare the performance of the system to human performance, we estimate the correlation with the hypothetical 'ground truth'—the averaged labels from N labellers for $N \to \infty$ [Hön 10b, Hön 12a]. First, our reference score (from the combined melody and rhythm scores from 62 labellers, with a pairwise correlation of $r = 0.44$) correlates with the ground truth with $r = 0.99$. That means that the system correlates to the ground truth with $r = 0.721 \cdot 0.99 = 0.71$. The average correlation of a single labeller to the ground truth is the square root of pairwise correlation: $r = \sqrt{0.44} = 0.66$. Thus, the system is slightly better than the average human labeller. Note that these estimates are based on the assumption of an interval scale; we have shown, however, that this assumption produces precise prediction for our data [Hön 10b].

For both pronunciation training and language testing, an assessment result aggregated over a number of productions is interesting. We study this scenario by averaging all reference and predicted scores per speaker. On the present material, these speaker-level results are formed from 5 sentences. The correlation of the predicted speaker scores with the reference speaker scores is $\rho = 0.854$. This result is visualized in Figure 8.6.

We also tried non-linear regression with the help of a radial basis function kernel, cf. (4.31). The two meta-parameters were optimized over a limited grid, cf. Table 8.15. rho did not improve; however, r was a little higher ($\rho = 0.764$, $r = 0.742$). Speaker level scores were worse than for the linear model ($\rho = 0.816$ vs. 0.854).

Information about the text spoken is used by our global features only to a very limited extent; the aggregation of stressed syllables is the best we did so far in this regard. This was the motivation for the divide and conquer approach described in Section 7.2.2 based on scoring syllables with context. Although that approach did not

---

[14]In the most comparable set-up, we use a 5-fold cross-validation, an SVR with a radial basis function kernel, and optimize meta-parameters to $C = 10$, $\gamma = 0.1$ on the whole data as was done for the sake of simplicity in [Hön 12a]. Then, we achieve $\rho = 0.774$ and $r = 0.761$ which is slightly better than the $r = 0.75$ reported in [Hön 12a] for the same data.

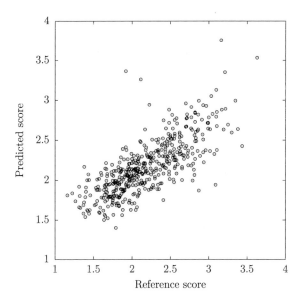

Figure 8.5: The best system for assessing non-native prosody ($\rho = 0.773, r = 0.704$) on C-AuDiT. Note that there is a single gross outlier at $(1.87, -1.05)$ which is not displayed in favour of a range that concentrates on the most interesting region of the scatter plot. (That outlier is the cause for r being considerably lower than ρ and could easily be fixed by clipping outputs to the known range of the scores.) Note that although the original rating scale ranges from 1 to 5 inclusive, the reference scores (averaged over 62 labellers) stay below 4. The range of the predicted values is smaller than that of the reference values ($\sigma = 0.378$ vs. 0.458) which is a consequence of the estimator being not perfectly confident ($r < 1$), thus preferring predictions closer to the mean.

		\multicolumn{3}{c}{C}		
		1	10	100
	0.0001			★
	0.001		★	★
γ	0.01	★	★	★
	0.1	★	★	
	1	★		

Table 8.15: Pairs of C and γ that were considered as meta-parameters for the SVR with an RBF kernel, marked by '★'. For both C and γ, higher values lead to a more complex model; therefore, pairs that set a low (upper left) or high (lower right) complexity for both parameters at the same time can be omitted. Note that restriction to this small grid is possible through the normalization of feature vectors to unity norm, cf. Section 8.2.

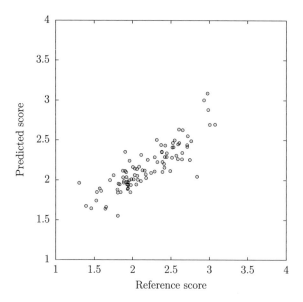

Figure 8.6: Performance of the best system on C-AuDiT for assessing non-native prosody, evaluated on speaker level by averaging 5 utterance scores: $\rho = 0.854$. Note that through the averaging, the range of the scores is even smaller than for utterance scores (cf. Figure 8.5). As in the case of the utterance level results, the range of the predicted values is smaller than that of the reference values ($\sigma = 0.287$ vs. 0.397).

Group	Features	Utterance	Speaker
Tempo	speechRate	0.402	0.435
	articulationRate	0.361	0.409
	pauseProportion	0.198	0.220
	all	0.388	0.420
PVI	rPVIv	0.080	0.091
	rPVIc	0.225	0.562
	nPVIv	-0.124	-0.109
	nPVIc	0.115	0.431
	all	0.455	0.641
GPI	percentV	0.032	0.114
	deltaV	0.137	0.191
	deltaC	0.107	0.190
	varcoV	-0.063	-0.063
	varcoC	0.030	0.103
	all	0.447	0.560
all	all	0.541	0.656

Table 8.16: Assessment of non-native prosody on C-AuDiT with the help of specialized rhythm features. The figure given is the Spearman correlation ρ between reference scores and predictions on utterance or speaker level.

lead to improvements (at least for the present task) in [Hön 12a], there was some hope because we are now including rich spectral information through the MFCC features. In order to be successful, the local scoring module needs to model some translational invariance; we therefore apply non-linear SVR with the help of a radial basis function kernel. So far, we did not gain improvements with the approach; we obtained (in just a two-fold cross-validation) $\rho = 0.617$ (vs. $\rho = 0.746$ for the linear model when using two folds). Also when combining the two approaches linearly (with weights w and $1 - w$, with $w \in \{0, 0.1, 0.2, \ldots, 1.0\}$) we observed no improvement.

Next, we have a look at specialized rhythm features, cf. Section 7.1.4. The results of these experiments are listed in Table 8.16. Speech rate correlates with $\rho = 0.402$ on utterance level, and is superior to articulation rate or pause ratio alone ($\rho = 0.361$ and 0.198, respectively); the combination of the three (redundant) measures does not improve results. Although ideally, ratings of the appropriateness of a speaker's prosody should be independent of tempo, tempo correlates with general proficiency and thus also prosodic proficiency. An explanation why speech rate is better than articulation could be that speech rate captures both articulation speed (related to motor proficiency) and fluency (related to planning/reading abilities).

None of the pairwise variability indices seems to be useful in isolation to predict utterance-level scores: their individual performances range between $\rho = -0.124$ for nPVIv and $\rho = 0.225$ for rPVIc. That changes soon as scores are aggregated over multiple utterances: on speaker level, rPVIc and nPVIc yield correlations of $\rho = 0.562$ and 0.431, respectively. Also combining all four PVI measures yields noticeable correlations ($\rho = 0.455$ on utterance level, and $\rho = 0.641$ on speaker level).

Global proportions of intervals lead to in substantial correlations only when combined: when all 5 are used, $\rho = 0.447$ on utterance level and $\rho = 0.560$ on speaker level result.

Combining all of the specialized features results in $\rho = 0.541$ on utterance and $\rho = 0.656$ on speaker level (last row, underlined). That performance is considerable, but clearly below the performance of our generic features ($\rho = 0.773$). Adding the specialized features to the latter improves results just a little bit (from $\rho = 0.773$ to $\rho = 0.774$ on utterance level, and from $\rho = 0.854$ to $\rho = 0.855$ on speaker level; not contained in Table 8.16).

Interestingly, if a non-linear model is applied to the rhythm features (neither contained in Table 8.16), correlation improves substantially from $\rho = 0.541$ to $\rho = 0.606$. On speaker level, the result even goes up from $\rho = 0.656$ to $\rho = 0.765$, which is quite a nice result. Possibly, the rhythm features are powerful but too noisy for short-term assessment.

When comparing the results obtained for the specialized rhythm and tempo features (up to $\rho = 0.541$, $r = 0.540$) with those obtained in [Hön 12a] for very similar features on the same data, there is a striking difference: there, $r = 0.73$ resulted for the combination of all rhythm features. Although using a more comparable setup (non-linear model, 5 folds, meta-parameters optimized on all data) improves results to $\rho = r = 0.610$, there is still a large gap. One possible reason is that the speech recognizer (trained with just 17 speakers) we are using for segmentation is not as good as the commercial speech recognizer used in [Hön 12a]. If that were true, it would speak in favour of our generic approach, which achieves slightly higher correlation than that of [Hön 12a] in spite of a possibly worse segmentation.

8.3.2   AUWL

Table 8.17 gives the results on the clean material (i. e. utterances without reading errors) of AUWL, which amounts to 3732 utterances from 31 non-native speakers. Generally, the obtained correlations between reference scores and predictions are considerably lower than on C-AuDiT, which is an indication that the task is more difficult on that data. This is corroborated by the fact that pair-wise labeller correlation is distinctly lower than for C-AuDiT ($r = 0.34$ vs. 0.44). Furthermore, the recording quality is very low for some speakers in AUWL.

Regarding individual subsets of features, the text features alone do not provide useful information. The duration features are again most important: using all segmentations, $\rho = 0.542$ is achieved. Similarly to the results on C-AuDiT, energy is more informative than f0, and MFCCs are more useful than energy: for the descriptor subsets 'statistics$^-$', 'shape$^-$' and 'frequency$^-$' (and all segmentations), f0 yields $\rho = 0.252$, 0.081, and 0.253, respectively, which is surpassed by energy with $\rho = 0.279$, 0.243, and 0.270, respectively, which in turn is surpassed by MFCCs with $\rho = 0.429$, 0.307, and 0.354, respectively.

Again, the combination of all descriptors (including duration) per short-time feature seems to outweigh the important duration features, leading to worse results than duration alone ($\rho = 0.508$ for f0, $\rho = 0.497$ for energy, $\rho = 0.523$ for MFCCs, vs. $\rho = 0.542$ for duration alone).

Short-time features	Descriptors	Segmentation				
		whole	syl	ssyl	tails	all
text		-	-0.027	-0.004	**0.005**	0.031
(any)	duration⁻	0.261	0.455	**0.524**	0.430	0.542
f0	statistics⁻	0.071	0.052	**0.143**	0.021	0.252
	shape⁻	-0.168	-0.014	**0.061**	-0.059	0.081
	frequency⁻	0.052	0.082	**0.195**	0.095	0.253
	all	0.252	0.442	**0.503**	0.413	0.508
ene	statistics⁻	-0.058	-0.058	**0.234**	0.181	0.279
	shape⁻	0.128	0.131	**0.253**	0.182	0.243
	frequency⁻	0.120	0.120	**0.222**	0.172	0.270
	all	0.298	0.471	**0.498**	0.406	0.497
mfcc1–4	statistics⁻	0.257	0.397	**0.406**	0.330	0.429
	shape⁻	-0.008	**0.328**	0.289	0.171	0.307
	frequency⁻	0.292	**0.407**	0.305	0.249	0.354
	all	0.379	**0.559**	0.516	0.405	0.523
all	statistics⁻	0.264	0.360	**0.366**	0.213	0.371
	shape⁻	0.259	**0.326**	0.292	0.213	0.323
	frequency⁻	0.306	**0.315**	0.242	0.234	0.326
	all	0.371	**0.549**	0.505	0.409	0.530

Table 8.17: Assessment of non-native prosody on AUWL for different configurations; cf. Table 8.14 for explanations. Typographic emphasis: see text.

Unlike the results on C-AuDiT, the combination of all short-time features per descriptor subset does improve results only for 'shape⁻' ($\rho = 0.323$), while it deteriorates results for 'statistics⁻' ($\rho = 0.371$ vs. 0.429 for just MFCCs) and 'frequency⁻' ($\rho = 0.326$ vs. 0.354 for just MFCCs).

Another difference to the results on C-AuDiT is that with regard to the descriptor subsets 'frequency⁻', 'shape⁻', and 'frequency⁻', (which should be independent of duration), shape is now the least important. In accord with C-AuDiT, however, statistics are better than frequency descriptors in the majority of cases. (For example: using MFCCs, $\rho = 0.307$ for 'shape⁻', 0.354 for 'frequency⁻' and 0.429 for 'statistics⁻'.)

Considering segmentation, the method of aggregating stressed syllables and their context (column 'ssyl') again contributes most: in 11 out of 17 cases (typeset in bold face), it leads to better results than 'whole', 'syl', or 'tails'. Aggregating all syllables without context (column 'syl') wins for MFCC and all short-time features (when using all descriptors). However, this time, these two results with 'syl' surpass even the results when using all segmentations: For MFCC, $\rho = 0.559$ (underlined), vs. 0.523 for all segmentations, and for all short-time features, $\rho = 0.549$ (underlined), vs. 0.530 for all segmentations. Using the whole speech interval now seems to contribute little: it is surpassed by other segmentations in all 16 cases.

As already encountered above, using all available features (all short-time features, all descriptors, and all segmentations) with $\rho = 0.530$ is now surpassed by smaller feature subsets in three cases (durations from all segmentations: 0.542, MFCC for 'syl': 0.559, and all short-time segments for 'syl': 0.549). However, when using a non-linear regressor (SVR with an RBF kernel; not contained in Table 8.17), that changes: Using all features leads to the best result with $\rho = 0.619$ and $r = 0.600$ (durations from all segmentations: $\rho = 0.572$, MFCC for 'syl': $\rho = 0.612$, and all short-time segments for 'syl': $\rho = 0.581$). This result is visualized in 8.7; it is slightly better than the one reported in [Hön 12a][15] and similar to the one reported in [Blac 15], the winner of the sub-challenge 'Nativeness' in the INTERSPEECH 2015 paralinguistic challenge [Schu 15][16].

After these experiments were finished, we realized that there is a large mismatch between the training data of the speech recognizer (used for segmentation) and parts of the non-native AUWL data: Audio quality is fine for all native speakers, while it is very low for several non-native speakers. This should have a negative effect on the quality of segmentations, and thus on features and system performance. Indeed, when using a well-matched speech recognizer[17], results improve for the linear system from $\rho = 0.530$ to $\rho = 0.577$ (the RBF system changes only little, from $\rho = 0.619$ to 0.616).

In order to compare to human performance, we first note that our reference labels for AUWL are generated by averaging over just 5 labellers with a pairwise correlation of only $r = 0.34$, which means that the estimated correlation between reference and ground truth is $r = 0.85$. Thus, we can only expect our automatic predictions (which are correlated to the reference scores with $r = 0.600$) to correlate to the ground truth with $r = 0.600 \cdot 0.85 = 0.51$. That is considerably lower than the correlation $r = \sqrt{0.34} = 0.58$ of the average human labeller to the ground truth.

As for C-AuDiT, we also study for AUWL what happens when scores are aggregated over several utterances of a speaker. Again, we just average reference scores and predictions over all utterances of each speaker. The number of utterances contributed by a speaker varies between 18 and 309. The resulting speaker-level correlation is $\rho = 0.821$; cf. Figure 8.8 for a visualization.

We test the suitability of the specialized rhythm features on AUWL, too. The results of these experiments are presented in Table 8.18. Tempo is again a relatively good predictor: speech rate correlates with $\rho = 0.362$ on utterance level, and with $\rho = 0.541$ on speaker level. Also consistent with the C-AuDiT results, speech rate is better than articulation rate or the proportion of pauses alone. This time, however,

---

[15]The most comparable set-up is 5-fold cross-validation with meta-parameters optimized on the whole data; here, we obtain (with $C = 10$, $\gamma = 0.01$) a correlation of $r = 0.603$, which is larger than the value $r = 0.57$ reported in [Hön 12a] for the same data.

[16] When evaluating on the same data (union of AUWL and the few sentences from ISLE used in the panel subset = training set of the challenge), and evaluating as Black and colleagues do, i. e. performing a 6-fold speaker-independent cross-validation, we obtain $\rho = 0.622$. That is higher than the $\rho = 0.605$ reported by [Blac 15]; however, since they also report the standard deviation of "model performance across training folds", the reported figure seems to be the average of the correlation obtained on the cross-validation folds (rather a single correlation computed on the combined test data). This figure is a little lower for our system ($\rho = 0.584$).

[17]For simplicity, we trained the recognizer using all (both native and non-native) material from C-AuDiT and AUWL. This could be regarded as cheating; however, we are just using the target text, plus the information that the speaker did not introduce word errors—which is what we use in our system anyway.

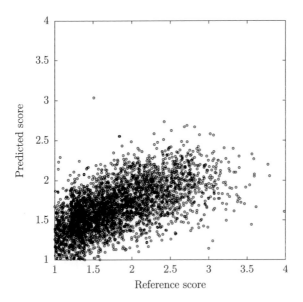

Figure 8.7: The best system for assessing non-native prosody on AUWL ($\rho = 0.619$). As the reference score is averaged from 5 labeller's integral scores, it is really discrete $(1, 1.2, 1.4, \dots)$; to reduce the overlap of the points and thus enhance visibility, scatter (uniform between 0 and 0.2) has been added to the reference values before plotting. As is to be expected from a regressor that is not perfectly confident, predictions near the mean are preferred, causing the spread of the predicted values to be considerably smaller than that of the reference values ($\sigma = 0.304$ vs. 0.528).

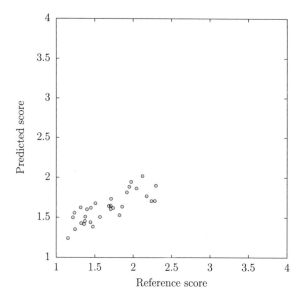

Figure 8.8: The best system on AUWL when averaging scores per speaker ($\rho = 0.821$, $r = 0.799$); Through the averaging over all utterances of each speaker, the spread of the reference scores is strongly reduced (from $\sigma = 0.528$, cf. Figure 8.7, to $\sigma = 0.341$). The spread of the predicted values is still smaller than that of the reference values ($\sigma = 0.182$ vs. 0.341), again the consequence of regressor not perfectly confident.

Group	Features	Utterance	Speaker
Tempo	speechRate	0.362	0.541
	articulationRate	0.223	0.437
	pauseProportion	0.247	0.001
	all	0.412	0.623
PVI	rPVIv	0.069	0.017
	rPVIc	-0.170	-0.220
	nPVIv	-0.194	-0.291
	nPVIc	-0.162	-0.144
	all	0.229	0.099
GPI	percentV	-0.009	-0.040
	deltaV	0.139	0.031
	deltaC	-0.039	-0.030
	varcoV	-0.229	-0.383
	varcoC	-0.150	-0.342
	all	0.238	0.318
all	all	0.442	0.625

Table 8.18: Assessment of non-native prosody on AUWL with the help of specialized rhythm features.

the combination of the three yields a little improvement ($\rho = 0.412$ and $\rho = 0.623$ for utterance and speaker level, respectively).

The pairwise variability indices are not very useful this time; the still best result is obtained by combining the four coefficients ($\rho = 0.229$), but the relevance is moot since results drop to $\rho = 0.099$ on speaker level. The global proportions of intervals are a bit better ($\rho = 0.238$ and $\rho = 0.318$ on utterance and speaker level, respectively).

Finally, the combination of all specialized features (last row, underlined) yields $\rho = 0.442$ on utterance and $\rho = 0.625$ on speaker level. Again, this performance is clearly below that of our generic features. Adding the specialized features to the latter did not change results.

Interestingly, when a non-linear model is applied to the specialized features, correlations improve quite a bit to $\rho = 0.507$. This does not approach the performance of the generic features ($\rho = 0.619$). However, when looking at the correlation on speaker level, $\rho = 0.834$ results, which is even better than the $\rho = 0.821$ obtained with the generic features. Thus, the rhythm features are useful features for long-term assessment, but they seem to be too noisy for short-term.

As in the case of C-AuDiT, there is a large gap between the present results ($\rho = 0.442$, $r = 0.404$ for all rhythm and tempo features) and those reported in [Hön 12a] for very similar features on the same data ($r = 0.56$). Although the gap gets smaller when comparable experimental conditions are used (non-linear model, 5 folds, meta-parameters optimized on all data), a difference remains ($\rho = 0.529$). Again, this could be explained by the possibly worse segmentation in the present experiments.

9

Discussion

Our approach of substituting the specialized Erlangen prosody module by a simpler and more generic architecture seems to have been successful: Although we dropped phoneme-specific normalizations, and increased dimensionality by exhaustively applying descriptors regardless of the type of short-time features used, results for both tasks studied are competitive both with regard to the ones previously obtained with the Erlangen prosody module and the general state of the art. Thus, the approach has proven useful for both local and global classification/assessment tasks. The big advantage of our approach is that it can flexibly and rapidly be adapted to new tasks—be it within paralinguistic speech processing, or other applications fields, even outside speech processing. All that is required for adaptation to a new domain is the selection of suitable short-time features, and definition of intervals to which the generic descriptors should be applied in order to compute local or global features. It has to be noted that the system is by far not as generic as openSMILE [Eybe 10, Eybe 13] in the sense that it cannot be applied usefully out-of-the box. That limits its ease of use for new tasks; on the other hand, only the facility for adaptation enabled state-of-the-art performance: for rhythm assessment, openSMILE without the possibility to incorporate phonetic knowledge cannot reach comparable performances [Hön 12b].

The descriptors that aggregate the properties of a short-time feature sequence during a given segment were designed to cope with missing values in a principled way. However, it turned out that this was not really necessary; linearly interpolating over the whole utterance (before cutting out the segment) was even a little better and avoids the missing values in the first place. Thus, the efforts seem vain in hindsight; nevertheless, the suggested methods could come in handy in other contexts. Also, an intelligent mixture of the two approaches (using the interpolated sequence for shape descriptors, and the original sequence for the other descriptors) might still improve results.

We made an effort to obtain unbiased estimates of the performance of our systems: As usual in machine learning, meta-parameters were estimated on held-out validation data to avoid overfitting to the test data. However, some overfitting probably happened during system development, which was at least partly done with the help of all, i.e. also test data. On the other hand, our cross-evaluation procedures were modest, using just 4x4 folds, which means that only $(3/4)^2 = 56\%$ of the data were used for model fitting at a time; thus, we can assume some performance gain when we train a final system with all data.

For comparison to human performance on the tasks studies, we also made an effort to obtain unbiased comparisons: Rather than comparing system performance with the training labels, which can lead to biased results, we measured (word accents) or extrapolated (rhythm) agreement to held-out labellers not used for training. That enabled us to draw valid comparisons between human and machine performance. The relatively high performance of our approaches (better than 2 out of 9 labellers for word accents; better than average human rhythm assessment at least for C-AuDiT) is a nice result; nevertheless, it should not deludes us: the systems are highly tailored to the present domains, and will perform clearly worse than humans when applied to mismatched data such as different speaking styles or acoustic mismatch; already application to new texts will have a noticeable impact.

In absolute terms, the correlations obtained for rhythm assessment are modest. Clearly, that is a difficult task, as the similarly low human performance shows. Also increasing difficulty is the fact that the speakers contained in our databases are relatively good speakers, which can be seen from the fact that the higher scores (= worse pronunciation) are rare in the reference labels. When speaker proficiencies are more heterogeneous, correlation are automatically higher for the same task [Cout 16]. Nevertheless, rhythm assessments—at least on utterance level—will always be uncertain to some extent, making it a challenge to apply them in CAPT. Maybe a two-fold strategy that checks rhythm on the more reliable medium term (rather than utterance level) combined with automatically suggested exercises for specific, concrete prosodic phenomena (word accents, placement of useful phrase boundaries, weakening of unstressed syllables etc.) could be successful.

Plenty of future work suggests itself: approaches similar to the one presented for detecting errors in word accent could be developed for phrase accents and boundaries; C-AuDiT could be used at least for initial studies. The present approach for word accents could be evaluated also for a text-independent setting, ideally resulting in suggestions of how much data is needed to obtain a virtually text-independent system. Also, it would be interesting to study if a native training corpus can lead to the performance of expensive, annotated non-native training data. The approach should also be evaluated together with an utterance verification module, ideally as fine-grained as to detect syllable insertions or deletions, in order to report them, or at least exclude the affected words from error feedback (which runs a high risk of being erroneous, as the underlying assumptions are violated).

For rhythm assessment, currently the most successful method seems to be the aggregation of (canonically) stressed syllables with their context. That is a bit twisted because it must necessarily mix up two things: (1) the average properties of actually stressed syllables, and (2) how well canonical word accent is produced. Therefore, an obvious possibility for improvement could be (1) to base that aggregation on actually stressed syllables (as identified by an automatic module), and/or (2) to use the word accent error probabilities as features for rhythm assessment. Also, it would be highly desirable to evaluate rhythm assessment together with an utterance verification module, or a speech recognizer that accounts for some word errors.

On the modelling side, a quite unpleasant property of the proposed system is its dependence on expensive annotated, non-native material— the 'wholy grale' of rhythm assessment would be a method that can be trained with native data only. Possibly, unsupervised learning techniques such as outlier detection could help; or methods that are based on the usefulness of appropriate prosody for human communication (easing listening and parsing effort).

Finally, with the recent advances in neuronal networks, the era of manual feature design seems to come to an end. It will be highly interesting to work out how to best substitute the traditional modules 'feature extraction + classifier/regressor' by suitable network architectures for the present task. If segmentation is obtained from external sources, that seems relatively straightforward for syllable accent classification: a convolutional neuronal network applied to a fixed-size interval, within which the short-time feature sequence of the current syllable is centred, could be a start. A more elegant way would be sliding a recurrent network over the individual short-time features, putting out either the empty word or a target labels, but many details (e. g. how to best encode knowledge about the target text) will have to be worked for that model to work well and finally supersede the current approaches. Another challenge is how to gain knowledge from the results obtained—for which interpretability is the key.

10

Summary

The present thesis studies methods for automatically assessing the prosody of non-native speakers, for the purpose of giving feedback in the context of computer-assisted language learning. In particular, word accent placement (as a prototypical concrete prosodic function) and assessment of speech rhythm (as the most important overall prosodic property) are studied. After introducing these tasks, the role of prosody in native language was discussed, followed by a review of the pertinent state of the art. Following that, the mathematical foundations for our approaches were presented: computing basic time-varying properties of speech such as loudness or fundamental frequency (which are the basis for the decisions of our system; we call them short-time features), over classification and regression techniques (which are the decision mechanisms of our system, using technologies from artificial intelligence/machine learning) to hidden Markov models, the classical model for time-varying events that is still used today in many speech recognition systems (which is used for segmentation—defining the scope of the system decisions, and sources of information).

Next, the speech corpora used were introduced: C-AuDiT, which features conventional read sentences, which play an important role in computer-assisted language learning, despite their unnaturalness (and difficulties often more related to reading and grapheme-phoneme conversion issues rather than pronunciation). AUWL represents an effort to obtain more 'natural' material, using the scenario of practising pre-scripted dialogues. This is still far from natural human-to-human communication but nevertheless highly relevant for computer-assisted language learning.

We collected manual reference values for feedback: for the word accent task, the actually produced word accent configuration, and for the rhythm task, quality ratings. We need these annotations for two purposes: most importantly, we need to estimate how well our system works. Secondly, we can use them to train our classifiers and regressors (i. e. construct decision algorithms in a data-driven way). We present the annotations collected for C-AuDiT and AUWL; note that for both corpora these annotations cover more aspects than the two approached here.

Next, we described our proposed approaches. First, we describe our method to extract higher-level prosodic *features* (acoustic parameters computed from speech that might be useful for our classification or regression task) from the short-time features. The key points of our method are (1) genericity which allows easy transfer to new tasks, (2) exhaustiveness which allows to exploit as much information as possible, (3) principled handling of missing values (e. g. fundamental frequency during unvoiced speech) and (4) interpretability. We describe how the algorithms can be used to obtain *local* features on syllable level (will be used for word accent classification) as well as global features (for rhythm assessment). The necessary segmentation into words and phonemes is obtained by using a speech recognizer under the assumption that the target text has indeed been produced.

For word accent recognition, we constructed a method that estimates the *probability of an acceptable word accent configuration*, given the canonical pronunciation according to the lexicon, and the acoustic realization. That probability can be thresholded suitably to adjust the system to a desired behaviour: a strict or courageous system that is more likely to report a possible pronunciation error (which will catch more actual errors but also produce more false alarms), or a lenient or careful system that is less likely to report a possible error (which will miss more actual errors but produce less false alarms). What an acceptable word accent configuration is can be chosen as desired: either all primary and secondary word accents need to match exactly to the canonical pronunciation, or secondary accents are ignored. A third alternative is the 'tolerant' version which allows (1) confusing secondary and primary accents and (2) converting secondary accents to un-accented syllables. The system for word accent error detection is ideally trained with annotated non-native data, but it can also work with (much cheaper) un-annotated native data, under the assumption that natives produce few pronunciations deviating from canonical word accent configuration.

For rhythm assessment, we do not identify a technique that works with native data only; rather, we train algorithms to directly predict prosody scores from our global prosodic features.

In the course of the experimental evaluations, we identify a number of design decisions that seem to be most useful for the tasks. These are: (1) The best way to approach normalization (normalization in the final logarithmic domain if speech/non-speech segmentation is available; otherwise, normalization in the original linear domain. This result may be useful elsewhere, especially for mel-frequency cepstral coefficients, MFCCs). (2) It is better to impute the short-time features via linear interpolation, rather than leaving it to the feature extraction module to cope with missing values. (3) Syllables and nuclei suffice as sources of information for extracting features; approaches with fixed-size intervals, aimed at introducing some invariance to (possibly erroneous) segmentations, were discarded. (4) When modelling context of syllables (which is necessary to obtain excellent results), it is better to use early imputation on the level of the short-time features rather than late imputation on the level of the higher-level features. (5) Explicitly providing context by concatenation was better than describing the evolution of features within the neighbourhood by mean and slope descriptors.

For word accent error detection, we compare performance when using either un-annotated native data, or native, annotated data, using subsets of the C-AuDiT corpus, chosen such that results are actually comparable (in terms of the cardinality of data used for training the classifiers). When adjusting the false positive rate (FPR) of the system to 5 %, the true positive rate (TPR) achieved is 34.3 % for native training data and 39.0 % for non-native training data. Thus, there is a little loss in reliability, but it might be possible to make that up by using more of the (much cheaper) native training data.

Humans err; therefore, human reference labels are necessarily imperfect. Merging multiple labellers can improve the situation; however, we identified a problem: annotated pronunciation errors are relatively rare events, and when applying naïve majority voting, the number of coinciding error annotations can decrease, leading to a reference that is actually worse than the annotation of a single labeller. We identified a strategy to cope with that problem and thus produce better reference labels.

The final best system for word accent error detection achieves a TPR of 71.5 % at 5 % FPR. This is a very nice result close to average human performance (TPR 61.9 % at 3.2 % FPR). The system is better than 2 out of 9 of our labellers, and very competitive to the state-of-the art.

For rhythm assessment, our best system on C-AuDiT achieves a Spearman correlation $\rho = 0.773$ to target labels. When comparing that (in an unbiased way) to human performance, we find that our system is actually slightly better than the human labellers (estimated Pearson correlation $r = 0.71$ to ground truth, vs. r=0.66 for the labellers). For language testing, a result aggregated over multiple utterances is interesting. We test this by averaging reference scores and predictions per speaker; then, a correlation of $\rho = 0.854$ results.

On AUWL, rhythm assessment turned out to be a much more difficult task than on C-AuDiT. Probable reasons are: (1) reading hesitations, an easy clue to proficiency on C-AuDiT, are less frequent, and (2) recording quality is very heterogeneous. Also for the labellers, AUWL is more difficult than C-AuDiT (pairwise $r = 0.34$ vs $r = 0.44$). As a consequence, the resulting correlations of our best system are lower ($\rho = 0.619$); on speaker level, $\rho = 0.821$ is obtained. Direct comparison with labeller performance reveals that the system is not as good as the average labeller here (estimated Pearson correlation to ground truth for human: $r = 0.58$ vs. 0.51 for our system). Both the results on C-AuDiT and AUWL are competitive to the state-of-the-art.

Regarding the importance of individual properties of the speech signal, on both databases duration is the most important. Although ideally, prosody scores should be invariant to tempo to some large extent, general proficiency is usually correlated to speaking rate, and thus also prosodic proficiency. Next important are spectral cues (which are encoded by MFCCs in our system), followed by energy and fundamental frequency as the least important clue to assessing non-native prosody.

With respect to the techniques to aggregate information over the whole utterance for our global features, the trick to use just stressed syllables (plus their context) proved most important. It is a method to provide some additional knowledge about the spoken text, or, viewed from a different perspective, it is a method to retain some information about locality and order that is lost otherwise (e. g. when just aggregating over all syllables).

Specialized rhythm measures were not as suitable for scoring single utterances as our exhaustive generic features. For example, the best result when using rhythm metrics on AUWL was $\rho = 0.507$ (vs. 0.619 for the generic features). However, when aggregating results over all utterances of a speaker, correlation rises to $\rho = 0.834$; even better than the corresponding result with the generic features ($\rho = 0.821$). Thus, the rhythm features are useful features for long-term assessment, but they seem to be too noisy for short-term.

Summing up, our approaches are very successful, even though they do without specializations such as phoneme-specific normalization of short-time features as employed in the Erlangen prosody module. Also, they are much more flexible and easily adapted and specialized to new tasks.

Appendix A

Corpora details

A.1 C-AuDiT corpus text material

This section details the texts that were used to elicit speech in the C-AuDiT corpus, cf. Table A.1.

Type	Exercise	Track	ISLE	Prompt
Short stories	642201	b		Please call Stella.
		c (*)		Ask her to bring these things with her from the store:
		d		Six spoons of fresh snow peas, five thick slabs of blue cheese, and maybe a snack for her brother Bob.
		e	`	We also need a small plastic snake and a big toy frog for the kids.
		f (*)		She can scoop these things into three red bags, and we will go meet her Wednesday at the train station.
	642204	b		Well, here's a story for you:
		c (*)		Sarah Perry was a veterinary nurse who had been working daily at an old zoo in a deserted district of the territory, so she was very happy to start a new job at a superb private practice in North Square near the Duke Street Tower.
		d		That area was much nearer for her and more to her liking.
		e		Even so, on her first morning, she felt stressed.
		f (*)		She ate a bowl of porridge, checked herself in the mirror and washed her face in a hurry.

continued ...

...continued

Type	Exercise	Track	ISLE	Prompt
		g		Then she put on a plain yellow dress and a fleece jacket, picked up her kit and headed for work.
		h		When she got there, there was a woman with a goose waiting for her.
		i		The woman gave Sarah an official letter from the vet.
		j (*)		The letter implied that the animal could be suffering from a rare form of foot and mouth disease, which was surprising, because normally you would only expect to see it in a dog or a goat.
		k		Sarah was sentimental, so this made her feel sorry for the beautiful bird.
		l (*)		Before long, that itchy goose began to strut around the office like a lunatic, which made an unsanitary mess.
		m		The goose's owner, Mary Harrison, kept calling, "Comma, Comma," which Sarah thought was an odd choice for a name.
		n (*)		Comma was strong and huge, so it would take some force to trap her, but Sarah had a different idea.
		o (*)		First she tried gently stroking the goose's lower back with her palm, then singing a tune to her.
		p		Finally, she administered ether.
		q		Her efforts were not futile.
		r		In no time, the goose began to tire, so Sarah was able to hold onto Comma and give her a relaxing bath.
		s (*)		Once Sarah had managed to bathe the goose, she wiped her off with a cloth and laid her on her right side.
		t		Then Sarah confirmed the vet's diagnosis.
		u		Almost immediately, she remembered an effective treatment that required her to measure out a lot of medicine.

continued ...

... continued

Type	Exercise	Track	ISLE	Prompt
		v		Sarah warned that this course of treatment might be expensive—either five or six times the cost of penicillin.
		w		I can't imagine paying so much, but Mrs. Harrison—a millionaire lawyer—thought it was a fair price for a cure.
Sentences with stress shift	642206	b		This is a house.
		c		This is a house?
		d		Yes, this is a house.
		e		Is this really a house?
		f		Yes, this is really a house! Wow!
	642235	b		They are lazy.
		c		Very lazy!
		d		They are very lazy people!
		e		A bunch of lazy people, that's what they are!
	642208	b		They went to India.
		c		They went to India?
		d		Yes, they went to India.
		e		You went to India?
		f		No, no, we went to Italy.
		h		Yeah, imagine, they went to India!
	642218	b		Dublin
		c		Dublin Airport
		d		Welcome to Dublin!
		e		Welcome to Dublin Airport!
		g		The Dublin Airport Authority welcomes you to Ireland.
		h		For more information, log on to the Dublin Airport Website.
		i		Or call the Dublin Airport Information Service.
	642219	b		This is Ryan.
		c		He founded Ryanair.
		d		Did you ever fly with Ryanair?
		e		Ryanair flights are really cheap!
		f		How's it goin', Ryan?
		g		Actually, my name's Ryan Anthony.
	642239	b		This is Peter.
		c		This is Peter?
		d		Yeah ... No, no, sorry, that's Peter over there!
		e		That's Peter?

continued ...

... continued

Type	Exercise	Track	ISLE	Prompt
		f		Yes, that's Peter.
		g		So, that's Peter, huh?
		h		He's ugly!
		i		Yeah!
	642240	b		Look, there's Lilly!
		c		Where's Lilly?
		d		There! That's her!
		e		That's her?
		f		Yeah, that's Lilly!
		g		That's Lilly?
		h		She's ... gorgeous!
		i		She is!
	642236	b		Rome
		c		The Romans
		d		A Roman citizen
		e		Roman architecture
		f		The Roman Empire
		g		Under Roman law
		h		A Roman Catholic
		i		Roman Catholicism
		j		The Roman alphabet
		k		A Roman numeral
		l		Friends! Romans! Countrymen!
		m		When in Rome, do as the Romans do.
	642212	b		Arabic
		c		Arabia
		d		The Arab World
		e		In Saudi-Arabia
		f		An Arab-speaking country
		g		1001 Arabian Nights
		h		He's Arab.
		i		I'm learning Arabic.
	642258	b		Our subject today is ... stress!
		c		Mary's boss is the subject of never-ending discussions.
		d		This special offer is subject to availability.
		e (∗)		It is inhumane to subject someone to this kind of ordeal.
		f		This is just your very subjective point of view.
		g (∗)		An entire nation was subjected to state surveillance.
		h		This subject matter is very delicate.

continued ...

... continued

Type	Exercise	Track	ISLE	Prompt
	642210	b		She's a symbol of hope for the whole nation.
		c		She gave an impressive speech in a very symbolic place.
		d		The symbolism of her words was just stunning.
		e (∗)		She rose like a phoenix from the ashes, symbolically speaking.
	643062	b	E_29	He's a photographer.
		c	E_32	He takes wonderful but strange photographs.
		d	E_05	He has his own photographic studio.
		e		And he's quite photogenic, too.
	643049	b (∗)(†)	E_11	The company expects to increase its workforce next year.
		c (∗)(†)	E_01	The referee needed a police escort after the match.
		d	E_41	There has been an increase in global temperatures.
		e	E_44	They produce more than they can consume.
		f (∗)(†)	E_40	They will have to transport the components overland.
		g		Their musical styles contrast very strongly.
		h	E_09	The prime suspect is the director.
		i	E_20	The UK imports most of its food.
		k	E_42	They had to reject his plan.
		l	E_04	They wanted to protest against student fees.
		m	E_59	Staff must record all accidents in the book.
	643050	b (∗)	E_34	Students staged a protest march outside parliament.
		c (∗)	E_24	The area's become a desert.
		d	E_51	The police suspect a conspiracy.
		e	E_49	The village looks quite deserted.
		f	E_52	They sell fresh farm produce.
		g	E_26	The team will present their results at the conference.
		h	E_54	She asked him to escort her to her car.
		i	E_39	She expects to graduate next summer.

continued ...

... continued

Type	Exercise	Track	ISLE	Prompt
		j	E_08	Singers learn how to project their voices.
		k	E_23	She's a graduate of Cambridge University.
		l	E_60	They have made record profits from the sale of computers.
Shorter and longer sentences	609311	b		How annoying!
		c		I'm very sorry.
		d		That's disappointing.
		e		I'm very disappointed.
	598114	b		I don't agree with you.
		c		I'm sorry, but that's not right.
		d		I totally agree with you.
		e		I totally agree with him on that.
		f		I believe in horoscopes.
		g		I don't believe in things like that.
	570910	b		I like bacon and eggs.
		c		I'd like a beer.
		d		I'd like a hamburger.
		e		I like chicken salad.
	643048	d	D01_12	I said got not goat.
		f	D01_01	I said white not bait.
		g	D01_19	I said psychology not pneumatic.
		h	D01_03	I said bad not bed.
	641881	b		I have attached a copy of the terms and conditions.
		c (*)		Please see the attachment for further details.
		d		I'll e-mail my report to you as an attachment.
		e		I wasn't able to open the attachment.
	443656	b		Sorry, but I'm out of the country that day.
		d		I'm afraid I won't be able to make it that day.
		e		Unfortunately, I can't come on Thursday.
		f		I'd much rather make it another day.
	443655	b		Shall we hold a meeting?
		c		When can we schedule a meeting?
		e		Who's going to chair the meeting?
	443653	b		Can I take a message?
		d		Could I give her a message?

continued ...

. . . continued

Type	Exercise	Track	ISLE	Prompt
		e		Let me take down your name and number.
		f		I'll pass on the message.
		g		I'll tell her you called.
Longer	643047	b (∗)(†)	F_05	Can I have soup, then lamb with boiled potatoes, green beans and a glass of red wine?
sentences		f		I'd like a prawn cocktail as a starter and then roast chicken.
and	643063	j	G_10	I would like to take a trip to Wales for a weekend.
tongue		k	G_06	I plan to go to the United States.
twisters		l (∗)(†)	G_03	We're planning to travel to Egypt for a week or so.
	442533	b		Could you agree to take over the transportation costs?
		c		I'll have to consult my boss on this.
		d		How would you feel about using an express service?
		e		Let me get back to you on this.
		f		We can offer you a discount of 12 percent.
		g		I cannot give you the last word on that.
		h		We could offer you the basic features in December.
		i		I need to talk to my team about this.
		j (∗)		The best I can do is agree to extend the warranty period.
		k		I'll have to run this by my boss.
	643061	f		What's she wearing?
		g (∗)		She's wearing a leather jacket and corduroy trousers.
	643056	b		Peter Piper picked a peck of pickled peppers.
		g		Where she sits she shines, and where she shines she sits.
		q		Will I always be so merry when I marry Mary Mac?
	643060	d (∗)		When I was in Arkansas I saw a saw that could outsaw any other saw I ever saw saw.

continued . . .

... continued

Type	Exercise	Track	ISLE	Prompt
		e		If you've got a saw that can outsaw the saw I saw saw then I'd like to see your saw saw.
		l		Red lorry, yellow lorry.
Words	642211	10434		China
(shuffled)		10436		Chinese
		10834		Japan
		10835		Japanese
		10666		Germany
		10665		German
		11048		Mexico
		11046		Mexican
		10381		Canada
		10382		Canadian
	642215	10205		America
		10206		American
		10207		American English
		112475		Americanism
		112476		americanize
		112477		americanization
		112478		Americana
		66361		Anglo-American
		112479		Mexican-American
	642214	10589		Europe
		10590		European
		112482		European Parliament
		10587		Euro
		112481		Euro zone
	642209	72624		symbol
		112486		symbolic
		112487		symbolical
		112488		symbolically
		112489		symbolism
	642216	11299		Roman
		112491		Romanesque
		16165		organize
		16164		organization
		18206		symphony
		112490		symphonic
		65816		poem
		112492		poetic
		112495		dessertspoon
	642217	16172		origin
		16173		original

continued ...

... continued

Type	Exercise	Track	ISLE	Prompt
		112496		original recording
		16174		originally
		16175		originate
		112497		originality
	642257	b		second
		c		secondhand
		d		second-hand furniture
		e		second class
		f		a second-class ticket
		g		on second thought ...
	642237	b		green
		c		greengrocer
		d		Mr. Greenbaum
		f		Fried Green Tomatoes
		g		greenhouse
		h		the greenhouse effect
		j		green-eyed
		k		a green-eyed monster
		l		Greenland
		m		Greenlandic
		n		Greenpeace
	642255	b		ice
		c		ice age
		d		iceberg
		e		iceberg lettuce
		f		icy
		g		icy roads
		h		ice cream
		i		ice cream parlor
		j		I scream for ice cream.
	642254	16434		photograph
		16861		radio
		112498		photographic
		112474		radioactive
		16436		photographer
		112499		radioactivity
		17247		romantic
		112500		co-op
		112501		romanticist
		96015		cooperate
		112493		romanticism
		13105		cooperation
		13420		desert
		14796		history

continued ...

... continued

Type	Exercise	Track	ISLE	Prompt
		112494		deserted
		95272		historian
		112503		desertion
		112504		historicity
Word pairs (shuffled, dubbed)	643335	a		the insult
		b		to insult
		c		the permit
		d		to permit
		e		the produce
		f		to produce
		g		the progress
		h		to progress
		i		the project
		j		to project
		k		the protest
		l		to protest
		m		the rebel
		n		to rebel
		o		the reject
		p		to reject
		q		the survey
		r		to survey
		s		the suspect
		t		to suspect
		u		the transfer
		v		to transfer
		w		the transport
		x		to transport
	643333	a		the abstract
		b		to abstract
		c		the conflict
		d		to conflict
		e		the contest
		f		to contest
		g		the contrast
		h		to contrast
		i		the convict
		j		to convict
		k		the escort
		l		to escort
		m		the estimate
		n		to estimate
		o		the export
		p		to export

continued ...

. . . continued

Type	Exercise	Track	ISLE	Prompt
		q		the graduate
		r		to graduate
		s		the import
		t		to import
		u		the increase
		v		to increase
	643044	a		the record
		b		to record
		c		the conduct
		d		to conduct
		e		the present
		f		to present
		g		the contract
		h		to contract
		i		the perfect
		j		to perfect

Table A.1: Prompts displayed for eliciting read speech in the C-AuDiT corpus, together with the type of exercise and identifiers used in the filenames of the recordings (second and third column). Promts in common with the ISLE corpus [Menz 00] are indicated in the fourth column. Prompts in the *reduced* set are marked with (∗); prompts in the *panel* set are marked with (†) (third column). The given order is the order of presentation, except for the prompts of type 'Words', which were presented in a different order for each speaker. Also the 'Word pairs' were randomized; additionally, the speaker here heard a pre-recorded realization by a native speaker before producing each item.

A.2 AUWL corpus text material

This section lists the dialogues that were used in the AUWL corpus.

A2.1: Two people talk about how to spend the evening. What will they decide to do?

Speaker 1: What should we do tonight?

Speaker 2: We could go to an Indian restaurant.

Speaker 1: I'm not that hungry. Besides, I don't like curry.

Speaker 2: Well, there's a nice bar near here, The King's Head. Maybe we could go there?

Speaker 1: I'd rather not. I don't drink.

Speaker 2: Okay then. What would you suggest?

Speaker 1: Well, we could go to the movies.

Speaker 2: That's a good idea.

––––––

A2.1: At the train station ticket office. What happens when the train is sold out?

Speaker 1: Good afternoon. How can I help you?

Speaker 2: I'd like a one-way ticket to London, please.

Speaker 1: I'm afraid there are no more seats available on the 8 o'clock train.

Speaker 2: Not a single one?

Speaker 1: I'm afraid not.

Speaker 2: And when is the next train?

Speaker 1: At 9 o'clock. Let me see if there are seats available. Ah, yes there are.

Speaker 2: Okay, that will have to do.

Speaker 1: That's twelve pounds fifty, please.

––––––

A2.3: Someone needs to ask for directions to get to the museum. Is it far?

Speaker 1: Excuse me, can you tell me how to get to the city museum?

Speaker 2: Sure. Just continue on along this street until you come to the traffic lights.

Speaker 1: Oh. I see the lights now.

Speaker 2: Exactly. Now, turn right at the lights. The museum will be on the left.

Speaker 1: Okay, great! Is it far?

Speaker 2: Not at all. It's about a 10-minute walk.

Speaker 1: Oh, that's not too bad. Thanks for your help.

Speaker 2: You're welcome.

A2.4: A customer and a salesperson in a shop. Will the customer buy or not?

Speaker 1: Good morning. Are you looking for something special?

Speaker 2: Oh, no ... I'm just browsing.

Speaker 1: If you need any assistance, just let me know.

Speaker 2: Yes, I will. Um ... Actually, these gloves here are nice. Could I try them on?

Speaker 1: Of course! They really are very nice.

Speaker 2: Yes, I like them. But they're a little expensive. Could you give me a discount?

Speaker 1: I'm afraid not. They're already reduced. They're a real bargain.

Speaker 2: Okay, I understand. No thanks then.

A2.5: A customer talks to the salesclerk about a broken laptop. Can it be repaired?

Speaker 1: Can I help you?

Speaker 2: Well, I hope so. I'd like to make a complaint. Just last week, I bought this laptop, and now it doesn't work.

Speaker 1: And what's the problem exactly?

Speaker 2: Well, when I turn it on, nothing happens!

Speaker 1: Yes, that is a problem. I'm very sorry about that. I'll have to send it back to the manufacturer for repair.

Speaker 2: How long will that take?

Speaker 1: It should be back in 2 weeks. Have you still got your receipt?

Speaker 2: Yes, here it is.

———

A2.6: Two friends talk about planning a trip. But will the trip even take place?

Speaker 1: Did you ask your boss about Friday yet?

Speaker 2: No, not yet. I wanted to speak to him this morning but he was too busy.

Speaker 1: Well, when are you going to ask him then?

Speaker 2: Don't worry, I'll talk to him today.

Speaker 1: Good, because we really need to plan our trip.

Speaker 2: I know. I'll speak to him today.

Speaker 1: Okay, it's just that Bob offered to pick us up at the airport.

Speaker 2: And you want to tell him what time we'll arrive?

Speaker 1: Exactly!

Speaker 2: I'll know for sure by noon, I promise.

———

B1.1: Two friends try to make plans. But will they find time?

Speaker 1: What are you doing this evening? Shall we do something together?

Speaker 2: I can't. I'm going to the theater with Jessica.

Speaker 1: Oh. Well, what are you doing tomorrow?

Speaker 2: I'm meeting friends.

Speaker 1: Hmm. What about Saturday? What are you doing then?

Speaker 2: I'm afraid I'm playing tennis on Saturday.

Speaker 1: You're really busy! Do you have anything planned for Sunday?

Speaker 2: I'm visiting my parents.

Speaker 1: When do you have time, then?

Speaker 2: Hmm ... I'm free next Tuesday!

B1.2: A real-estate agent and client discuss a potential office. Will they find a suitable location?

Speaker 1: So, what exactly did you have in mind?

Speaker 2: Someplace bright, centrally located, and big enough to accommodate at least 60 people.

Speaker 1: I think I have just the place for you. There's a new office building opposite the opera house that would suit you.

Speaker 2: Oh, that's a very prestigious address.

Speaker 1: Here, take a look at some of these photos.

Speaker 2: It looks great. But I need open-plan offices for some of my personnel. Well, actually, we need a mix of open-plan and small offices.

Speaker 1: Well, how about this building? 2nd floor, a mix of open plan and small offices. And lots of glass!

Speaker 2: Hmm ... I don't know. We're a law firm. I think our clients would feel uncomfortable.

Speaker 1: Oh yes, I understand. Well, let me see what I can do.

B1.3: One person asks a friend for a ride to work. What time do they need to leave?

Speaker 1: Could you give me a ride to work tomorrow?

Speaker 2: Of course. What time do you need to be there?

Speaker 1: I have a meeting at 9, so I need to be there no later than 8:30.

Speaker 2: Okay. Should I pick you up at 8 then?

Speaker 1: Yes, that should be enough time.

Speaker 2: You know, if I pick you up at 7:30, we could go get a coffee first.

Speaker 1: Oh, that would be wonderful, thanks! And I'm buying!

Speaker 2: Great. Then I'll see you tomorrow morning!

———

B1.4: A new employee is getting a tour. But how long does it take to fit in?

Speaker 1: Hi, welcome to the company! Shall I show you around?

Speaker 2: Yes, please. It's great to be here. I'm a bit nervous, though— you know, first day and all.

Speaker 1: Oh, don't worry. You'll fit in in no time. Everyone is very nice here.

Speaker 2: Well, that's good to know.

Speaker 1: And here's sales and marketing. You'll be sharing an office with Mary Bennette.

Speaker 2: Yes, I've met her already.

Speaker 1: And here's the human resources department. You'll need to talk to Mr Waldron in HR later.

Speaker 2: I think I'm supposed to drop by this afternoon.

Speaker 1: Yes, that's right.

———

B1.5: Two people are talking about a company. Do they rent or own the building?

Speaker 1: What a nice building.

Speaker 2: Thanks. We're very comfortable here.

Speaker 1: Do you own or lease your premises?

Speaker 2: Well, we're actually leasing these offices, but we usually buy.

Speaker 1: Does your company have any subsidiaries abroad?

Speaker 2: Oh yes, we have several in Europe.

Speaker 1: Where do you manufacture your products?

Speaker 2: Mostly in Newark, New Jersey. But we ship all over the world.

Speaker 1: Really? I didn't know that.

―――――

B1.6: Making an appointment at the doctor's. When is the best time?

Speaker 1: Good morning, Dr Brown's office. How may I help you?

Speaker 2: I'd like to make an appointment, please.

Speaker 1: Certainly. When would you like to come?

Speaker 2: This afternoon would be best.

Speaker 1: Would three o'clock be alright?

Speaker 2: I'll check my schedule. ...No, I'm afraid I've got another appointment then.

Speaker 1: What about five o'clock?

Speaker 2: That sounds fine.

Speaker 1: Okay, I'll put you down for 5, then. Goodbye.

Speaker 2: Thank you. Bye!

―――――

B2.1: Two people talk about working conditions. Is head of sales satisfied?

Speaker 1: Hi, I'm conducting a survey about people working in the area. Are you employed?

Speaker 2: Yes, I'm an employee at a local software company.

Speaker 1: Okay. Are there more than twenty, fifty, one hundred or five hundred people on the payroll?

Speaker 2: Hmmm, I'd say there are a couple of hundred—but not more than 500.

Speaker 1: Do you hold a management position at your company?

Speaker 2: Yes, I do. I'm head of sales.

Speaker 1: Terrific. And how would you rate your working conditions? With 1 being very poor and 10 excellent?

Speaker 2: Well, I'd say working conditions are an 8. It's a stressful job, but I work with great people.

––––––

B2.2: Two people talking about moving to a new city. But what about the house?

Speaker 1: So, you're really serious about moving to New York?

Speaker 2: Yes, I am. I'm looking forward to being closer to my family, and I love the city. Plus I've got that house there.

Speaker 1: I didn't know you owned your own house!

Speaker 2: Well, I inherited my grandfather's old place in upstate New York. It's just a small cottage, really.

Speaker 1: Lucky you. But, the market is awful right now. Will you have to sell your house here?

Speaker 2: I think if I rent an apartment in New York, I should be able to rent out my house here, and then I won't have to sell.

Speaker 1: That's a good idea. So ... this house in upstate New York. Can I come visit?

Speaker 2: Of course! Like I said, it's just a small cottage, so it's a bit ... rustic.

Speaker 1: Rustic? It sounds great to me!

––––––

B2.3: Two employees talk about an investor report. Was it a lot of work?

Speaker 1: Did you finish that expansion report yet? Bob needs it by three.

Speaker 2: It's already done. Don't worry!

Speaker 1: May I see it?

Speaker 2: Here you go. ... What do you think?

Speaker 1: Hmm ... hey, this is really fantastic. You did a lot of research!

Speaker 2: Thanks. But Jane helped me. She was able to provide me with a lot of figures.

Speaker 1: How long did it take you to put it all together?

Speaker 2: Quite a while, actually. But this kind of thing is right down my alley!

———

B2.4: A boss and an employee talk about a pay raise. Has the employee earned one?

Speaker 1: Excuse me, is this a good time to talk?

Speaker 2: Yes, of course. Come in. Take a seat.

Speaker 1: Thanks.

Speaker 2: So, what is it you would like to talk to me about?

Speaker 1: Well, not to beat around the bush, I'd like a pay raise.

Speaker 2: Ah, ... it's a really bad time. You know what business has been like this year.

Speaker 1: Yes, I realize the timing is bad, but my work isn't. The feedback on all my accounts is excellent and many of our clients are continuing with us as a result of my personal commitment to these projects.

Speaker 2: I am aware of this, but I'm afraid my hands are tied right now. What I would propose is that we discuss this again in 3 months. I'll be in a better position to offer you something then.

Speaker 1: Okay, I understand. Shall we arrange another meeting for the middle of March then?

Speaker 2: That sounds fine.

———

B2.5: After arriving in Hawaii, two tourists try to decide what to do. Where should they go?

Speaker 1: Funny, isn't it? I've been dreaming about coming to Hawaii my whole life. Now I'm here, and I don't know what to do.

Speaker 2: That's the truth! Well, my sister said there's a really nice beach on the other side of the island.

Speaker 1: Oh! I love the beach. But I really want to go out on a boat.

Speaker 2: Hmm. Well, this brochure says that we can take a sunset cruise from the harbor any night of the week.

Speaker 1: Terrific. Let's do that tomorrow night. Maybe we can go to a hula show, too.

Speaker 2: Now that I think of it, the lady at check-in said there's a great hula show near that beach my sister mentioned. Maybe we could go to the show and the beach on Wednesday.

Speaker 1: Yes! And look here! This map shows a trail through the jungle, and it's not far from the hotel.

Speaker 2: Oh, I want to see that! Come on, put your shoes on! Let's go look for it.

–––––––

B2.6: An important client changed its requirements at the last minute. Will the company find a suitable solution?

Speaker 1: Okay, will someone fill me in on the Baxter problem?

Speaker 2: Well, basically, Baxter is not sticking to its side of the deal.

Speaker 1: How so?

Speaker 2: The agreement was that we would develop a data management system for their product data. We asked them to send us all their data and an outline of what they wanted.

Speaker 1: Which they did, right?

Speaker 2: Right! The data looked complete, so we designed the system. Then last week, Baxter sent us a new list of criteria.

Speaker 1: I see. So, these new requirements mean that you can't install the system this week.

Speaker 2: Exactly. Which means we're going to break the contract terms.

Speaker 1: Well, I'll talk to them. I'm confident that if we explain the situation, they'll give us more time. After all, these new details are for their benefit.

Speaker 2: I sure hope you're right!

List of Figures

List of Tables

Bibliography

[Aach 01]   T. Aach and V. H. Metzler. "Defect interpolation in digital radiography: how object-oriented transform coding helps". In: *Proceedings of SPIE Medical Imaging, San Diego, CA, USA, Vol. 4322*, pp. 824–835, 2001.

[Aber 49]   D. Abercrombie. "Teaching Pronunciation". *English Language Teaching*, Vol. 3, No. 5, pp. 113–122, 1949.

[Aber 67]   D. Abercrombie. *Elements of General Phonetics*. University Press, Edinburgh, 1967.

[Ahme 74]   N. Ahmed, T. Natarajan, and K. R. Rao. "Discrete cosine transform". *Computers, IEEE Transactions on*, Vol. 100, No. 1, pp. 90–93, 1974.

[Alla 07]   C. Allauzen, M. Riley, J. Schalkwyk, W. Skut, and M. Mohri. "OpenFst: A general and efficient weighted finite-state transducer library". In: *Implementation and Application of Automata*, pp. 11–23, Springer, 2007.

[Anan 07]   S. Ananthakrishnan and S. Narayanan. "Improved speech recognition using acoustic and lexical correlates of pitch accent in a n-best rescoring framework". In: *Proceedings of ICASSP, IEEE International Conference on Acoustics, Speech and Signal Processing*, pp. 873–876, Honolulu, Hawaii, USA, 2007.

[Ande 92]   J. Anderson-Hsieh. "Using electronic visual feedback to teach suprasegmentals". *System*, Vol. 20, No. 1, pp. 51–62, 1992.

[Anth 63]   E. M. Anthony. "Approach, method, technique". *English Language Teaching*, Vol. 17, pp. 63–67, 1963.

[Aria 10]   J. P. Arias, N. B. Yoma, and H. Vivanco. "Automatic intonation assessment for computer aided language learning". *Speech communication*, Vol. 52, No. 3, pp. 254–267, 2010.

[Asak 05]   S. Asakawa, N. Minematsu, T. Isei-Jaakkola, and K. Hirose. "Structural representation of the non-native pronunciations.". In: *Proceedings of INTERSPEECHs*, pp. 165–168, Lisbon, Portugal, 2005.

[Asso 99]   I. P. Association. *Handbook of the International Phonetic Association: A guide to the use of the International Phonetic Alphabet*. Cambridge University Press, 1999.

[Aull 85]   A. M. Aull and V. W. Zue. "Lexical stress determination and its application to large vocabulary speech recognition". In: *Proceedings of ICASSP, IEEE International Conference on Acoustics, Speech, and Signal Processing*, pp. 1549–1552, IEEE, ampa, Florida, USA, 1985.

[Bach 90]   L. Bachmann. *Fundamental Considerations in Language Testing.* Oxford University Press, 1990.

[Bags 94]   P. C. Bagshaw. *Automatic prosodic analysis for computer aided pronunciation teaching.* PhD thesis, University of Edinburgh, 1994.

[Batl 00]   A. Batliner, J. Buckow, H. Niemann, E. Nöth, and V. Warnke. "The Prosody Module". In: W. Wahlster, Ed., *Verbmobil: Foundations of Speech-to-Speech Translations*, pp. 106–121, Springer, 2000.

[Batl 01]   A. Batliner, J. Buckow, R. Huber, V. Warnke, E. Nöth, and H. Niemann. "Boiling down Prosody for the Classification of Boundaries and Accents in German and English". In: *Proceedings of EUROSPEECH*, pp. 2781–2784, Aalborg, Denmark, 2001.

[Batl 05]   A. Batliner and B. Möbius. *The Integration of Phonetic Knowledge in Speech Technology*, Chap. Prosodic Models, Automatic Speech Understanding, and Speech Synthesis: Towards the Common Ground?, pp. 21–44. Springer, 2005.

[Batl 10]   G. Batliner and A. Batliner. "'Der Ton macht die Musik': Prosodie - die zweite Ebene der Kommunikation". *Schnecke*, Vol. 68, pp. 42–44, 2010.

[Batl 89]   A. Batliner and E. Nöth. "The Prediction of Focus". In: *Proceedings of EUROSPEECH, 1st European Conference on Speech Communication and Technology*, Paris, France, 1989.

[Batl 91]   A. Batliner, W. Oppenrieder, E. Nöth, and G. Stallwitz. "The intonational marking of focal structure: Wishful thinking or hard fact?". In: *Proceedings of ICPhS, 12th International Congress of Phonetic Sciences*, pp. 278–281, Aix-en-Provence, France, 1991.

[Batl 96]   A. Batliner, R. Kompe, A. Kiessling, H. Niemann, and E. Nöth. "Syntactic-prosodic labeling of large spontaneous speech data-bases". In: *Proceedings of ICSLP, 4th International Conference on Spoken Language Processing*, pp. 1720–1723, Philadelphia PA, USA, 1996.

[Batl 98]   A. Batliner, R. Kompe, A. Kießling, M. Mast, H. Niemann, and E. Nöth. "M = Syntax + Prosody: A syntactic–prosodic labelling scheme for large spontaneous speech databases". *Speech Communication*, Vol. 25, pp. 193–222, 1998.

[Batl 99]   A. Batliner, J. Buckow, R. Huber, V. Warnke, E. Nöth, and H. Niemann. "Prosodic Feature Evaluation: Brute Force or Well Designed?". In: *Proceedings of ICPhS, International Congress of Phonetic Sciences*, pp. 2315–2318, San Francisco, USA, 1999.

[Baum 68]   L. E. Baum, G. R. Sell, *et al.* "Growth transformations for functions on manifolds". *Pacific J. Math*, Vol. 27, No. 2, pp. 211–227, 1968.

[Bear 90]   J. Bear and P. Price. "Prosody, syntax and parsing". In: *Proceedings of the 28th annual meeting on Association for Computational Linguistics*, pp. 17–22, 1990.

[Beck 86]   M. Beckman. *Stress and Non–stress Accent.* Foris Publications, Dordrecht, 1986.

[Benr 97] M. Benrabah. "Word-stress – a source of unintelligibility in English". *International Review of Applied Linguistics in Language Teaching*, Vol. 35, No. 3, pp. 157–166, 1997.

[Bern 07] J. Bernstein and J. Cheng. *The path of speech technologies in computer assisted language learning: From research toward practice*, Chap. Logic and validation of fully automatic spoken English test, pp. 174–194. Routledge Florence, KY, 2007.

[Bern 10] J. Bernstein, A. Van Moere, and J. Cheng. "Validating automated speaking tests". *Language Testing*, 2010.

[Bern 96] L. Bernstein and B. Christian. "For speech perceptions by humans or machines, three senses are better than one". In: *Proceedings of ICSLP, 4th International Conference on Spoken Language Processing*, Philadelphia PA, USA, 1996.

[Bial 99] E. Bialystok and K. Hakuta. "Confounded Age: Linguistic and Cognitive Factors in Age Differences for Second Language Acquisition". In: D. Birdsong, Ed., *Second Language Acquisition and the Critical Period Hypothesis*, Lawrence Erlbaum Associates, 1999.

[Bird 92] D. Birdsong. "Ultimate Attainment in Second Language Acquisition". *Language*, Vol. 68, No. 4, pp. 706–755, 1992.

[Bird 99] D. Birdsong, Ed. *Second Language Acquisition and the Critical Period Hypothesis*. Lawrence Erlbaum Associates, 1999.

[Bish 06] C. M. Bishop. *Pattern Recognition and Machine Learning*. Springer, 2006.

[Blac 15] M. Black, D. Bone, Z. I. Skordilis, R. Gupta, W. Xia, P. Papadopoulos, S. Nallan, Chakravarthula, B. Xiao, M. V. Segbroeck, J. Kim, P. Georgiou, and S. Narayanan. "Automated evaluation of non-native English pronunciation quality: combining knowledge- and data-driven features at multiple time scales". In: *Proceedings of INTERSPEECH, 16th Annual Conference of the International Speech Communication Association*, Dresden, Germany, 2015.

[Bloo 84] B. S. Bloom. "The 2 Sigma Problem: The Search for Methods of Group Instruction as Effective as One-to- One Tutoring". *Educational Researcher*, Vol. 13, pp. 4–16, 1984.

[Boli 61] D. L. Bolinger. "Contrastive accent and contrastive stress". *Language*, pp. 83–96, 1961.

[Bona 00] P. Bonaventura, D. Herron, and W. Menzel. "Phonetic rules for diagnosis of pronunciation errors". In: *Proceedings of KONVENS, 5. Konferenz zur Verarbeitung nat
"urlicher Sprache*, pp. 225–230, Ilmenau, Germany, 2000.

[Bord 05] A. Bordes, S. Ertekin, J. Weston, and L. Bottou. "Fast kernel classifiers with online and active learning". *The Journal of Machine Learning Research*, Vol. 6, pp. 1579–1619, 2005.

[Bord 79] G. J. Borden. "An interpretation of research on feedback interruption in speech". *Brain and language*, Vol. 7, No. 3, pp. 307–319, 1979.

[Bot 82]   K. de Bot and K. Mailfert. "The teaching of intonation: Fundamental research and classroom applications". *TESOL Quarterly*, Vol. 16, No. 1, pp. 71–77, 1982.

[Bot 83]   K. de Bot. "Visual Feedback of Intonation I: Effectiveness and Induced Practice Behavior.". *Language and Speech*, Vol. 26, No. 4, pp. 331–50, 1983.

[Boyd 04]   S. Boyd and L. Vandenberghe. *Convex Optimization*. Cambridge University Press, 7th printing with corrections Ed., 2004. Available at http://web.stanford.edu/~boyd/cvxbook/bv_cvxbook.pdf, last visited September 8th, 2017.

[Bran 06]   K. V. den Branden, Ed. *Task-Based Language Educatation: From theory to practice*. Cambridge University Press, 2006.

[Braz 84]   D. Brazil. *Intonation, Accent and Rhythm. Studies in Discourse Phonology*, Chap. The Intonation of Sentences Read Aloud, pp. 46–66. de Gruyter, 1984.

[Brow 90]   G. Brown. *Listening to spoken English*. Longman, 2nd Ed., 1990.

[Brun 08]   J. Bruner. *Wie das Kind sprechen lernt*. Huber, Bern, 2008.

[Burg 98]   C. J. Burges. "A tutorial on support vector machines for pattern recognition". *Data mining and knowledge discovery*, Vol. 2, No. 2, pp. 121–167, 1998.

[Busn 92]   M. Busnel, O. C. Granier-Deferre, and J. P. Lecanuet. "Fetal Audition". *Annals of the New York Academy of Sciences*, Vol. 662, No. 1, pp. 118–134, 1992.

[Camp 03a] N. Campbell and P. Mokhtari. "Voice quality: the 4th prosodic dimension". In: *Proceedings of ICPhS, International Congress of Phonetic Sciences*, Barcelona, Spain, 2003.

[Camp 03b] P. S. Campillo. "An analysis of implicit and explicit feedback on grammatical accuracy". *miscelánea: a journal of english and american studies*, No. 27, pp. 209–228, 2003.

[Camp 06]   W. Campbell, D. Sturim, and D. Reynolds. "Support Vector Machines Using GMM Supervectors for Speaker Verification". *Signal Processing Letters, IEEE*, Vol. 13, pp. 308–311, 2006.

[Camp 93]   N. Campbell. "Automatic detection of prosodic boundaries in speech". *Speech communication*, Vol. 13, No. 3, pp. 343–354, 1993.

[Care 04]   M. Carey. "CALL visual feedback for pronunciation of vowels: Kay Sona-Match". *CALICO Journal*, Vol. 21, No. 3, pp. 571–601, 2004.

[Cass 10]   E. D. Casserly and D. B. Pisoni. "Speech perception and production". *Wiley Interdisciplinary Reviews: Cognitive Science*, Vol. 1, No. 5, pp. 629–647, 2010.

[Celc 96]   M. Celce-Murcia, D. M. Brinton, and J. M. Goodwin. *Teaching pronunciation: A reference for teachers of English to speakers of other languages*. Cambridge University Press, 1996.

[Chel 08]   B. Chela-Flores. "Pronunciation and language learning: An integrative approach". *International Review of Applied Linguistics in Language Teaching*, Vol. 39, No. 2, pp. 85–101, 2008.

[Chen 04a] K. Chen and M. Hasegawa-Johnson. "How prosody improves word recognition". In: *Proceedings of Speech Prosody*, Nara, Japan, 2004.

[Chen 04b] K. Chen, M. Hasegawa-Johnson, and A. Cohen. "An automatic prosody labeling system using ANN-based syntactic-prosodic model and GMM-based acoustic-prosodic model". In: *Proceedings of ICASSP, International Conference on Acoustics, Speech, and Signal Processing*, pp. I-509, Montreal, Quebec, Canada, 2004.

[Chen 07a] J.-C. Chen, J.-S. R. Jang, and T.-L. Tsai. "Automatic pronunciation assessment for Mandarin Chinese: approaches and system overview". *Computational Linguistics and Chinese Language Processing*, Vol. 12, No. 4, pp. 443–458, 2007.

[Chen 07b] N. Chen and Q. He. "Using nonlinear features in automatic english lexical stress detection". In: *Proceedings of CISW, International Conference on Computational Intelligence and Security Workshops*, pp. 328–332, IEEE, Harbin, Heilongjiang, China, 2007.

[Chen 10]   J.-Y. Chen and L. Wang. "Automatic lexical stress detection for Chinese learners of English". In: *Proceedings of ISCSLP, IEEE International Symposium on Chinese Spoken Language Processing*, pp. 407–411, IEEE, Sun Moon Lake, Taiwan, 2010.

[Chen 11a] L. Chen and S.-Y. Yoon. "Detecting structural events for assessing nonnative speech". In: *Proceedings of the 6th workshop on Innovative Use of NLP for Building Educational Applications*, pp. 38–45, Association for Computational Linguistics, Portland, OR, USA, 2011.

[Chen 11b] L. Chen and K. Zechner. "Applying Rhythm Features to Automatically Assess Non-Native Speech.". In: *Proceedings of INTERSPEECH, 12th Annual Conference of the International Speech Communication Association*, pp. 1861–1864, Florence, Italy, 2011.

[Chen 12]   S.-H. Chen, J.-H. Yang, C.-Y. Chiang, M.-C. Liu, and Y.-R. Wang. "A New Prosody-Assisted Mandarin ASR System". *IEEE Transactions on Audio, Speech and Language Processing*, Vol. 20, pp. 1669–1684, 2012.

[Chev 02]   A. de Cheveigne and H. Kawahara. "YIN, a fundamental frequency estimator for speech and music". *Journal of Acoustical Society of America*, Vol. 111, No. 4, pp. 1917–1930, 2002.

[Chin 06]   G. M. Chinnery. "Emerging technologies. Going to the mall: mobile assisted language learning". *Language learning & technology*, Vol. 10, No. 1, pp. 9–16, 2006.

[Chom 59]   N. Chomsky. "A Review of B. F. Skinner's Verbal Behavior". *Language*, Vol. 1, pp. 26–58, 1959.

[Chom 62]   N. Chomsky. "Explanatory Models in Linguistics". In: P. S. Ernest Nagel and A. Tarski, Eds., *Logic, Methodology and Philosophy of Science of the 1960 International Conference*, Stanford University Press, 1962.

[Chri 03]   M. H. Christiansen and S. Kirby. "Language Evolution: The Hardest Problem in Science?". In: M. Christiansen and S. Kirby, Eds., *Language Evolution: The States of the Art*, Oxford University Press, 2003.

[Clar 06]   M. Clark. *A practical guide to quality interaction with children who have a hearing loss*. Plural Publishing, 2006.

[Cont 89]   M. E. Conte, Ed. *Kontinuität und Diskontinuität in Texten und Sachverhalts- Konfigurationen. Diskussion über Konnexität, Kohäsion und Kohärenz*. Buske Helmut Verlag, 1989.

[Cool 65]   J. W. Cooley and J. W. Tukey. "An algorithm for the machine calculation of complex Fourier series". *Mathematics of computation*, Vol. 19, No. 90, pp. 297–301, 1965.

[Cord 67]   S. P. Corder. "The Significance of Learner's Errors". *International Review of Applied Linguistics in Language Teaching*, Vol. 5, No. 4, pp. 161–170, 1967.

[Cort 95]   C. Cortes and V. Vapnik. "Support-vector networks". *Machine learning*, Vol. 20, No. 3, pp. 273–297, 1995.

[Coun 01]   Council of Europe, Ed. *Common European Framework of Reference for Languages: Learning, Teaching, Assessment*. Cambridge University Press, 2001. Available from http://www.coe.int/portfolio; direct link: https://rm.coe.int/1680459f97; last visited September 8th, 2017.

[Cout 16]   E. Coutinho, F. Hönig, Y. Zhang, S. Hantke, A. Batliner, E. Nöth, and B. Schuller. "Assessing the Prosody of Non-Native Speakers of English: Measures and Feature Sets.". In: *Proceedings of LREC, 10th International Conference on Language Resources and Evaluation*, Portoroz, Slovenia, 2016.

[Cram 02]   K. Crammer and Y. Singer. "On the algorithmic implementation of multiclass kernel-based vector machines". *The Journal of Machine Learning Research*, Vol. 2, pp. 265–292, 2002.

[Crys 03]   D. Crystal. *A Dictionary of Linguistics & Phonetics*. Blackwell, 5 Ed., 2003.

[Crys 94]   D. Crystal. "Documenting rhythmical change". In: J. W. Lewis, Ed., *Studies in general and English phonetics*, pp. 174–179, Routledge, 1994.

[Cucc 00]   C. Cucchiarini, H. Strik, and L. Boves. "Quantitative assessment of second language learners' fluency by means of automatic speech recognition technology". *Journal of the Acoustical Society of America*, Vol. 107, No. 2, pp. 989–999, 2000.

[Cucc 02]   C. Cucchiarini, H. Strik, and L. Boves. "Quantitative assessment of second language learners' fluency: Comparisons between read and spontaneous speech". *The Journal of the Acoustical Society of America*, Vol. 111, No. 6, pp. 2862–2873, 2002.

[Cucc 09]   C. Cucchiarini, A. Neri, and H. Strik. "Oral proficiency training in Dutch L2: The contribution of ASR-based corrective feedback". *Speech Communication*, Vol. 51, No. 10, pp. 853–863, 2009.

[Cucc 98]   C. Cucchiarini, H. Strik, and L. Boves. "Quantitative assessment of second language learners' fluency: an automatic approach". In: *Proceedings of ICSLP, 5th International Conference on Spoken Language Processing*, Sydney, Australia, 1998.

[Cutl 81]   A. Cutler and C. J. Darwin. "Phoneme-monitoring reaction time and preceding prosody: Effects of stop closure duration and of fundamental frequency". *Perception & Psychophysics*, Vol. 29, No. 3, pp. 217–224, 1981.

[Cutl 84]   A. Cutler. *Intonation, Accent and Rhythm. Studies in Discourse Phonology*, Chap. Stress and Accent in Language Production and Understanding, pp. 77–90. de Gruyter, 1984.

[Cutl 86]   A. Cutler, J. Mehler, D. Norris, and J. Segui. "The syllable's differing role in the segmentation of French and English". *Journal of Memory and Language*, Vol. 25, pp. 385–400, 1986.

[Dahl 13]   G. E. Dahl, T. N. Sainath, and G. E. Hinton. "Improving deep neural networks for LVCSR using rectified linear units and dropout". In: *Acoustics, Speech and Signal Processing (ICASSP), 2013 IEEE International Conference on*, pp. 8609–8613, IEEE, 2013.

[Dalt 94]   C. Dalton and B. Seidlhofer. "Is pronunciation teaching desirable? Is it feasible?". In: *Proceedings of the 4th International NELLE Conference*, Hamburg, Germany, 1994.

[Darw 71]   C. Darwin. *The Descent of Man and Selection in Relation to Sex*. Vol. Volume 1, John Murray, 1871.

[Daue 11]   R. M. Dauer. "The Lingua Franca Core: A New Model for Pronunciation Instruction?". *TESOL Quarterly*, Vol. 39, pp. 543–550, 2011.

[Daue 83]   R. M. Dauer. "Stress-timing and syllable-timing reanalyzed". *Journal of Phonetics*, Vol. 11, No. 1, pp. 51–62, 1983.

[Davi 06]   J. Davis and M. Goadrich. "The relationship between Precision-Recall and ROC curves". In: *Proceedings of the 23rd international conference on Machine learning*, pp. 233–240, ACM, 2006.

[Davi 80]   S. Davis and P. Mermelstein. "Comparison of parametric representations for monosyllabic word recognition in continuously spoken sentences". *Acoustics, Speech and Signal Processing, IEEE Transactions on*, Vol. 28, No. 4, pp. 357–366, 1980.

[Dell 03]   V. Dellwo. "Rhythm and Speech Rate: A varation coefficient for ΔC". In: *Proceedings of the 38th linguistic Colloquium, Budapest, Hungary*, 2003.

[Delm 00]   R. Delmonte. "SLIM prosodic automatic tools for self-learning instruction". *Speech Communication*, Vol. 30, No. 2, pp. 145–166, 2000.

[Delm 02]   R. Delmonte. "Feedback generation and linguistic knowledge in 'SLIM'automatic tutor". *ReCALL*, Vol. 14, No. 2, pp. 209–234, 2002.

[Delm 97]   R. Delmonte, M. Petrea, and C. Bacalu. "SLIM Prosodic Module for Learning Activities in a Foreign Language". In: *Proceedings of EUROSPEECH, 5th European Conference on Speech Communication and Technology*, Rhodes, Greece, 1997.

[Demp 77]   A. P. Dempster, N. M. Laird, and D. B. Rubin. "Maximum likelihood from incomplete data via the EM algorithm". *Journal of the royal statistical society. Series B (methodological)*, pp. 1–38, 1977.

[Dewe 07]   M. Dewey. "English as a lingua franca and globalization: an interconnected perspective". *International Journal of Applied Linguistics*, Vol. 17, No. 3, pp. 332–354, 2007.

[Dill 78]   K. C. Diller. *The Language Teaching Controversy*. Newbury House Publishers, 1978.

[Dowd 98]   A. Dowd, J. Smith, and J. Wolfe. "Learning to pronounce vowel sounds in a foreign language using acoustic measurements of the vocal tract as feedback in real time". *Language and Speech*, Vol. 41, No. 1, pp. 1–20, 1998.

[Druc 96]   H. Drucker, C. J. Burges, L. Kaufman, A. Smola, and V. Vapnik. "Support vector regression machines". In: *Proceedings of the Neural Information Processing Systems Conference*, pp. 155–161, 1996.

[Duda 01]   R. O. Duda, P. E. Hart, and D. G. Stork. *Pattern classification*. Wiley, 2001.

[Dyru 01]   L. O. Dyrud. *Hindi-Urdu: Stress Accent or Non-Stress Accent?* Graduate Faculty of the University of North Dakota, 2001.

[Educ 11]   Educational Testing Service. "Validity Evidence Supporting the Interpretation and Use of TOEFL iBT TM Scores". *TOEFL iBT Research Insight*, Vol. 4, 2011.

[Ehsa 98]   F. Ehsani and E. Knodt. "Speech technology in computer-aided language learning: Strengths and limitations of a new CALL paradigm". *Language Learning & Technology*, Vol. 2, No. 1, pp. 45–60, 1998.

[El T 06]   M. El Tatawy. "Corrective feedback in second language acquisition". *Teachers College, Columbia University Working Papers in TESOL & Applied Linguistics*, Vol. 2, No. 2, 2006.

[Elli 97]   R. Ellis. *Second Language Acquisition*. Oxford Univesity Press, 1997.

[Eske 07]   M. Eskenazi, A. Kennedy, C. Ketchum, R. Olszewski, and G. Pelton. "The NativeAccent(TM) Pronunciation Tutor: Measuring Success in the Real World". In: *Proceedings of SLaTE, Workshop on Speech and Language Technology in Education*, Farmington Pennsylvania, USA, 2007.

[Eske 09]   M. Eskenazi. "An overview of spoken language technology for education". *Speech Communication*, Vol. 51, No. 10, pp. 832–844, 2009.

[Eske 13]   M. Eskenazi, G.-A. Levow, H. Meng, G. Parent, and D. Suendermann, Eds. *Crowdsourcing for Speech Processing: Applications to Data Collection, Transcription and Assessment*. John Wiley & Sons, 2013.

[Eule 09]   H. Euler, A. W. v. Gudenberg, K. Jung, and K. Neumann. "Computergestützte Therapie bei Redeflussstörungen: Die langfristige Wirksamkeit der Kasseler Stottertherapie (KST)". *Sprache Stimme Gehör*, Vol. 33, pp. 193–202, 2009.

[Eybe 10]   F. Eyben, M. Wöllmer, and B. Schuller. "openSMILE - The Munich Versatile and Fast Open-Source Audio Feature Extractor". In: *Proc. of ACM Multimedia*, pp. 1459–1462, ACM, Florence, Italy, 2010.

[Eybe 13]   F. Eyben, F. Weninger, F. Gross, and B. Schuller. "Recent developments in openSMILE, the Munich open-source multimedia feature extractor". In: *Proceedings of the 21st ACM international conference on Multimedia*, pp. 835–838, ACM, 2013.

[Falk 04]   D. Falk. "Prelinguistic evolution in early hominins: Whence motherese?". *Behavioral and Brain Sciences*, Vol. 27, No. 04, pp. 491–503, 2004.

[Fan 08]   R.-E. Fan, K.-W. Chang, C.-J. Hsieh, X.-R. Wang, and C.-J. Lin. "LIB-LINEAR: A Library for Large Linear Classification". *Journal of Machine Learning Research*, Vol. 9, pp. 1871–1874, 2008.

[Fawc 04]   T. Fawcett. "ROC graphs: Notes and practical considerations for researchers". *Machine learning*, Vol. 31, pp. 1–38, 2004.

[Fels 11]   A. Felstiner. "Working the Crowd: Employment and Labor Law in the Crowdsourcing Industry.". *Berkeley journal of employment & labor law*, Vol. 32, No. 1, pp. 143–203, 2011.

[Fern 78]   C. Fernando and J. Basmajian. "Biofeedback in physical medicine and rehabilitation". *Biofeedback and Self-regulation*, Vol. 3, No. 4, pp. 435–455, 1978.

[Ferr 15]   L. Ferrer, H. Bratt, C. Richey, H. Franco, V. Abrash, and K. Precoda. "Classification of lexical stress using spectral and prosodic features for computer-assisted language learning systems". *Speech Communication*, Vol. 69, pp. 31–45, 2015.

[Fitc 00]   W. T. Fitch. "The evolution of speech: a comparative review". *Trends in Cognitive Sciences*, Vol. 4, pp. 258–267, 2000.

[Fitc 05]   W. T. Fitch. "The evolution of language: A comparative review". *Biology and Philosophy*, Vol. 20, pp. 193–230, 2005.

[Fitc 10]   W. T. Fitch. *The Evolution of Language*. Cambridge University Press, 2010.

[Fleg 88]   J. Flege. "Using Visual Information to Train Foreign-Language Vowel Production". *Language Learning*, Vol. 38, No. 3, pp. 365–407, 1988.

[Fleg 89]   J. E. Flege and O.-S. Bohn. "An instrumental study of vowel reduction and stress placement in Spanish-accented English". *Studies in second language acquisition*, Vol. 11, No. 01, pp. 35–62, 1989.

[Fox 00]   A. Fox. *Prosodic Features and Prosodic Structure*. Oxford University Press, 2000.

[Frei 88]   G. J. Freij and F. Fallside. "Lexical stress recognition using hidden Markov models". In: *Proceedings of ICASSP, International Conference on Acoustics, Speech, and Signal Processing*, pp. 135–138, IEEE, New York, New York, USA, 1988.

[Fuji 94]   H. Fujisaki. "Foreword". In: H. Fujisaki, Ed., *Proceedings of the International Symposium on Prosody*, Yokohama, Japan, 1994.

[Fuji 98]   Y. Fujisawa, N. Minematsu, and S. Nakagawa. "Evaluation of Japanese
              manners of generating word accent of English based on a stressed syl-
              lable detection technique.". In: *Proceedings of ICSLP, 5th International
              Conference on Spoken Language Processing*, Sydney, Australia, 1998.

[Gall 01]   F. Gallwitz. *Integrated Stochastic Models for Spontaneous Speech
              Recognition.* PhD thesis, Friedrich-Alexander-Universtität Erlangen-
              Nürnberg, 2001.

[Gall 02]   F. Gallwitz, H. Niemann, E. Nöth, and V. Warnke. "Integrated recogni-
              tion of words and prosodic phrase boundaries". *Speech Communication*,
              Vol. 36, No. 1, pp. 81–95, 2002.

[Ghah 14]   P. Ghahremani, B. BabaAli, D. Povey, K. Riedhammer, J. Trmal, and
              S. Khudanpur. "A pitch extraction algorithm tuned for automatic speech
              recognition". In: *Proceedings of ICASSP, International Conference on
              Acoustics, Speech, and Signal Processing*, pp. 2494–2498, Florence, Italy,
              2014.

[Ghit 11]   O. Ghitza. "Linking speech perception and neurophysiology: speech de-
              coding guided by cascaded oscillators locked to the input rhythm". *Fron-
              tiers in Psychology*, Vol. 2, p. Article 130, 2011.

[Ghit 12]   O. Ghitza. "On the role of theta-driven syllabic parsing in decoding
              speech: intelligibility of speech with a manipulated modulation spec-
              trum". *Frontiers in Psychology*, Vol. 3, p. Article 238, 2012.

[Gibb 98]   D. Gibbon. *Intonation systems: A survey of twenty languages*, Chap. In-
              tonation in German, pp. 78–96. Cambridge University Press, 1998.

[Gilb 91]   J. B. Gilbert. *Teaching English Pronunciation. A Book of Readings*,
              Chap. Gadgets: Non-verbal tools for teaching pronunciation, pp. 308–
              322. Routledge, London, 1991.

[Gims 01]   A. C. Gimson and A. Cruttenden. *Pronunciation of English.* Hodder
              Arnold, 6th Ed., 2001.

[Glas 12]   J. Glass. "Towards unsupervised speech processing". In: *Proceedings
              of ISSPA, International Conference on Information Science, Signal Pro-
              cessing and their Applications*, pp. 1–4, Montreal, Quebec, Canada, 2012.

[Glus 10]   A. Gluszek and J. F. Dovidio. "The way they speak: A social psycholo-
              gical perspective on the stigma of non-native accents in communication".
              Personality and Social Psychology Review, Vol. 14, No. 2, pp. 214–237,
              2010.

[Goui 80]   F. Gouin. *L'art d'enseigner et d'étudier les langues.* Librairie Fischba-
              cher, 1880.

[Grab 02]   E. Grabe and E. L. Low. "Durational variability in speech and the rhythm
              class hypothesis". In: C. Gussenhoven and N. Warner, Eds., *Laboratory
              Phonology VII*, pp. 515–546, Mouton de Gruyter, Berlin, 2002.

[Grah 01]   C. Graham, A. W. Hamblin, and S. Feldstein. "Recognition of emotion
              in English voices by speakers of Japanese, Spanish and English". *Inter-
              national Review of Applied Linguistics in Language Teaching*, Vol. 39,
              No. 1, pp. 19–37, 2001.

[Gree 97]   D. D. Greenwood. "The Mel Scale's disqualifying bias and a consistency of pitch-difference equisections in 1956 with equal cochlear distances and equal frequency ratios". *Hearing research*, Vol. 103, No. 1-2, pp. 199–224, 1997.

[Grop 12]   M. Gropp. *Smart Combination of Individual Predictions for the Assessment of Non-Native Prosody*. Friedrich-Alexander-Universität Erlangen-Nürnberg, 2012.

[Guin 11]   C. Guinaudeau and J. Hirschberg. "Accounting for prosodic information to improve ASR-based topic tracking for TV broadcast news". In: *Proceedings of INTERSPEECH, 12th Annual Conference of the International Speech Communication Association*, Florence, Italy, 2011.

[Gut 09]   U. Gut. *Introduction to English Phonetics and Phonology*. Peter Lang, 2009.

[Hahn 04]   L. D. Hahn. "Primary stress and intelligibility: Research to motivate the teaching of suprasegmentals". *TESOL quarterly*, Vol. 38, No. 2, pp. 201–223, 2004.

[Hall 11]   G. Hall. *Exploring English Language Teaching: Language in Action*. Routledge, 2011.

[Hans 13]   T. K. Hansen. "The Danish Simulator-Exploring the Cost-cutting Potential of Computer Games in Language Learning". In: *Proceedings of the International Conference ICT for Language Learning, 6th edition*, Florence, Italy, 2013.

[Hard 04]   D. Hardison. "Generalization of Computer-Assisted Prosody Training: Quantitative and Qualitative Findings (1).". *Language, Learning & Technology*, Vol. 8, No. 1, pp. 34–52, 2004.

[Hast 08]   T. Hastie, R. Tibshirani, and J. Friedman. *The Elements of Statistical Learning. Data Mining, Inference, and Prediction*. Springer, 2008. Available online: `https://web.stanford.edu/~hastie/ElemStatLearn/download.html`, last visited September 8th, 2017.

[Haza 05]   V. Hazan, A. Sennema, M. Iba, and A. Faulkner. "Effect of audiovisual perceptual training on the perception and production of consonants by Japanese learners of English". *Speech Communication*, Vol. 47, No. 3, pp. 360–378, 2005.

[Haza 98]   V. Hazan and A. Simpson. "The effect of cue-enhancement on consonant perception by non-native listeners: preliminary results". In: *Proceedings of STiLL, Speech Technology in Language Learning*, Marholmen, Sweden, 1998.

[He 15]   K. He, X. Zhang, S. Ren, and J. Sun. "Delving deep into rectifiers: Surpassing human-level performance on imagenet classification". *arXiv preprint arXiv:1502.01852*, 2015.

[Higg 88]   J. Higgins. *Language, learners, and computers: Human intelligence and artificial unintelligence*. Longman, 1988.

[Hill 94]   S. Hiller, E. Rooney, R. Vaughan, M. Eckert, J. Laver, and M. Jack. "An Automated System for Computer-Aided Pronunciation Learning". *Computer Assisted Language Learning*, Vol. 7, No. 1, pp. 51–63, 1994.

[Hoch 97]   S. Hochreiter and J. Schmidhuber. "Long short-term memory". *Neural computation*, Vol. 9, No. 8, pp. 1735–1780, 1997.

[Hoeq 83]   C. E. Hoequist, Jr. "Durational Correlates of Linguistic Rhythm Categories". *Phonetica*, Vol. 40, pp. 19–31, 1983.

[Howa 84]   A. Howatt. *A History of English Language Teaching*. Oxford University Press, 1984.

[Howe 06]   J. Howe. "Crowdsourcing: A Definition". `http://crowdsourcing.typepad.com/cs/2006/06/crowdsourcing_a.html`, 2006. Last visited September 8th, 2017.

[Huan 01]   X. Huang, A. Acero, and H.-W. Hon. *Spoken Language Processing*. Prentice-Hall, 2001.

[Husb 11]   O. Husby, Å. Øvregaard, P. Wik, Ø. Bech, E. Albertsen, S. Nefzaoui, E. Skarpnes, and J. C. Koreman. "Dealing with L1 background and L2 dialects in Norwegian CAPT.". In: *Proceedings of SLaTE, Workshop on Speech and Language Technology in Education*, pp. 133–136, Venice, Italy, 2011.

[Hön 05]   F. Hönig, G. Stemmer, C. Hacker, and F. Brugnara. "Revising Perceptual Linear Prediction (PLP)". In: *Proceedings of INTERSPEECHs*, Lisbon, Portugal, 2005.

[Hön 09]   F. Hönig, A. Batliner, K. Weilhammer, and E. Nöth. "Islands of Failure: Employing word accent information for pronunciation quality assessment of English L2 learners". In: *Proceedings of SLATE*, Wroxall Abbey Estate, Warwickshire, England, 2009.

[Hön 10a]   F. Hönig, A. Batliner, K. Weilhammer, and E. Nöth. "Automatic Assessment of Non-Native Prosody for English as L2". In: *Proceedings of Speech Prosody*, Chicago IL, USA, 2010.

[Hön 10b]   F. Hönig, A. Batliner, K. Weilhammer, and E. Nöth. "How Many Labellers? Modelling Inter-Labeller Agreement and System Performance for the Automatic Assessment of Non-Native Prosody". In: *Proceedings of SLaTE, Workshop on Speech and Language Technology in Education*, Tokyo, Japan, 2010.

[Hön 11]   F. Hönig, A. Batliner, and E. Nöth. "How many labellers revisited – naives, experts and real experts". In: *Proceedings of SLaTE, Workshop on Speech and Language Technology in Education*, pp. 137–140, Venice, Italy, 2011.

[Hön 12a]   F. Hönig, A. Batliner, and E. Nöth. "Automatic Assessment of Non-Native Prosody – Annotation, Modelling and Evaluation". In: *IS ADEPT, International Symposium on Automatic Detection of Errors in Pronunciation Training*, Stockholm, Sweden, 2012.

[Hön 12b]   F. Hönig, T. Bocklet, K. Riedhammer, A. Batliner, and E. Nöth. "The Automatic Assessment of Non-Native Prosody: Combining Classical Prosodic Analysis with Acoustic Modelling". In: *Proceedings of INTERSPEECH, 13th Annual Conference of the International Speech Communication Association*, pp. 823–826, Portland Oregon, USA, 2012.

[Hön 15] F. Hönig, A. Batliner, and E. Nöth. "How Many Speakers, How Many Texts – The Automatic Assessment of Non-Native Prosody". In: *Proceedings of SLaTE, Workshop on Speech and Language Technology in Education*, Leipzig, Germany, 2015.

[Imot 02] K. Imoto, Y. Tsubota, A. Raux, T. Kawahara, and M. Dantsuji. "Modeling and automatic detection of English sentence stress for computer-assisted English prosody learning system.". In: *Proceedings of INTERSPEECH, 3rd Annual Conference of the International Speech Communication Association*, Jeju Island, Korea, 2002.

[Jame 40] A. L. James. *Speech Signals in Telephony*. Pitman, 1940.

[Jame 76] E. F. James. "The Acquisition of Prosodic Features of Speech Using a Speech Visualizer". *International Review of Applied Linguistics in Language Teaching*, Vol. 14, No. 3, pp. 227–244, 1976.

[Jang 09] T.-Y. Jang. "Automatic assessment of non-native prosody using rhythm metrics: Focusing on Korean speakers' English pronunciation". In: *Proceedings of the 2nd International Conference on East Asian Linguistics*, 2009.

[Jans 13] A. Jansen, E. Dupoux, S. Goldwater, M. Johnson, S. Khudanpur, K. Church, N. Feldman, H. Hermansky, F. Metze, R. Rose, M. Seltzer, P. Clark, I. McGraw, B. Varadarajan, E. Bennett, B. Borschinger, J. Chiu, E. Dunbar, A. Fourtassi, D. Harwath, C. Lee, K. Levin, A. Norouzian, V. Peddinti, R. Richardson, T. Schatz, and T. Samuel. "A Summary of the 2012 JHU CLSP Workshop on Zero Resource Speech Technologies and Models of Early Language Acquisition". In: *Proceedings of ICASSP, International Conference on Acoustics, Speech, and Signal Processing*, Vancouver, Canada, 2013.

[Jenk 00] J. Jenkins. *The Phonology of English as an International Language*. Oxford University Press, 2000.

[Jenk 02] J. Jenkins. "A Sociolinguistically Based, Empirically Researched Pronunciation Syllabus for English as an International Language". *Applied Linguistics*, Vol. 23, No. 1, pp. 83–103, 2002.

[Jenk 96] K. L. Jenkin and M. S. Scordilis. "Development and comparison of three syllable stress classifiers". In: *Proceedings of ICSLP, 4th International Conference on Spoken Language Processing*, pp. 733–736, Philadelphia PA, USA, 1996.

[Jenk 98] J. Jenkins. "Which pronunciation norms and models for English as an International Language?". *ELT Journal Volume*, Vol. 52, No. 2, pp. 119–126, 1998.

[John 08] W. L. Johnson and S. Wu. "Assessing aptitude for learning with a serious game for foreign language and culture". In: *Proceedings of ITS, 9th International Conference on Intelligent Tutoring Systems*, pp. 520–529, Springer, Montreal, Canada, 2008.

[John 12] W. L. Johnson. "Error Detection for Teaching Communicative Competence". In: *IS ADEPT, International Symposium on Automatic Detection of Errors in Pronunciation Training*, Stockholm, Sweden, 2012.

[Jone 06] D. Jones, P. Roach, J. Hartman, and J. Setter, Eds. *Cambridge English Pronouncing Dictionary*. Cambridge University Press, 2006.

[Jong 01] J. H. A. L. de Jong and J. Bernstein. "Relating Phonepass Overall Scores to the Council of Europe Framework Level Descriptors". In: *Proceedings of INTERSPEECH, 2nd Annual Conference of the International Speech Communication Association*, pp. 2803–2806, Aalborg, Denmark, 2001.

[Juff 90] A. Juffs. "TONE, SYLLABLE STRUCTURE AND INTERLAN-GUAGE PHONOLOGY: CHINESE LEARNERS'STRESS ERRORS". *IRAL-International Review of Applied Linguistics in Language Teaching*, Vol. 28, No. 2, pp. 99–118, 1990.

[Kagl 10] A. Kaglik and P. B. de Mareüil. "Polish-accented French prosody in perception and production: transfer or universal acquisition process?". In: *Proceedings of Speech Prosody*, Chicago IL, USA, 2010.

[Kell 69] L. G. Kelly. *25 centuries of language teaching*. Newbury House Publishers, 1969.

[Kenn 09] S. Kennedy. "L2 Proficiency: Measuring the Intelligibility of Words and Extended Speech". In: A. G. Benati, Ed., *Issues in Second Language Proficiency*, pp. 132–146, Continuum International Publishing Group, 2009.

[Kenw 87] J. Kenworthy. *Teaching English Pronunciation*. Longman, 1987.

[Kies 97] A. Kießling. *Extraktion und Klassifikation prosodischer Merkmale in der automatischen Sprachverarbeitung. Berichte aus der Informatik*, Shaker, Aachen, Germany, 1997.

[Kim 11] Y.-J. Kim and M. C. Beutnagel. "Automatic assessment of american English lexical stress using machine learning algorithms". In: *Proceedings of SLaTE, Workshop on Speech and Language Technology in Education*, pp. 93–96, Venice, Italy, 2011.

[Koch 05] G. Kochanski, E. Grabe, J. Coleman, and B. Rosner. "Loudness predicts Prominence; Fundamental Frequency lends little". *Journal of Acoustical Society of America*, Vol. 11, pp. 1038–1054, 2005.

[Koch 10] G. Kochanski, A. Loukina, E. Keane, C. Shih, and B. Rosner. "Long-Range Prosody Prediction and Rhythm". In: *Proceedings of Speech Prosody*, Chicago IL, USA, 2010.

[Kohl 94] K. J. Kohler, G. Lex, M. Pätzold, M. T. M. Scheffers, A. P. Simpson, and W. Thon. "Handbuch zur Datenaufnahme und Transliteration in TP14 von Verbmobil - 3.0". Tech. Rep., IPDS, Kiel, 1994.

[Kola 06] J. Kolář, E. Shriberg, and Y. Liu. "On speaker-specific prosodic models for automatic dialog act segmentation of multi-party meetings". In: *Proceedings of INTERSPEECH – ICSLP, 9th International Conference on Spoken Language Processing*, Pittsburgh, PA, USA, 2006.

[Komp 94a] R. Kompe, A. Batliner, A. Kiessling, U. Kilian, H. Niemann, E. Nöth, and P. R. Brietzmann. "Automatic classification of prosodically marked phrase boundaries in German". In: *Proceedings of ICASSP, International Conference on Acoustics, Speech, and Signal Processing*, pp. II–173, IEEE, Adelaide, South Australia, Australia, 1994.

[Komp 94b] R. Kompe, E. Nöth, A. Kießling, T. Kuhn, M. Mast, H. Niemann, K. Ott, and A. Batliner. "Prosody takes over: Towards a prosodically guided dialog system". *Speech Communication*, Vol. 15, No. 1, pp. 155–167, 1994.

[Komp 96] R. Kompe. *Prosody in Speech Understanding Systems*. PhD thesis, Friedrich-Alexander-Universität Erlangen-Nürnberg, 1996.

[Kore 11] J. Koreman, Ø. Bech, O. Husby, and P. Wik. "L1-L2map: a tool for multilingual contrastive analysis". In: *Proceedings of ICPhS, International Congress of Phonetic Sciences*, pp. 599–602, Hong Kong, 2011.

[Kral 12] A. Kral and A. Sharma. "Developmental neuroplasticity after cochlear implantation". *Trends in neurosciences*, Vol. 35, No. 2, pp. 111–122, 2012.

[Kras 82] S. D. Krashen. *Principles and practice in second language acquisition*. Pergamon, 1982.

[Kras 85] S. D. Krashen. *The input hypothesis: Issues and implications*. Longman, 1985.

[Kras 89] S. D. Krashen. "We Acquire Vocabulary and Spelling by Reading: Additional Evidence for the Input Hypothesis". *The Modern Language Journal*, Vol. 73, No. 4, pp. 440–464, 1989.

[Krau 16] C. A. Krause. *The direct method in modern languages: contributions to methods and didactics in modern languages*. C. Scribner's Sons, 1916.

[Kuhl 00] P. K. Kuhl. "A new view of language acquisition". *PNAS*, Vol. 97, No. 22, pp. 11850–11857, 2000.

[Kuhl 04] P. K. Kuhl. "Early language acquisition: cracking the speech code.". *Nature Reviews: Neuroscience*, Vol. 5, pp. 831–843, 2004.

[Ladd 96] D. R. Ladd. *International Phonology*. Cambridge Univ Press, 1996.

[Lai 13] C. Lai, K. Evanini, and K. Zechner. "Applying Rhythm Metrics to Nonnative Spontaneous Speech". In: *Proceedings of SLaTE, Workshop on Speech and Language Technology in Education*, Grenoble, France, 2013.

[Lars 00] D. Larsen-Freeman. *Techniques and Principles in Language Teaching*. Oxford University Press, 2000.

[Lash 51] K. S. Lashley. "The problem of serial order in behavior". In: L. A. Jeffress, Ed., *Cerebral Mechanisms in Behavior*, Wiley, 1951.

[Lea 72] W. A. Lea. "Use of Syntactic Segmentation and Stressed Syllable Location in Phonetic Recognition". In: *ERIC Number: ED088288, presented at the 84th Meeting of the Acoustical Society of America*, Miami, Florida, USA, 1972.

[Lea 73a] W. A. Lea. "An Algorithm for Locating Stressed Syllables in Continuous Speech.". In: *ERIC Number: ED088286, presented at the 86th Meeting of the Acoustical Society of America*, Los Angeles, Californica, USA, 1973.

[Lea 73b] W. A. Lea. "Perceived Stress as the "Standard" for Judging Acoustical Correlates of Stress". In: *ERIC Number: ED088287, presented at the 86th Meeting of the Acoustical Society of America*, Los Angeles, Californica, USA, 1973.

[Lea 73c]   W. A. Lea, M. F. Medress, and T. E. Skinner. "Prosodic Aids to Speech Recognition. II. Syntactic Segmentation and Stressed Syllable Location". Tech. Rep., DTIC Document, 1973.

[LeCu 15]   Y. LeCun, Y. Bengio, and G. Hinton. "Deep Learning". *Science*, Vol. 521, pp. 436–444, 2015.

[LeCu 98]   Y. LeCun, L. Bottou, Y. Bengio, and P. Haffner. "Gradient-based learning applied to document recognition". *Proceedings of the IEEE*, Vol. 86, No. 11, pp. 2278–2324, 1998.

[Ledo 04]   O. Ledoit and M. Wolf. "A well-conditioned estimator for large-dimensional covariance matrices". *Journal of multivariate analysis*, Vol. 88, No. 2, pp. 365–411, 2004.

[Lehi 70]   I. Lehiste. *Suprasegmentals*. MIT Press, 1970.

[Lehi 73]   I. Lehiste. "Phonetic Disambiguation of Syntactic Ambiguity". *Journal of Acoustical Society of America*, Vol. 53, No. 1, p. 380, 1973.

[Lehi 76]   I. Lehiste, J. P. Olive, and L. A. Streeter. "Role of duration in disambiguating syntactically ambiguous sentences". *The Journal of the Acoustical Society of America*, Vol. 60, No. 5, pp. 1199–1202, 1976.

[Leic 07]   R. Leicht. "Claudia Roths Silben haben eine Hacke". online, June 2007. Available: `http://www.tagesspiegel.de/meinung/kommentare/` `leichts-sinn-claudia-roths-silben-haben-eine-hacke/967234.` `html`; last visited September 8th, 2017.

[Lenn 67]   E. H. Lenneberg. *Biological foundations of language*. Wiley, 1967.

[Lev 10]   S. Lev-Ari and B. Keysara. "Why don't we believe non-native speakers? The influence of accent on credibility". *Journal of Experimental Social Psychology*, Vol. 46, No. 6, pp. 1093–1096, 2010.

[Levi 83]   S. E. Levinson, L. R. Rabiner, and M. M. Sondhi. "An introduction to the application of the theory of probabilistic functions of a Markov process to automatic speech recognition". *Bell System Technical Journal*, Vol. 62, No. 4, pp. 1035–1074, 1983.

[Levo 09]   G.-A. Levow. "Investigating pitch accent recognition in non-native speech". In: *Proceedings of the ACL-IJCNLP 2009 Conference Short Papers*, pp. 269–272, Association for Computational Linguistics, 2009.

[Levy 97]   M. Levy. *Computer-Assisted Language Learning: Context and Conceptualization*. Oxford University Press, 1997.

[Leyt 83]   F. Leyton. *The extent to which group instruction supplemented by mastery of the initial cognitive prerequisitesapproximatesthe learning effectiveness of one-to-one tutorial instruction*. PhD thesis, University of Chicago, 1983.

[Li 11]   K. Li, S. Zhang, M. Li, W. K. Lo, and H. M. Meng. "Prominence Model for Prosodic Features in Automatic Lexical Stress and Pitch Accent Detection.". In: *Proceedings of INTERSPEECH, 12th Annual Conference of the International Speech Communication Association*, pp. 2009–2012, Florence, Italy, 2011.

[Li 12]   K. Li and H.-Y. Meng. "Perceptually-motivated assessment of automatically detected lexical stress in L2 learners' speech". In: *Proceedings of ISCSLP, IEEE International Symposium on Chinese Spoken Language Processing*, pp. 179–183, IEEE, Hong Kong, 2012.

[Li 13]   K. Li, X. Qian, S. Kang, and H. Meng. "Lexical stress detection for L2 English speech using deep belief networks.". In: *Proceedings of INTER-SPEECH, 14th Annual Conference of the International Speech Communication Association*, pp. 1811–1815, Lyon, France, 2013.

[Lieb 60]   P. Lieberman. "Some Acoustic Correlates of Word Stress in American English". *JASA*, Vol. 32, pp. 451–454, 1960.

[Ligh 99]   P. M. Lightbown and N. Spada. *How languages are learned*. Oxford University Press, 1999.

[Litt 81]   W. Littlewood. *Communicative Language Teaching: An Introduction*. Cambridge University Press, 1981.

[Liu 06]   Y. Liu, E. Shriberg, A. Stolcke, D. Hillard, M. Ostendorf, and M. Harper. "Enriching speech recognition with automatic detection of sentence boundaries and disfluencies". *IEEE Transactions on Audio, Speech, and Language Processing*, Vol. 14, No. 5, pp. 1526–1540, 2006.

[Long 00]   M. Long and J. Norris. "Task-based teaching and assessment". In: M. Byram, Ed., *Encyclopedia of Language Teaching*, pp. 597–603, Routledge, 2000.

[Long 92]   M. Long and G. Crookes. "Three approaches to task-based syllabus design". *TESOL Quarterly*, Vol. 26, No. 1, pp. 27–56, 1992.

[Lope 11]   J. Lopes, I. Trancoso, and A. Abad. "A Nativeness Classifier for TED Talks". In: *Proceedings of ICASSP, International Conference on Acoustics, Speech, and Signal Processing*, pp. 5672–5675, Prague, Czech Republic, 2011.

[Louk 11]   A. Loukina, G. Kochanski, B. Rosner, E. Keane, and C. Shih. "Rhythm measures and dimensions of durational variation in speech". *The Journal of the Acoustical Society of America*, Vol. 129, No. 5, pp. 3258–3270, 2011.

[Lyst 97]   R. Lyster and L. Ranta. "Corrective feedback and learner uptake". *Studies in second language acquisition*, Vol. 19, No. 01, pp. 37–66, 1997.

[Maie 09a] A. Maier, F. Hönig, V. Zeißler, A. Batliner, E. Körner, N. Yamanaka, P. Ackermann, and E. Nöth. "A Language-Independent Feature Set for the Automatic Evaluation of Prosody". In: *INTERSPEECH, 10th Annual Conference of the International Speech Communication Association*, Brighton, United Kingdom, 2009.

[Maie 09b] A. Maier, T. Haderlein, U. Eysholdt, F. Rosanowski, A. Batliner, M. Schuster, and E. Nöth. "PEAKS – A system for the automatic evaluation of voice and speech disorders". *Speech Communication*, Vol. 51, pp. 425–437, 2009.

[Mark 96]   D. J. Markham and Y. Nagano-Madsen. "Input modality effects in foreign accent". In: *Proceedings of ICSLP, 4th International Conference on Spoken Language Processing*, pp. 1473–1476, Philadelphia PA, USA, 1996.

[Mart 97]   A. Martin, G. Doddington, T. Kamm, M. Ordowski, and M. Przybocki. "The DET curve in assessment of detection task performance". In: *Proceedings of EUROSPEECH, 5th European Conference on Speech Communication and Technology*, Rhodes, Greece, 1997.

[Matt 92]   C. Matthews. "Going AI. Foundations of ICALL". *Computer Assisted Language Learning*, Vol. 5, No. 1-2, pp. 13–31, 1992.

[McAl 98]   R. McAllister. "Second Language Perception and the Concept of Foreign Accent". In: *Proceedings of STiLL, Speech Technology in Language Learning*, Marholmen, Sweden, 1998.

[McAr 02]   T. McArthur. *The Oxford guide to World English*. Oxford University Press, 2002.

[McGu 76]   H. McGurk and J. MacDonald. "Hearing lips and seeing voices". *Nature*, Vol. 264, No. 5588, pp. 746–748, 1976.

[McNe 92]   M. McNerney and D. Mendelsohn. "Suprasegmentals in the pronunciation class: Setting priorities". In: *Teaching American English pronunciation*, Oxford University Press, 1992.

[Medr 78]   M. F. Medress, T. C. Diller, D. R. Kloker, L. L. Lutton, H. N. Oredson, and T. E. Skinner. "An automatic word spotting system for conversational speech". In: *Proceedings of ICASSP, IEEE International Conference on Acoustics, Speech, and Signal Processing*, pp. 712–717, IEEE, Tulsa, Oklahoma, USA, 1978.

[Mehl 88]   J. Mehler, P. Jusczyk, G. Lambertz, N. Halsted, J. Bertoncini, and C. Amiel-Tison. "A precursor of language acquisition in young infants". *Cognition*, Vol. 29, No. 2, pp. 143–178, 1988.

[Mehl 96]   J. Mehler, E. Dupoux, T. Nazzi, and G. Dehaene-Lambertz. "Coping with linguistic diversity: the infant's viewpoint". In: J. L. Morgan and K. Demuth, Eds., *Signal to Syntax: Bootstrapping from Speech to Grammar in Early Acquisition*, pp. 101–116, Lawrence Erlbaum Associates., 1996.

[Meng 00]   M. Meng and M. Bader. "Ungrammaticality detection and garden path strength: Evidence for serial parsing". *Language and Cognitive Processes*, Vol. 15, No. 6, pp. 615–666, 2000.

[Meng 09]   H. Meng, C. yu Tseng, M. Kondo, A. Harrison, and T. Viscelgia. "Studying L2 Suprasegmental Features in Asian Englishes: A Position Paper". In: *INTERSPEECH, 10th Annual Conference of the International Speech Communication Association*, Brighton, United Kingdom, 2009.

[Menz 00]   W. Menzel, E. Atwell, P. Bonaventura, D. Herron, P. Howarth, R. Morton, and C. Souter. "The ISLE Corpus of Non-native Spoken English". In: *Proceedings of LREC, 2nd International Conference on Language Resources and Evaluation*, pp. 957–963, Athens, Greece, 2000.

[Menz 01]   W. Menzel, D. Herron, R. Morton, D. Pezzotta, P. Bonaventura, and P. Howarth. "Interactive pronunciation training". *ReCALL*, Vol. 13, No. 01, pp. 67–78, 2001.

[Merc 09]   J. Mercer. "Functions of positive and negative type, and their connection with the theory of integral equations". *Philosophical transactions of the Royal Society of London, Series A*, pp. 415–446, 1909.

[Meye 09]   B. T. Meyer. *Human and automatic speech recognition in the presence of speech-intrinsic variations*. PhD thesis, Fakultät für Mathematik und Naturwissenschaften der Carl-von-Ossietzky-Universität Oldenburg, 2009.

[Mild 15]   B. Milde and C. Biemann. "Using Representation Learning and Out-of-domain Data for a Paralinguistic Speech Task". In: *Proceedings of INTERSPEECH, 16th Annual Conference of the International Speech Communication Association*, Dresden, Germany, 2015.

[Mill 65]   G. A. Miller. "Some preliminaries to psycholinguistics". *American Psychologist*, Vol. 20, No. 1, pp. 15–20, 1965.

[Mine 97]   N. Minematsu, N. Ohashi, and S. Nakagawa. "Automatic detection of accent in English words spoken by Japanese students". In: *Proceedings of EUROSPEECH, 5th European Conference on Speech Communication and Technology*, Rhodes, Greece, 1997.

[Miss 07]   F. Missaglia. "Prosodic training for adult Italian learners of German: the Contrastive Prosody Method". In: J. Trouvain and U. Gut, Eds., *Non-Native Prosody. Phonetic Description and Teaching Practice*, pp. 236–258, Mouton de Gruyter, 2007.

[Miss 97]   F. Missaglia. *Studi sul bilinguismo scolastico italo-tedesco*. La Scuola, 1997.

[Miss 99a]   F. Missaglia. "Contrastive prosody in SLA – An empirical study with adult Italian learners of German". In: *Proceedings of ICPhS, International Congress of Phonetic Sciences*, pp. 551–554, San Francisco, USA, 1999.

[Miss 99b]   F. Missaglia. *Phonetische Aspekte des Erwerbs von Deutsch als Fremdsprache durch italienische Muttersprachler*. T. Hector, 1999.

[Moed 08]   M. Moedjito. "Priorities in English Pronunciation Teaching in EFL Classrooms". *K@ta - a biannual publication on the study of language and literature*, Vol. 10, No. 2, pp. 129–142, 2008.

[Mohr 02]   M. Mohri, F. Pereira, and M. Riley. "Weighted finite-state transducers in speech recognition". *Computer Speech & Language*, Vol. 16, No. 1, pp. 69–88, 2002.

[Mont 15]   C. Montacié and M.-J. Caraty. "Phrase Accentuation Verification and Phonetic Variation Measurement for the Degree of Nativeness Sub-Challenge". In: *Proceedings of INTERSPEECH, 16th Annual Conference of the International Speech Communication Association*, Dresden, Germany, 2015.

[Moor 83]   B. C. Moore and B. R. Glasberg. "Suggested formulae for calculating auditory-filter bandwidths and excitation patterns". *The Journal of the Acoustical Society of America*, Vol. 74, No. 3, pp. 750–753, 1983.

[Muka 05]   J. C. Mukalel. *Approaches To English Language Teaching*. iscovery Publishing House, 2005.

[Murr 71]   J. Murray, Ed. *The Compact Edition of the Oxford English Dictionary*. Oxford University Press, 1971.

[Naka 02]   A. Nakamichi, A. Jogan, M. Usami, and D. Erickson. "Perception by native and non-native listeners of vocal emotion in a bilingual movie". *Gifu City Women's College Research Bulletin*, Vol. 52, pp. 87–91, 2002.

[Nati 04]   National Institute of Standards and Technology. "Fall 2004 Rich Transcription (RT-04F) Evaluation Plan". Tech. Rep., National Institute of Standards and Technology, 2004.

[Nazz 98]   T. Nazzi, J. Bertoncini, and J. Mehler. "Language discrimination by newborns: Toward an understanding of the role of rhythm.". *Journal of Experimental Psychology: Human perception and performance*, Vol. 24, No. 3, p. 756, 1998.

[Neri 02]   A. Neri, C. Cucchiarini, and H. Strik. "Feedback In Computer Assisted Pronunciation Training: Technology Push Or Demand Pull?". In: *Proceedings of INTERSPEECH, 3rd Annual Conference of the International Speech Communication Association*, pp. 1209–1212, Jeju Island, Korea, 2002.

[Neri 06]   A. Neri, C. Cucchiarini, and H. Strik. "ASR-based corrective feedback on pronunciation: Does it really work?". In: *Proceedings of INTERSPEECH – ICSLP, 9th International Conference on Spoken Language Processing*, Pittsburgh, PA, USA, 2006.

[Neri 08]   A. Neri, C. Cucchiarini, and H. Strik. "The effectiveness of computer-based speech corrective feedback for improving segmental quality in L2 Dutch". *ReCALL*, Vol. 20, No. 2, pp. 225–243, 2008.

[Nesp 03]   M. Nespor, M. Pena, and J. Mehler. "On the different roles of vowels and consonants in speech processing and language acquisition". *Lingue e Linguaggio*, Vol. 2, pp. 221–247, 2003.

[Nick 13]   S. Nickels, B. Opitz, and K. Steinhauer. "ERPs show that classroom-instructed late second language learners rely on the same prosodic cues in syntactic parsing as native speakers". *Neuroscience letters*, Vol. 557, pp. 107–111, 2013.

[Nicu 05]   A. Niculescu-Mizil and R. Caruana. "Predicting good probabilities with supervised learning". In: *Proceedings of the 22nd international conference on Machine learning*, pp. 625–632, ACM, Bonn, Germany, 2005.

[Nieb 09]   O. Niebuhr. "F0-Based Rhythm Effects on the Perception of Local Syllable Prominence". *Phonetica*, Vol. 66, No. 1-2, pp. 95–112, 2009.

[Niem 13]   T. Nieminen and M. L. O'Dell. "Visualizing speech rhythm: A survey of alternatives.". In: E.-L. Asu and P. Lippus, Eds., *Proceedings of the XIth Conference on Nordic Prosody*, p. 265–274, Peter Lang, Frankfurt am Main, Tartu, Estonia, 2013.

[Niem 83]   H. Niemann. *Klassifikation von Mustern*. Springer, 1983. 2nd Edition available online: `http://www5.cs.fau.de/fileadmin/Persons/NiemannHeinrich/klassifikation-von-mustern/m00links.html`, last visited September 8th, 2017.

[Nöt 00]   E. Nöth, A. Batliner, A. Kießling, R. Kompe, and H. Niemann. "Verbmobil: The use of prosody in the linguistic components of a speech understanding system". *IEEE Transactions on Speech and Audio Processing*, Vol. 8, No. 5, pp. 519–532, 2000.

[Nöt 88]   E. Nöth, H. Niemann, and S. Schmölz. "Prosodic features in German speech: stress assignment by man and machine". In: H. Niemann, M. Lang, and G. Sagerer, Eds., *Recent Advances in Speech Understanding and Dialog Systems*, pp. 101–106, Springer, 1988.

[Nöt 91]   E. Nöth. *Prosodische Information in der automatischen Spracherkennung: Berechnung und Anwendung.* Niemeyer, Tübingen (Germany), 1991.

[OSha 87]   D. O'Shaughnessy. *Speech communication: human and machine.* Addison-Wesley, 1987.

[Otak 93]   T. Otake, G. Hatano, A. Cutler, and J. Mehler. "Mora or syllable? Speech segmentation in Japanese". *Journal of Memory and Language*, Vol. 32, pp. 258–278, 1993.

[Part 13]   E. Partanen, T. Kujala, R. Näätänen, A. Liitola, A. Sambeth, and M. Huotilainen. "Learning-induced neural plasticity of speech processing before birth". *Proceedings of the National Academy of Sciences*, Vol. 110, No. 37, pp. 15145–15150, 2013.

[Pask 72]   G. Pask and B. Scott. "Learning strategies and individual competence". *International Journal of Man-Machine Studies*, Vol. 4, No. 3, pp. 217–253, 1972.

[Pedr 11]   F. Pedregosa, G. Varoquaux, A. Gramfort, V. Michel, B. Thirion, O. Grisel, M. Blondel, P. Prettenhofer, R. Weiss, V. Dubourg, J. Vanderplas, A. Passos, D. Cournapeau, M. Brucher, M. Perrot, and E. Duchesnay. "Scikit-learn: Machine Learning in Python". *Journal of Machine Learning Research*, Vol. 12, pp. 2825–2830, 2011.

[Pell 12]   B. Pellom. "Rosetta Stone ReFLEX: Toward Improving English Conversational Fluency in Asia". In: *IS ADEPT, International Symposium on Automatic Detection of Errors in Pronunciation Training*, Stockholm, Sweden, 2012.

[Penf 59]   W. Penfield and L. Roberts. *Speech and Brain Mechanisms.* Princeton University Press, 1959.

[Penn 12]   N. D. Penna and M. D. Reid. "Crowd & prejudice: An impossibility theorem for crowd labelling without a gold standard". In: *Proceedings of Collective Intelligence*, Cambridge, MA, USA, 2012.

[Pike 45]   K. L. Pike. *The intonation of American English.* University of Michigan Press, 1945.

[Pink 90]   S. Pinker and P. Bloom. "Natural language and natural selection". *Behavioral and Brain Sciences*, Vol. 13, No. 4, pp. 707–784, 1990.

[Plat 00]   J. C. Platt. *Advances in Large Margin Classifiers*, Chap. Probabilities for SV Machines, pp. 61–74. MIT Press, 2000.

[Plat 98]   J. C. Platt. "Sequential Minimal Optimization: A Fast Algorithm for Training Support Vector Machines". Tech. Rep. MSR-TR-98-14, Microsoft Research, April 1998.

[Pols 77]   L. C. W. Pols. *Spectral Analysis and Identification of Dutch Vowels in Monosyllabic Words.* PhD thesis, University of Amsterdam, 1977.

[Pove 11]   D. Povey, A. Ghoshal, G. Boulianne, L. Burget, O. Glembek, N. Goel, M. Hannemann, P. Motlicek, Y. Qian, P. Schwarz, J. Silovsky, G. Stemmer, and K. Vesely. "The Kaldi Speech Recognition Toolkit". In: *IEEE 2011 Workshop on Automatic Speech Recognition and Understanding*, IEEE Signal Processing Society, Dec. 2011. IEEE Catalog No.: CFP11SRW-USB.

[Powe 12]   A. J. Power, N. Mead, L. Barnes, and U. Goswami. "Neural entrainment to rhythmically presented auditory, visual, and audio-visual speech in children". *Frontiers in Psychology*, Vol. 3, p. Article 216, 2012.

[Prec 00]   K. Precoda, C. A. Halverson, and H. Franco. "Effects of speech recognition-based pronunciation feedback on second-language pronunciation ability". In: *Proceedings of InSTIL – Integrating Speech Technology in (Language) Learning*, pp. 102–105, Dundee, Scotland, 2000.

[Putn 67]   H. Putnam. "The 'Innateness Hypothesis' and Explanatory Models in Linguistics". *Synthese*, Vol. 17, No. 1, pp. 12–22, 1967.

[Rabi 07]   L. R. Rabiner and R. W. Schafer. *Introduction to Digital Speech Processing*. Now Publishers Inc, 2007.

[Rabi 89]   L. R. Rabiner. "A tutorial on hidden Markov models and selected applications in speech recognition". *Proceedings of the IEEE*, Vol. 77, No. 2, pp. 257–286, 1989.

[Rade 68]   C. Rader. "Discrete Fourier transforms when the number of data samples is prime". *Proceedings of the IEEE*, Vol. 56, No. 6, pp. 1107–1108, 1968.

[Ramu 02]   F. Ramus. "Acoustic correlates of linguistic rhythm: Perspectives". In: *Proceedings of Speech Prosody*, pp. 115–120, Aix-en-Provence, France, 2002.

[Ramu 99]   F. Ramus, M. Nespor, and J. Mehler. "Correlates of linguistic rhythm in the speech signal". *Cognition*, Vol. 73, pp. 265–292, 1999.

[Rayk 12]   V. C. Raykar and S. Yu. "Eliminating Spammers and Ranking Annotators for Crowdsourced Labeling Tasks". *Journal of Machine Learning Research*, Vol. 13, pp. 491–518, 2012.

[Ren 04]   Y. Ren, S.-S. Kim, M. Hasegawa-Johnson, and J. Cole. "Speaker-independent automatic detection of pitch accent". In: *Proceedings of Speech Prosody*, Nara, Japan, 2004.

[Rich 01]   J. C. Richards and T. S. Rodgers. *Approaches and Methods in Language Teaching*. Cambridge University Press, 2001.

[Rich 82]   J. C. Richards and T. Rodgers. "Method: Approach, Design, and Procedure". *TESOL Quarterly*, Vol. 16, No. 2, pp. 153–168, 1982.

[Rose 03]   E. Rosenfeld, D. Massaro, and J. Bernstein. "Automatic analysis of vocal manifestations of apparent mood or affect". In: *Proceedings of the MAVEBA, 3rd International Workshop Models and analysis of vocal emissions for biomedical applications, Florence, Italy*, p. 3, 2003.

[Rose 09]   A. Rosenberg and J. Hirschberg. "Detecting pitch accents at the word, syllable and vowel level". In: *Proceedings of Human Language Technologies: Annual Conference of the North American Chapter of the Association for Computational Linguistics, Companion Volume: Short Papers*, pp. 81–84, 2009.

[Rose 10a] A. Rosenberg. "AuToBI-a tool for automatic ToBI annotation.". In: *Proceedings of INTERSPEECH, 11th Annual Conference of the International Speech Communication Association*, pp. 146–149, Makuhari, Chiba, Japan, 2010.

[Rose 10b] A. Rosenberg and J. B. Hirschberg. "Production of english prominence by native mandarin chinese speakers". In: *Proceedings of Speech Prosody*, Chicago IL, USA, 2010.

[Sala 96] M. R. Salaberry. "A theoretical foundation for the development of pedagogical tasks in computer mediated communication". *Calico Journal*, Vol. 14, No. 1, pp. 5–34, 1996.

[Schm 97] R. A. Schmidt and G. Wulf. "Continuous concurrent feedback degrades skill learning: Implications for training and simulation". *Human Factors*, Vol. 39, No. 4, pp. 509–525, 1997.

[Schn 06] E. Schneiderman, J. Bourdages, and C. Champagne. "Second-Language Accent: The Relationship Between Discrimination and Perception in Acquisition". *Language Learning*, Vol. 38, No. 1, pp. 1–19, 2006.

[Scho 00] B. Sch"olkopf. "The kernel trick for distances". In: *Proceedings of the Neural Information Processing Systems Conference*, 2000.

[Scho 99] B. Schölkopf, R. C. Williamson, A. J. Smola, J. Shawe-Taylor, and J. C. Platt. "Support Vector Method for Novelty Detection". In: *Proceedings of the Neural Information Processing Systems Conference*, pp. 582–588, 1999.

[Schu 06] M. Schuster, T. Haderlein, E. Nöth, J. Lohscheller, U. Eysholdt, and F. Rosanowski. "Intelligibility of laryngectomees' substitute speech: automatic speech recognition and subjective rating". *European Archives of Oto-Rhino-Laryngology and Head & Neck*, Vol. 263, No. 2, pp. 188–193, 2006.

[Schu 08] B. Schuller, M. Wimmer, L. Mösenlechner, C. Kern, D. Arsic, and G. Rigoll. "Brute-forcing hierarchical functionals for paralinguistics: A waste of feature space?". In: ICASSP08, Ed., *Proceedings of ICASSP, International Conference on Acoustics, Speech, and Signal Processing*, pp. 4501–4504, Las Vegas, Nevada, 2008.

[Schu 09] B. Schuller, S. Steidl, and A. Batliner. "The INTERSPEECH 2009 Emotion Challenge". In: *INTERSPEECH, 10th Annual Conference of the International Speech Communication Association*, Brighton, United Kingdom, 2009.

[Schu 13] B. Schuller and A. Batliner. *Computational paralinguistics: emotion, affect and personality in speech and language processing.* John Wiley & Sons, 2013.

[Schu 15] B. Schuller, S. Steidl, A. Batliner, S. Hantke, F. Hönig, J. R. Orozco-Arroyave, E. Nöth, Y. Zhang, and F. Weninger. "The INTERSPEECH 2015 Computational Paralinguistics Challenge: Nativeness, Parkinson's & Eating Condition". In: *Proceedings of INTERSPEECH, 16th Annual Conference of the International Speech Communication Association*, Dresden, Germany, 2015.

[Schu 95]   E. G. Schukat-Talamazzini. *Automatische Spracherkennung. Grundlagen, statistische Modelle und effiziente Algorithmen.* Vieweg, 1995. Available online: `http://www.minet.uni-jena.de/fakultaet/schukat/asebuch.html`, last visited September 8th, 2017.

[Schw 90]   C. B. Schwind. "An intelligent language tutoring system". *International Journal of Man-Machine Studies*, Vol. 33, No. 5, pp. 557–579, 1990.

[Seid 04]   B. Seidlhofer. "RESEARCH PERSPECTIVES ON TEACHING ENGLISH AS A LINGUA FRANCA". *Annual Review of Applied Linguistics*, Vol. 24, pp. 209–239, 2004.

[Seli 72]   L. Selinker. "Interlanguage". *International Review of Applied Linguistics in Language Teaching*, Vol. 10, pp. 209–231, 1972.

[Shen 90]   X.-N. S. Shen. *The Prosody of Mandarin Chinese.* University of California Press, 1990.

[Shi 10]   Q. Shi, K. Li, S. Zhang, S. M. Chu, J. Xiao, and Z. Ou. "Spoken English assessment system for non-native speakers using acoustic and prosodic features". In: *Proceedings of INTERSPEECH, 11th Annual Conference of the International Speech Communication Association*, pp. 1874–1877, Makuhari, Chiba, Japan, 2010.

[Shri 00]   E. Shriberg, A. Stolcke, D. Hakkani-Tür, and G. Tür. "Prosody-based automatic segmentation of speech into sentences and topics". *Speech communication*, Vol. 32, No. 1, pp. 127–154, 2000.

[Shri 04]   E. Shriberg and A. Stolcke. "Prosody modeling for automatic speech recognition and understanding". In: *Mathematical Foundations of Speech and Language Processing*, pp. 105–114, Springer, 2004.

[Shri 98]   E. Shriberg, A. Stolcke, D. Jurafsky, N. Coccaro, M. Meteer, R. Bates, P. Taylor, K. Ries, R. Martin, and C. Van Ess-Dykema. "Can prosody aid the automatic classification of dialog acts in conversational speech?". *Language and speech*, Vol. 41, No. 3-4, pp. 443–492, 1998.

[Silv 92]   K. E. Silverman, M. E. Beckman, J. F. Pitrelli, M. Ostendorf, C. W. Wightman, P. Price, J. B. Pierrehumbert, and J. Hirschberg. "TOBI: a standard for labeling English prosody.". In: *Proceedings of ICSLP, the Second International Conference on Spoken Language Processing*, Banff, Alberta, Canada, 1992.

[Slan 03]   M. Slaney. "ESPS Pitch Tracker Available!!!!". `http://www.auditory.org/mhonarc/2003/msg00407.html`, last visited September 8th, 2017, July 2003.

[Slaw 99]   E. B. Slawinski. "Acquisition of /r-l/ phonemic contrast by Japanese children and adults". In: *Proceedings of the 5th International Congress of the International Society of Applied*, pp. 583–590, Porto, Portugal, 1999.

[Slui 96]   A. M. Sluijter and V. J. Van Heuven. "Spectral balance as an acoustic correlate of linguistic stress". *The Journal of the Acoustical society of America*, Vol. 100, No. 4, pp. 2471–2485, 1996.

[Smol 04]   A. J. Smola and B. Schölkopf. "A tutorial on support vector regression". *Statistics and computing*, Vol. 14, No. 3, pp. 199–222, 2004.

[Stan 70]   K. Stange. *Angewandte Statistik I*. Springer, 1970.

[Stee 75]   J. Steele. *An essay towards establishing the melody and measure of speech to be expressed and perpetuated by peculiar symbols*. W. Bowyer and J. Nichols, 2nd Ed., 1775.

[Stei 09]   K. Steinhauer, E. J. White, and J. E. Drury. "Temporal dynamics of late second language acquisition: Evidence from event-related brain potentials". *Second Language Research*, Vol. 25, No. 1, pp. 13–41, 2009.

[Stem 05]   G. Stemmer. *Modeling Variability in Speech Recognition*. PhD thesis, Friedrich-Alexander-Universtität Erlangen-Nürnberg, 2005.

[Stev 37]   S. S. Stevens, J. Volkmann, and E. B. Newman. "A scale for the measurement of the psychological magnitude pitch". *The Journal of the Acoustical Society of America*, Vol. 8, No. 3, pp. 185–190, 1937.

[Stri 10]   H. Strik, J. van de Loo, J. van Doremalen, and C. Cucchiarini. "Practicing syntax in spoken interaction: Automatic detection of syntactical errors in non-native utterances". In: *Proceedings of SLaTE, Workshop on Speech and Language Technology in Education*, Tokyo, Japan, 2010.

[Suzu 05]   M. Suzuki. "Corrective feedback and learner uptake in adult ESL classrooms". *Teachers College, Columbia University Working Papers in TESOL & Applied Linguistics*, Vol. 4, No. 2, 2005.

[Talk 95]   D. Talkin. *Speech Coding and Synthesis*, Chap. A robust algorithm for pitch tracking (RAPT), pp. 495–518. Vol. 495, Elsevier Science, 1995.

[Tayl 81]   D. S. Taylor. "Non-native speakers and the rhythm of English". *IRAL-International Review of Applied Linguistics in Language Teaching*, Vol. 19, No. 1-4, pp. 219–226, 1981.

[Teix 00]   C. Teixeira, H. Franco, E. Shriberg, K. Precoda, and K. Sönmez. "Prosodic Features for Automatic Text-Independent Evaluation of Degree of Nativeness for Language Learners". In: *Proceedings of INTERSPEECH, 1st Annual Conference of the International Speech Communication Association*, pp. 187–190, Beijing, 2000.

[Tepp 05]   J. Tepperman and S. Narayanan. "Automatic syllable stress detection using prosodic features for pronunciation evaluation of language learners". In: *Proceedings of ICASSP, International Conference on Acoustics, Speech, and Signal Processing*, pp. 937–940, Philadelphia, USA, 2005.

[Tepp 08]   J. Tepperman and S. Narayanan. "Better Nonnative Intonation Scores through Prosodic Theory". In: *Proceedings of INTERSPEECH*, pp. 1813–1816, Brisbane, Australia, 2008.

[Tepp 10]   J. Tepperman, T. Stanley, K. Hacioglu, and B. Pellom. "Testing suprasegmental English through parroting". In: *Proceedings of Speech Prosody*, pp. 11–14, Chicago IL, USA, 2010.

[Thie 05]   E. D. Thiessen. "Infant-Directed Speech Facilitates Word Segmentation". *Infancy*, Vol. 7, No. 1, pp. 53–71, 2005.

[Thie 07]   E. D. Thiessen and J. R. Saffran. "Learning to learn: Infants' acquisition of stress-based strategies for word segmentation". *Language learning and development*, Vol. 3, No. 1, pp. 73–100, 2007.

[Thom 14]   W. F. Thompson. *Music in the Social and Behavioral Sciences: An Encyclopedia*. Sage Publications, 2014.

[Till 97]   H. G. Tillmann. "Die Mensch-Maschine-Kommunikation". In: P. Hoole, Ed., *Forschungsberichte des Instituts für Phonetik und Sprachliche Kommunikation der Universität München (FIPKM)*, pp. 3–15, München, 1997.

[Tito 68]   R. Titone. *Teaching Foreign Languages: An Historical Sketch*. Georgetown University Press, 1968.

[Toro 05]   J. M. Toro, J. B. Trobalon, and N. Sebastián-Gallés. "Effects of backward speech and speaker variability in language discrimination by rats.". *Journal of Experimental Psychology: Animal Behavior Processes*, Vol. 31, No. 1, p. 95, 2005.

[Town 85]   J. Townsend. "Paralinguistics: How the non-verbal aspects of speech affect our ability to communicate". *Journal of European Industrial Training*, Vol. 9, No. 3, pp. 27–31, 1985.

[Town 98]   B. Townshend, J. Bernstein, O. Todic, and E. Warren. "Estimation of spoken language proficiency". In: *Proceedings of STiLL, Speech Technology in Language Learning*, Marholmen, Sweden, 1998.

[Tram 01]   M. J. Tramo, P. A. Cariani, B. Delgutte, and L. D. Braida. "Neurobiological foundations for the theory of harmony in western tonal music". *Annals of the New York Academy of Sciences*, Vol. 930, No. 1, pp. 92–116, 2001.

[Truo 05]   K. P. Truong, A. Neri, F. De Wet, C. Cucchiarini, and H. Strik. "Automatic detection of frequent pronunciation errors made by L2-learners". In: *Proceedings of INTERSPEECHs*, pp. 1345–1348, Lisbon, Portugal, 2005.

[Tsub 02]   Y. Tsubota, T. Kawahara, and M. Dantsuji. "Recognition and verification of English by Japanese students for computer-assisted language learning system". In: *Proceedings of INTERSPEECH, 3rd Annual Conference of the International Speech Communication Association*, pp. 1205–1208, Jeju Island, Korea, 2002.

[Vaki 15]   A. S. Vakil and J. Trouvain. "Automatic classification of lexical stress errors for German CAPT". In: *Proceedings of SLaTE, Workshop on Speech and Language Technology in Education*, Leipzig, Germany, 2015.

[Van 10]   B. Van Patten and A. G. Benati. *Key Terms in Second Language Acquisition*. Continuum International Publishing Group, 2010.

[Vapn 74]   V. Vapnik and A. Y. Chervonenkis. *Teoriya raspoznavaniya obrazov: Statisticheskie problemy obucheniya. (Russian) [Theory of pattern recognition: Statistical problems of learning]*. Nauka., 1974.

[Vapn 82]   V. N. Vapnik. *Estimation of Dependences Based on Empirical Data*. Springer, 1982.

[Vapn 95]   V. Vapnik. *The Nature of Statistical Learning Theory*. Springer, 1995.

[Vite 67]   A. J. Viterbi. "Error bounds for convolutional codes and an asymptotically optimum decoding algorithm". *IEEE Transactions on Information Theory*, Vol. 13, No. 2, pp. 260–269, 1967.

[Vrie 10] B. P. de Vries, C. Cucchiarini, R. van Hout, and H. Strik. *Interdisciplinary Approaches to Adaptive Learning: A Look at the Neighbours*, Chap. Adaptive Corrective Feedback in Second Language Learning, pp. 1–14. Springer, 2010.

[Wach 99] K. A. Wachowicz and B. Scott. "Software That Listens: It's Not a Question of Whether, It's a Question of How". *CALICO Journal*, Vol. 16, No. 3, pp. 253–276, 1999.

[Waib 86] A. Waibel. "Recognition of lexical stress in a continuous speech understanding system-a pattern recognition approach". In: *Proceedings of ICASSP, IEEE International Conference on Acoustics, Speech, and Signal Processing*, pp. 2287–2290, IEEE, Tokyo, Japan, 1986.

[Wang 01] C. Wang. *Prosodic Modeling for Improved Speech Recognition and Understanding*. PhD thesis, Massachusetts Institute of Technology, 2001.

[Wang 92] M. Q. Wang and J. Hirschberg. "Automatic classification of intonational phrase boundaries". *Computer Speech & Language*, Vol. 6, No. 2, pp. 175–196, 1992.

[Weld 12] D. S. Weld, E. Adar, L. Chilton, R. Hoffmann, E. Horvitz, M. Koch, J. Landay, C. H. Lin, and M. Mausam. "Personalized online education - a crowdsourcing challenge". In: *Workshops at the Twenty-Sixth AAAI Conference on Artificial Intelligence*, 2012.

[Werk 84] J. F. Werker and R. C. Tees. "Cross-Language Speech Perception: Evidence for Perceptual Reorganization During the First Year of Life". *Infant Behavior and Development*, Vol. 7, pp. 49–63, 1984.

[Whit 07a] L. White and S. L. Mattys. "Calibrating rhythm: First language and second language studies". *Journal of Phonetics*, Vol. 35, No. 4, pp. 501–522, 2007.

[Whit 07b] L. White and S. L. Mattys. *Segmental and prosodic issues in Romance phonology*, Chap. Rhythmic typology and variation in first and second languages, pp. 237–257. Vol. 282, John Benjamins, 2007.

[Wigh 92] C. W. Wightman and M. Ostendorf. "Automatic recognition of intonational features". In: *Proceedings of ICASSP, International Conference on Acoustics, Speech, and Signal Processing*, pp. 221–224, San Francisco, California, USA, 1992.

[Witt 99] S. M. Witt. *Use of Speech Recognition in Computer-assisted Language Learning*. PhD thesis, University of Cambridge, 1999.

[Yumo 82] E. Yumoto, W. J. Gould, and T. Baer. "Harmonics-to-noise ratio as an index of the degree of hoarseness". *The journal of the Acoustical Society of America*, Vol. 71, No. 6, pp. 1544–1550, 1982.

[Zadr 02] B. Zadrozny and C. Elkan. "Transforming classifier scores into accurate multiclass probability estimates". In: *Proceedings of the eighth ACM SIGKDD international conference on Knowledge discovery and data mining*, pp. 694–699, ACM, Edmonton, AB, Canada, 2002.

[Zech 07] K. Zechner, D. Higgins, and X. Xi. "Speechrater(TM): A Construct-Driven Approach to Scoring Spontaneous Non-Native Speech". In: *Proceedings of SLaTE, Workshop on Speech and Language Technology in Education*, Farmington Pennsylvania, USA, 2007.

[Zech 11]   K. Zechner, X. Xi, and L. Chen. "Evaluating prosodic features for auto-
              mated scoring of non-native read speech". In: *Proceedings of ASRU,
              IEEE workshop on Automatic Speech Recognition and Understanding*,
              pp. 461–466, Waikoloa, HI, USA, 2011.

[Zeis 12]   V. Zeißler. *Robuste Erkennung der prosodischen Phänomene und der
              emotionalen Benutzerzustände in einem multimodalen Dialogsystem.*
              PhD thesis, Friedrich-Alexander-University Erlangen-Nuremberg, 2012.

[Zhao 11]   J. Zhao, H. Yuan, J. Liu, and S. Xia. "Automatic lexical stress detection
              using acoustic features for computer assisted language learning". *Proceed-
              ings of APSIPA ASC, the Annual Summit and Conference of Asia Pacific
              Signal and Information Processing Association*, pp. 247–251, 2011.

[Zhao 12]   J. Zhao, W.-Q. Zhang, H. Yuan, J. Liu, and S. Xia. "Automatic pitch
              accent detection using auto-context with acoustic features". In: *Pro-
              ceedings of ISCSLP, IEEE International Symposium on Chinese Spoken
              Language Processing*, pp. 247–251, Hong Kong, 2012.

[Zhao 13]   J. Zhao, J. Xu, W.-q. Zhang, H. Yuan, J. Liu, and S. Xia. "Exploiting
              articulatory features for pitch accent detection". *Journal of Zhejiang
              University SCIENCE C (Computers & Electronics)*, Vol. 14, No. 11,
              pp. 835–844, 2013.

[Zhu 13]   Y. Zhu. *Expression and recognition of emotion in native and foreign
              speech : the case of Mandarin and Dutch.* PhD thesis, Faculteit der
              Letteren, Leiden University, Netherlands, 2013.

[Zirp 08]   H. Zirpins. *Modesprache – Sprachmoden.* Wagner Verlag, 2008.

[Zoln 03]   A. Zolnay, R. Schlüter, and H. Ney. "Extraction Methods of
              Voicing Feature for Robust Speech Recognition". In: *Proceedings of
              EUROSPEECH/INTERSPEECH, 8th European Conference on Speech
              Communication and Technology*, Geneva, Switzerland, 2003.

In der Reihe *Studien zur Mustererkennung,*
herausgegeben von
Prof. Dr. Ing Heinricht Niemann und Herrn Prof. Dr. Ing. Elmar Nöth
sind bisher erschienen:

1   Jürgen Haas   Probabilistic Methods in Linguistic Analysis

                         ISBN 978-3-89722-565-7, 2000, 260 S.   40.50 €

2   Manuela Boros   Partielles robustes Parsing spontansprachlicher
                         Dialoge am Beispiel von Zugauskunftdialogen

                         ISBN 978-3-89722-600-5, 2001, 264 S.   40.50 €

3   Stefan Harbeck   Automatische Verfahren zur Sprachdetektion,
                         Landessprachenerkennung und Themendetektion

                         ISBN 978-3-89722-766-8, 2001, 260 S.   40.50 €

4   Julia Fischer   Ein echtzeitfähiges Dialogsystem mit iterativer
                         Ergebnisoptimierung

                         ISBN 978-3-89722-867-2, 2002, 222 S.   40.50 €

5   Ulrike Ahlrichs   Wissensbasierte Szenenexploration auf der Basis
                         erlernter Analysestrategien

                         ISBN 978-3-89722-904-4, 2002, 165 S.   40.50 €

6   Florian Gallwitz   Integrated Stochastic Models for Spontaneous
                         Speech Recognition

                         ISBN 978-3-89722-907-5, 2002, 196 S.   40.50 €

7   Uwe Ohler   Computational Promoter Recognition in
                         Eukaryotic Genomic DNA

                         ISBN 978-3-89722-988-4, 2002, 206 S.   40.50 €

8   Richard Huber   Prosodisch-linguistische Klassifikation
                         von Emotion

                         ISBN 978-3-89722-984-6, 2002, 293 S.   40.50 €

Alle erschienenen Bücher können unter der angegebenen ISBN im Buchhandel oder direkt beim Logos Verlag Berlin (www.logos-verlag.de, Fax: 030 - 42 85 10 92) bestellt werden.